LEGALIZED GAMBLING

A Reference Handbook

Second Edition

Other Titles in ABC-CLIO's
CONTEMPORARY
WORLD ISSUES
Series

LEGALIZED
GAMBLING

A Reference Handbook

Second Edition

William N. Thompson

**CONTEMPORARY
WORLD ISSUES**

ABC-CLIO

Santa Barbara, California
Denver, Colorado
Oxford, England

Library of Congress Cataloging-in-Publication Data

Thompson, William Norman.
    Legalized gambling : a reference handbook / William N. Thompson.—2nd ed.
        p.   cm.—(Contemporary world issues series)
    Includes bibliographical references and index.
    ISBN 0-87436-947-9 (alk. paper)
    1. Gambling—Handbooks, manuals, etc.   2. Gambling—United States—Handbooks, manuals, etc.   3. Gambling—United States—Canada—Handbooks, manuals, etc.   I. Title.   II. Series.
    HV6710.T48   1997   97-23954
    795—dc21   CIP

02 01 00 99 98 97   10 9 8 7 6 5 4 3 2 1

ABC-CLIO, Inc.
130 Cremona Drive, P.O. Box 1911
Santa Barbara, California 93116-1911

This book is printed on acid-free paper ∞.
Manufactured in the United States of America

This book is dedicated to Tim, Laura, and Steve—fun people to be around

Contents

List of Figures

List of Tables

Acknowledgments

Many persons have contributed to the completion of this revised book. I offer my dedication of this volume to my three children, Steve, Tim, and Laura. I suspect that they are an overriding motivating force for much of what I do. After all, I do feel a sense of deep responsibility for overseeing their development, as do all parents with their children. But they have made that task so much easier by venturing off on their own and doing neat things. One might say that "the nest was full" as I launched my academic career. As that career progressed, I dragged the children along to many places where I am sure they did not care to go. Their parents might have enjoyed travel and sightseeing that was tied to dad's "academic agenda," but children don't necessarily care to have friendships and personal agendas disrupted on so many occasions, especially when it involves long relocation times during sabbaticals or a permanent relocation from "home" in Michigan to Las Vegas. I know that such disruptions were not always (and probably not often—if ever) fair to them. But they went along with the program, and that "going along" certainly made the academic ventures much easier and seemingly more worthwhile.

While I never want to pressure my children with thoughts that I will live my dreams through their deeds, I am very happy with many things they have done. Such dreams have been more than fulfilled by their support—especially by their simply being "good kids." Steve is completing a music major at the University of Nevada–Reno. I may write words, but he gives music to people, and I look up to him for developing his music-giving talents. My son Tim is completing a civil and environmental engineering degree at Purdue University, and he looks forward to ways in which he can apply his grasp of technical knowledge to the betterment of all society—a youthful enthusiasm that he has maintained while surrounded by technocrats and a typical contemporary student body that may emphasize securing jobs as its top priority. I have confidence that his enthusiasm will persist. My daughter graduated with a communications degree from the University of San Diego, and she is finishing a master's degree in counseling at the University of Nevada–Reno (UNR). She has been an academic counselor for athletes on the UNR teams, making sure they are eligible so that they can beat my University of Nevada–Las Vegas (UNLV) teams in most major sports. I hate to say it, but I take some of that UNR success personally, and I enjoy it. I am proud that she is pursuing a profession devoted to helping others. My delight in dedicating this book to my children is shared with the one who has been my partner in helping—and not hindering—them along on their way. My wife, Kay, has been a wonderful mother in the home but also a fantastic role model for our children in the workplace, and always a "neat friend." Over the course of my academic career she has done more than her share in the work world as a Spanish teacher and a school guidance counselor. I thank these four special people for their support in this project and in all my work.

In the first edition I recognized many of my academic colleagues with a dedication. To them I still owe a debt of gratitude. I wish to recognize several academic colleagues here as well. Ricardo Gazel of the Economics Department at UNLV and economics professor Dan Rickman of Oklahoma State University have been my coresearchers in several studies of the impacts of gaming over the past three years. I have also worked with Henry Lesieur, perhaps the leading U.S. scholar on problem gambling, and I have appreciated the opportunity to have his insights. Materials on Native American gaming were first generated in research projects made in collaboration with Professor Diana Dever of Mohave Community College in Arizona. I also appreciate the help that I have received from economist and Native American scholar Gary Anders of Arizona State University–West in Phoenix. I continue to appreciate the support of other colleagues at UNLV: Vern Mattson, Gene Moehring, and Hal Rothman of the History Department; Jim Frey in Sociology; Bob Boehm in Engineering; Shirley Emerson in Counseling; Bob Aalberts and Mike Clauretie in Finance; Vince Eade and Shannon Bybee in the Hotel School; Carole Case and Ron Farrel in Criminal Justice; Susan Jarvis, Tom Mirkovich, Sidney Watson, and Maria White of the University Library Staff; Keith Schwer of the Business and Economic Research Center; my Public Administration colleagues Doug Imig, Delores Brosnan, Pat Goodall, and Rick Tilman; Sharolyn Craft of the Nevada Small Business Development Center; Tom Guthrie of the Southern Nevada Small Business Development Company; and our College of Business support staff members, Sharon Green, Donna Evans, Patricia Ray Roach, Cecelia Romero, Peggy Jackman, Diane Sjoberg, and Cara Lary.

I have learned much about the gaming industry by venturing outside the walls of my local academic setting. I especially am thankful for the opportunity I have had to work as a expert witness for many Indian gaming tribes, an opportunity that was facilitated by attorney Bruce Greene of Boulder, Colorado. Jack Binion of the Horseshoe Casino enterprise invited me to work for his staff on several projects. I learned much from him and others on the Horseshoe team—Don Schupan, Gary Border, Dennis Piotrowski, and John Schriber. My coeditors of *International Casino Law*, Las Vegas attorney Anthony Cabot and London consultant Andrew Tottenham, remain supportive and helpful in my research tasks. I am also grateful for the help of the coeditor of the forthcoming edition of that book, Professor Carl Braunlich of Purdue University. I appreciate the assistance of Marian Green of *International Gaming and Business Research* for providing useful materials. I treasure the friendship and support of Joe Richardson of "The Great Gamble" in Fargo, North Dakota. Joe is an incurable "net" surfer, and his help in searching out web sites that could be included in Chapter 6 has been invaluable. I also extend thanks to my "Michigan research staff," friends John and Carol Holms of Kalamazoo; Tony and Linda Juliano of Lansing; Leo Kennedy, director of the Michigan State Legislative Research Council; John Tarras of Michigan State University; my brother, Fred Thompson, of Ann Arbor; and my friend Professor Fred Wacker of Wayne State University. I continue to welcome sage advice as well as research tidbits from I. Nelson Rose of Whittier Law College in

Los Angeles, and I appreciate the help of Roger Dunstan of the California Research Bureau.

I have appreciated opportunities to speak on gambling issues in many places. Roy Kawaguchi of Las Vegas introduced me to the major players in Japan's pachinko industry. Ana Lemos invited me to be a professor in the summer gambling program at the University of Madrid. I am grateful for the support of Bill Eadington and Judy Cornelius of UNR in organizing many gaming conferences in which I have been able to share my research with others; I especially enjoyed the chance to participate in the European Gaming conference they cosponsored at Cambridge, England, in 1995. Reno gaming researcher Ken Adams was also of assistance, as were Mike Vargo of the "No Dice" campaign in Pittsburgh and David Hanson of Duquesne University. Tom Peacock of the Luxor Casino, Mary Winter of the Santa Fe, and Kim Stein of Casino Data Systems have been helpful as well.

I am thankful for the assistance of several Canadian friends. Kathie Maher-Wolbaum of Casino Regina provided the photograph used for the book. Ron Sheppard, formerly of the Crystal Casino in Winnipeg and Casino du Montreal, invited me to develop a customer service program along with Michele Comeau. As a result we were able to write *Casino Customer Service*. Professors Colin Campbell of Malaspina University and Christian Marfels of Dalhousie University were also helpful. I genuinely appreciate the help of members of the Ontario Consortium on Casino Training, each of whom hosted me for presentations. The members include Shirley Mary Tomovic and Dave Taylor of Niagara College, Warren Howes and Bill Gordon of Georgian College, and Kelly Bevan, Neil Chartrand, and Margaret Jeffrey of St. Clair College.

I appreciate the hard work of the editorial staff of ABC-CLIO, especially Todd Hallman and Allan Sutton, in guiding this revision toward completion and in enduring the difficult editorial task of making sense out of many of my rambling statements. I think Todd, Allan, and the ABC-CLIO staff are to be commended for doing a great job. However, if anyone notices any loose ends, maybe a few facts out of place, or questionable academic judgments, I have no one to blame but myself. I accept all responsibility for this volume. I cannot accept all or even most of the credit; it is shared with those mentioned above, especially Laura, Steve, Tim—and Kay.

Preface

On New Year's Eve 1996, Las Vegas Boulevard South sought to outdo Times Square itself as the place to be to ring in the New Year. Over 500,000 people gathered at the lower end of the famous casino Strip to witness a planned display of fireworks, the likes of which had not been seen anywhere before. They gathered to see a fantastic array of bursting streams of colored light followed by the implosion of an entire casino complex. The pyrotechnics provided the prelude. The main movement was executed by 1,125 pounds of explosives scientifically placed to level the 900-room, 11-story-tall Hacienda Hotel and Casino. After 40 seconds of internal eruptions, a fireball went skyward, and in one collective fall the structure disintegrated into a 30-foot-high pile of rubble. In actuality, one corner remained and had to be removed by a traditional wrecking ball on New Year's Day. The show was spectacular nonetheless.

Some might have seen the show as a symbolic one. Opponents of the spread of legalized gambling have been gathering their strength over the past two or three years. They have formed a National Coalition Against Legalized Gambling. They have lobbied hard on Capitol Hill in Washington, trying to persuade the national government to institute a special tax on gambling along with a new set of federal regulations. They claimed credit for a new act creating a national commission to study gambling. They also claimed credit for bringing about the defeat of many measures seeking to legalize gambling in new jurisdictions. The opponents of gambling would like to suggest that the implosion of the Hacienda Casino portends a future when our nation will reject gambling and make illegal an activity that is now legal in one form or another in 48 states. They would like to suggest that casino operations can come to an end. The reality, however, may be quite the opposite. After all, the 900-room Hacienda Hotel and Casino did not come down in order to make a parking lot, nor will its rubble remain long as a symbol to the past. No, the owners of the hotel remain active at the location. In 1997, they will be laying the foundations of a new 4,000-room casino project built around a surfing theme. For them and for the industry, the implosion of the Hacienda signifies a renewal and a continued growth for the fastest-growing industry in the United States.

Indeed, the implosion of the Hacienda is itself a new symbol of Las Vegas. In the three years since the publication of the first edition of this book, Las Vegas has seen several of its traditional casinos evaporate into dust at the hands of demolition crews. Two towers of the Dunes came imploding down. One of the falling towers was featured in the movie *Casino*. A super luxurious casino hotel—the 3,000-room Belagio—is being built at the site. The famous Sands Casino, scene of the movie *Oceans Eleven* and the antics of Frank Sinatra and his "rat pack" of Hollywood stars (Sammy Davis Jr., Dean Martin, Peter Lawford, Shirley Maclaine, Joey Bishop), came crashing down to make way for a new 6,000-room hotel casino. To be sure, the Landmark was imploded to create a parking lot. But the parking lot was needed to ease the congestion around the ever-expanding Las Vegas Convention Center, the world's largest exhibition complex on a single level. The scene of the destruction of the Landmark is being preserved forever as part of the movie *Mars Attack*. The spokesmen for the destruction companies suggest that more implosions are on their way, all to make way for more growth in the gambling industry's capital city.

To be sure, the growth in the legalized gambling industry that has occurred over the past decade has generated a national political opposition not in evidence before now. People are being alerted to the fact that with gambling come problems. Certainly there is support for claims that some crime is associated with the presence of gambling. Certainly there is support for claims that gambling sometimes ruins lives and that it can carry enormous social costs. Gambling enterprises also can divert people's expenditure patterns away from one kind of products to another, in some cases from products needed for daily existence—food and shelter for families—to frivolous entertainment and risk taking. A political opposition is gathering the evidence and presenting it in political campaigns against further legalization of gambling. However, the opposition's record of success is debatable. It may be effective in some campaigns, but the suggestion that it has generated a backlash that will stop the spread of gambling is premature, to say the least.

The proponents of the further spread of gambling have won some major campaigns in recent years. They continue to ride a crest of national feelings favorable to their cause: a population that shows a willingness to prefer gambling taxation revenues over new or increased personal taxation; a population that accepts the idea that gambling enterprise can create employment in communities where other business enterprise has evaporated; a population that is still rejecting the notion that the state (government) should regulate morals by banning all forms of "victimless crimes." The population is also becoming older. The baby boomers—the post–World War II babies born between 1945 and 1960—are now approaching or already in their fifties. Each day over 10,000 baby boomers become 50 years old. People in the post-50 age group are great customers for gaming entertainment. Most have "emptied the nest," that is, their children have grown up and left their care; they are at the peak of their earning power; they have maximum vacation time from their jobs prior to a time when they can retire. Moreover the proponents of gambling are supported by the gambling industry itself, and the industry—with its ever-expanding player base—has a lot of money. That money has been put to use in political campaigns, and that money has also been directed toward the creation of a Washington interest group—the American Gaming Association—that has as its major goal the prevention of federal regulation and taxation of the gambling industry as well as the prevention of antigambling measures in the various states.

The years remaining in the twentieth century will be years of serious debate over gambling. The federal government will be studying the issues involved in legalized gambling in detail and pondering what role Washington should play in overseeing activity of the gambling industry in the future. The issues are moving toward the center stage of the national domestic political agenda.

The forces are still gathering and jockeying for position; there is as yet no national consensus on the issues. The two political parties each have serious divisions on the issues. Indeed, there is no liberal or conservative position on gambling, per se. In 1996, both parties and most candidates for statewide election did the political thing: They accepted campaign funds from both sides on the issue, and they avoided taking sides. That luxury will not be open to all political "leaders" in the future. Many of the issues will have to be faced for one reason or another. In some states, governors and legislators will have to implement gambling policies determined by popular referenda. In other states, leaders will have to decide whether or not to renew agreements with Indian gambling establishments. Nationally, a commission will be asked to make recommendations on a new national policy on gambling. A secretary of the interior will be asked to take a stand for or against Indian casinos, and the secretary (presently Bruce Babbitt) may not have the luxury of ducking the issue—silence itself will constitute a position on the issues.

It is to be hoped that students of North American political issues will see gambling as an exciting issue. I moved to Las Vegas in 1980 and became interested in the subject because I taught courses in the field of public administration—a field that is concerned with the regulation of commercial activities. And gambling was *the* commercial activity of my adopted state. At that time I recognized an irony—the United States was accepting gambling, and lotteries were spreading to a majority of states and all the provinces of Canada, yet people were consistently rejecting proposals to legalize casino gambling. I joined with criminologist John Dombrink of the University of California–Irvine, and we wrote a book analyzing casino gambling campaigns and comparing these with lottery campaigns. Since I began gathering research for the first edition of *Legalized Gambling*, the distinctions between lotteries and casinos have become very much blurred. The issue of the legalization of gambling was explored in the first edition, and it is treated in more depth here, as events have continued to unfold since 1994. Most of the material presented in this second edition builds upon the 1994 book. Many additions are sequential—that is, they record events since 1994. A simple update is essential, as this is a dynamic industry and dynamic political issue, but this edition seeks to go further than simply updating.

As with the first edition, it is vital that a book on legalized gambling in America consider gambling in Canada as well as in the

United States. The phenomenon of legalized gambling is a *North American* phenomenon. What happens to the north affects the south, and what happens to the south affects the north. Political boundaries do not stop the impacts of gambling phenomena.

Over the course of the history of the continent, two great democratic nations have approached social issues with different governmental structures and political processes. Yet they have acted almost in tandem, as if on a bicycle built for two, and invariably Canada has been found riding on the backseat. So it has been with gambling—at least for a while. After several New England states, New York, and New Jersey started lotteries, Canada followed. A national law in 1969 opened the door for provincial activity. The 1969 law also opened up possibilities for forms of casino gambling. At first the provinces were slow to act on this front, but in the 1990s it appears that provincial activity is moving quickly ahead of activity south of the international border.

As we approach the end of a century, Canadian casino activity has taken a lead, with major casinos aiming directly at the United States for their customer bases. The first casinos in Winnipeg and Montreal were not able to exploit international— that is, over the border—markets. The casino in Windsor, Ontario, was different. The provincial government planned for the casino to appeal to a Michigan clientele. The casino was very, very successful. Soon it was "winning" a million dollars a day from its U.S. customers. Perhaps it was too successful. Michigan voters retaliated and legalized casinos for Detroit specifically with the rationale that they needed to keep the gambling money in Michigan.

But Ontario marches on. A new casino in Niagara Falls, Ontario, attracts crowds in excess of 50,000 people a day, and collectively they bring most of their gambling dollars from the Buffalo metropolitan area. If the new casino's success matches or even exceeds that in Windsor, New York political forces will surely organize and make casino legalization a major political agenda issue in the Empire State. Casino and gambling machine activity in the Maritime Provinces may influence similar activity in the New England states. Canada appears to be in a leadership role today.

A future edition of this book might have to include Mexico. In 1995, serious discussions about casino legalization began among the political elite. As of early 1997, the discussions had generated considerable interest among casino gambling companies, but they remained on hold as other matters, which are probably more serious, dominated national politics south of the southern border of the United States. A consideration of gaming in Mexico is left for a future time.

In the first edition I talked about the force of "legalized gambling" as if it were a powerful train set loose down the tracks. There can be little doubt that the gambling train is on those tracks and is still in motion. Society will not be able to stop the train. However, with vigilance and with serious analysis of the issues—pro and con—the public and, more importantly, the political actors in charge of decision making on the issues will be able to keep the speed of the train under control. Most importantly, they will be able to keep the train on the tracks.

The second edition follows the format of the first. In Chapter 1, expanded attention is given to the political concerns that move the gambling issue. The economics of gambling is highlighted in new ways, as a regional input-output model is offered as a means to help understand where gambling can help the cause of economic development and where it may be adverse to the interests of economic expansion. More attention is also given to the social costs of gambling, the costs of crimes that may be related to legalized gambling, and costs associated with compulsive gambling.

Chapter 2 is a chronology of gambling events, with an emphasis on events in the middle of the 1990s. Chapter 3 provides biographies of leading figures in the gambling industry and in the arenas that control policymaking for gambling issues.

Chapter 4 reviews legislation and court decisions regarding gambling and presents statistics on major aspects of the gambling industry. Chapter 5 lists major gambling organizations in the United States and Canada. Chapters 6 and 7 review major research resources on gambling issues in both printed materials and film media. As before, the book ends with a glossary of major terms. I appreciate the interest readers expressed in the first edition and their desire to have this updated revision. It is hoped that the changes offered will help readers gain knowledge about gambling and encourage their continued exploration of what I have found to be a fascinating subject.

Introduction

1

The editors of *Esquire* magazine have called it "the World's Second Oldest Diversion" (Newman et al. 1962). *Business Week* ("Gambling—The Newest Growth Industry" 1978) said that it was the "newest growth industry" in the United States and pronounced in a cover story that a fever for it was sweeping the nation (Welles 1989). Indeed, the figures bear this out. Voters and politicians endorse it more and more. *It* is gambling, an industry that today is embroiled in governmental controversies from coast to coast in both the United States and Canada.

Gambling became a "front burner" political issue in the early 1990s for many reasons, which persist as the decade winds down toward the new century. State, local, provincial, and territorial governments have faced serious budget shortfalls of a kind that had not been witnessed since the Great Depression of the 1930s, and the public has been engulfed in a general antitaxation movement that has blocked political approval of traditional sources for new revenues. The public has also softened its objections to a variety of "sins," such as gambling and adult consensual nonmarital sexual activities, that were formerly categorized as "victimless crimes."

In November 1996, voters in two states, liberal California and conservative Arizona, actually voted for limited legalization of the use of marijuana. Moreover, the gaming industry has attracted entrepreneurs eager for new markets and high yields on their investments. The gaming industry now willingly sponsors political campaigns for gambling legalization.

Just a few decades ago, legalized gambling was confined to the casinos found in one isolated state, plus a few other places that allowed wagers on horse races or charity bingo games. Then came the 1960s, and starting with New Hampshire, state after state turned to public lotteries as a way of generating tax revenue. Canadian provinces and territories followed suit. In addition, many jurisdictions began to open doors wider for charity gambling, and horse tracks began to penetrate all parts of the continent. When voters in New Jersey authorized casinos for Atlantic City in 1976, many felt the lid of restriction had come off.

Casino gaming was not accepted in the same way that other forms of gambling were until the late 1980s (Dombrink and Thompson 1990). During this period South Dakota and Colorado opened certain historical locations to casino activity with limited betting, and Iowa and Illinois approved casino games on riverboats. These examples became models for duplication elsewhere. Indian reservations entered the gambling picture when they began to recognize a unique legal status that exempted them from many state restrictions. Reservation leaders discovered that bingo and even casino-type games could generate large sums of money for tribal programs.

Although the legalization of gambling in its many forms still continues to be a subject of contentious debate in many places, people throughout the North American continent are more and more accepting of gambling activity. Las Vegas, clearly the world center of the gambling industry, fought for over six decades to establish an honorable name among U.S. communities. Its residents have always tried to argue that "people in Las Vegas are just like people anywhere else" and that "Las Vegas is no different than any other city." Though such emotions were long rejected by others as being rather absurd, a recent change of opinion has occurred. Now, instead of trying to show that Las Vegas "is just like everywhere else," some rather powerful voices have suggested that "everywhere else" has become quite like Las Vegas. *Time* magazine presented a cover story entitled "Las Vegas: The New All-American City." The author of the story, Kurt Anderson, found that the rest of the United States was trying to imitate the values of Las Vegas in terms of "glitz," "architecture," "entertainment," and, yes, "gambling" (Anderson 1994).

This handbook examines the phenomenon of legalized gambling in North American society today. Gambling may be defined as an activity in which a person subjects something of value—usually money—to a risk involving a large element of chance in the hopes of winning something of greater value, which is usually more money. The types of gambling addressed in this handbook have all been addressed by policymakers: bingo, lotteries, raffles, dice, card games, slot machines, and sporting events, including team games, individual contests, and horse or dog races. Although gambling encompasses all these activities, the term *gaming* is usually associated with the activities found in casinos. Betting on sports and races is commonly referred to as *wagering*. Herein, the terms *gambling, gaming,* and *wagering* will be used somewhat interchangeably.

Throughout our lives we take chances in the hopes of obtaining certain rewards. We do this when we select our study areas in college, when we accept jobs, and when we go into business. Certainly we are taking chances when we invest in the stock markets or even when we deposit money into savings accounts. All these enterprises involve the risks of losing valuable time, money, and opportunity in exchange for the chances of reaping rewards, which often are financial ones. On the nonfinancial front, we may risk our health—even our lives—in the pursuit of recreational thrills. These risks include such activities as skiing, mountain climbing, contact sports, scuba diving, bungee jumping, or car racing. We also assume risks as we seek the pleasures of food or the fulfillment of other appetites. This research handbook does not concern itself with these types of gambles, although the information presented may contribute to the understanding of such activity. Our attention, rather, will be focused on commercial (including charitable and government-sponsored) financial games involving a considerable element of chance.

Some form of gambling is now legal in 48 states in the United States and in each of the Canadian provinces as well as the Yukon and Northwest Territories. Bingo games are legal in 47 states, the District of Columbia, and all Canadian provinces and territories (Christiansen 1996; Thompson 1994). Lotteries are conducted by 37 state governments, the District of Columbia, and all the provinces and territories. Horse race betting is permitted in 42 states, 19 states allow dog race wagering, and 4 states permit betting on jai alai games. All the Canadian provinces have some form of horse race betting. Nevada, New Jersey, and more than 20 other states and all of the provinces plus the Yukon offer some form of slot machines, card-rooms, or casino-type games. Major (high stakes) land-based commercial casinos operating on a permanent basis nearly every day of the year are in place throughout the state of Nevada and in Atlantic City, New Jersey; Halifax and Sydney, Nova Scotia; Winnipeg, Manitoba; Regina, Saskatchewan; Windsor and Niagara Falls, Ontario; and Montreal, Charlevoix, and Hull, Quebec. Such casinos have also been authorized for New Orleans, Louisiana, and Detroit, Michigan.

If all the gaming activities permitted in U.S. jurisdictions were brought together under a single holding company, that company would collect revenues making it the nation's eleventh largest corporation. More than $550 billion is gambled each year in the United States (Canadians wager an additional $10 billion), and legal gaming organizations—lotteries, tracks, casinos, and bingo halls—retain over $44 billion gross in gaming wins (Christiansen 1996). Considering that win figure as representative of "gross product sales," the holding company would lag behind the three biggest auto makers, IBM, and AT&T but would be well ahead of corporate giants like K-Mart and American Express. More money is gambled and lost in the United States than is spent on all recorded music and all motion pictures combined. There are more visits to gambling facilities than the combined attendance of all professional sports events. In 1995, there were 154 million visits to casinos in the United States. Those casino visits equal 87 percent of all the visits to all professional and amateur sports events (Dunstan 1997). More people visit casinos than visit amusement parks (Harrah's Entertainment, Inc. 1996). Atlantic City and Las Vegas each attract over 30 million visitors a year. Gambling enterprises produce over $16 billion in special taxes for state and local governments in the United States and were responsible for the employment of an estimated 650,000 workers (Christiansen 1996). U.S. casinos directly employed 367,000 people in 1995 (Harrah's Entertainment, Inc. 1996).

Although gambling has always existed, public involvement in the activity has not occurred evenly throughout history. There have been eras of gambling suppression and prohibition and eras of permissiveness. Today, we are most certainly experiencing a movement away from suppression and toward greater leniency. How did we arrive at this condition, and why is legalized gambling expanding and receiving more and more political attention?

Gambling throughout History

The editors of *Esquire* wrote that the "oldest diversion...is the same as the oldest profession, but it's odds-on that gambling came next, perhaps even immediately afterwards" (Newman et al. 1962). Others may disagree with this placement of gambling on the time line of humankind. Abt, Smith, and Christiansen, the authors of *The Business of Risk: Commercial Gambling in Mainstream America*, suggest that gambling should be listed as the starting point of "sinful" activity. They portray Adam and Eve's choice to eat forbidden fruit in the Garden of Eden as humankind's first real gamble. The price of this failed wager, they say, was a loss of innocence: "To many, man's fall from grace and subsequent history are proof [that] it [eating fruit] was immoral, or a sucker bet, the first step down the road to ruin. To others, the wager was an act of self-actualization." Through the Garden of Eden gamble, they assert, "Adam and Eve acquired humanity," and society began (Abt, Smith, and Christiansen 1985).

The mortal souls of all societies throughout history have known gambling. Compulsive gamblers in biblical Egypt were sent to quarries to work off their debts. It is likely that many of the workers who built the pyramids were among this group. It is appropriate, then, that when archaeologists excavated the pyramids, they found dice beside the mummified bodies of pharaohs. Interestingly, the dice were shaved, that is, they were "crooked." Greek history contains stories of soldiers who shot craps to while away the monotonous hours during the siege of Troy, and the Bible documents the story of Roman centurions gambling for the robes of Christ following the crucifixion. The Old and New Testaments, indeed, contain many references to gambling.

Roman society generally precluded the masses from gaming, except during festivals. However, gambling was a regular part of life in retirement communities established near hot springs and natural bath waters for career military personnel in the far reaches of Europe. Long before the Renaissance period, Germans and Englishmen wagered at Spa, Baden, and Bath. The privileged classes in Rome also gambled away their considerable leisure time. It is just as likely that Nero was raffling off slaves or villas to his palace guests as it is that he was playing a fiddle when Rome burned in A.D. 64 (Scarne 1961).

During the Middle Ages, pilgrims traveling to Canterbury, traders, and soldiers moving east to the Crusades utilized old

Roman roads. Inns along the way provided for their comfort, food, lodging, and entertainment. These inns also became centers for gambling in communities on these routes. Monarchs during the Middle Ages wagered on the speed of their horses. It is known that England's infamous King John (1199–1216) kept special racing horses in his royal stables (Scarne 1961).

Various kinds of gambling implements, such as sticks and dice, existed in the earliest societies, but the origin of playing cards is more recent. Cards probably appeared in Asia shortly after the Chinese invented paper in the first or second century A.D. The first European card decks date to fourteenth-century Italy and France. The popularity of card games spread rapidly throughout Europe after that time, and there is no doubt but that Columbus brought cards to the Western Hemisphere on his first voyage in 1492.

Continental lotteries financed public improvements prior to European migrations to North America. The first lotteries probably were held during the Roman Empire, and the first government-organized lottery took place in Florence in 1530. Soon afterward, lottery drawings occurred in Venice and Genoa. The Italians introduced lotteries to the French in 1533 when Catherine de Medici traveled to Versailles to marry King Henry II. Queen Elizabeth authorized England's first lottery in 1566, although the drawing was not held until 1569 (Blanche 1950). The money secured by the queen was dedicated "towards the reparation of the havens (harbors for ships) and strength of the Realme and towards such other publique good works" (Scarne 1961).

When European settlers came to the New World, they brought gambling paraphernalia and a gambling tradition. They quickly discovered that the indigenous people of the continent participated in a variety of gaming activities as well. Native Americans wagered heavily on sporting events. Favorite team games included lacrosse and a precursor of modern football. The teams comprised young males from neighboring villages or tribes. Supporters of each team wagered their possessions by placing blankets, clothing, jewelry, pottery, weapons, and livestock on a line near the middle of a playing field. Native Americans also bet on footraces, horse races, and athletic contests involving various hunting and warring skills. A popular contest involved shooting arrows into a rolling hoop.

Dice games were also popular. Early American dice typically was played with flat stones or bones painted with different colors on each side. Players would choose colors as the dice were thrown in the air. Also prevalent were guessing games involving deception. In one, a team would conceal a small object behind its collective back and pass it from member to member. The opposite team would then try to guess which member possessed the object.

These games and contests could last for days, with players and bettors engaged until they fell over from exhaustion. Although no "credit" gambling was allowed, a player's total possessions could be put at risk in the betting. Often, a series of double-or-nothing wagers would "wipe out" a participant. However, winners normally returned sufficient possessions so that losers would not face destitution or injury from exposure to the elements.

Gambling activity has ebbed and flowed with varying intensities throughout history. In what has appeared to be a love-hate relationship between the public and gambling promoters, several "waves" of permissiveness have rippled through North America, only to subside with prohibitionary regulation.

Gaming authority I. Nelson Rose suggests that we are now in the "third wave" of gaming in European–North American history (Rose 1980). The first occurred during the colonial era and early years of nationhood. Lotteries, horse racing, and gentlemanly card games punctuated this phase. Captain John Smith's Virginia encountered financial problems almost immediately after European settlers arrived at Jamestown Colony, and in his desperation for funding, Smith obtained a charter from King James in 1612 to conduct a lottery in London (Chafetz 1960). Soon, lotteries were being played in the colonies as well and becoming an integral element in colonial development. Lotteries were used to supplement government treasuries and were engaged by private organizations. Churches as well as colleges such as Harvard, Princeton, Columbia, and Rutgers used lotteries to finance construction projects. In fact, the Revolutionary War itself was financed in part by a lottery established by the Continental Congress.

The young Thomas Jefferson reportedly spent his first year in attendance at the College of William and Mary amusing himself with nonacademic entertainment such as card playing and attendance at horse racing—gambling at both pursuits (Burns 1997). Although Jefferson settled down to serious studies during his subsequent years at the Williamsburg campus, gambling by no means was out of his mind. At what might be considered the most glorious time for the United States as a nation, Jefferson may have allowed gambling to be a diversion from the critical tasks that had been thrust upon his shoulders. His diary indicates that during June 1776, he and his wife engaged in many games of backgammon as well as lotteries and that they incurred both wins and losses (Rosecrance 1988).

Newly formed state governments used lotteries to fund military activity and later turned to this funding mechanism for internal improvements after winning independence from the Crown. One report estimates that between 1790 and 1860, 24 of 33 states financed buildings, roads, and bridges from lottery revenues. This era peaked in 1831, when 8 states ran 420 lottery games that sold more than $66 million in tickets. This sum was five times that of the federal budget that year.

Thomas Jefferson, one of our most prominent founding fathers, spoke to the issue of the costs and benefits of lotteries on more than one occasion. Unfortunately, he seems to have spoken from both sides of his mouth. Clotfelter and Cook (1989) recite his words in their seminal study of lotteries (*Selling Hope*, p. 299). Obviously putting out of his conscious mind the activities of his younger days, Jefferson penned these words in an 1810 letter: "Having myself made it a rule *never* to engage in a lottery or any other adventure of mere chance, I cannot, with less candor or effect, urge it on others, however laudable or desirable its objectives may be." Ken Burns's 1997 television documentary "Thomas Jefferson" records his financial difficulties after leaving the presidency. Jefferson had monumental debts that precluded him from keeping up the maintenance of his beloved home, Monticello. His creditors allowed him to remain in his home only out of deep personal respect for his deeds on behalf of the nation. Perhaps because of his financial situation he was denied the opportunity to grant freedom to his slaves, placing him for eternity on the wrong side of the saddest issue in the nation's history. In any event, in his last year of life he desperately needed funds, and he applied to the Virginia legislature for permission to conduct a sale of many of his possessions through the use of a lottery. He was give permission, but the lottery was far from successful. When Jefferson died on 4 July 1826, 50 years to the day after the Declaration of Independence was approved by Congress, he was a major debtor. As he looked toward the use of a lottery as a tool for extracting himself from his financial burdens, he looked upon the gambling enterprise somewhat differently than he had only 16 years before. He wrote these words in a February 1826 essay that he called "Thoughts on Lotteries":

> The money is here a salutary instrument for disposing of it (his property), where many run small risks for the chance of obtaining a high prize.... Money is wanting for a useful undertaking for which a direct tax would

be disapproved. It is raised therefore by a lottery, wherein the tax is laid on the willing only, that is to say, on those who can risk the price of a ticket without sensible injury for the possibility of a higher prize. (Clotfelter and Cook, 1989)

Thomas Jefferson notwithstanding, in the 1820s and 1830s lotteries were exposed to the general public as being rife with scandals and swindles. The public became disgruntled with lottery activity, and soon movements to end the activity spread across the land.

The emergence of Andrew Jackson as the dominant national leader and promoter of governmental reform also energized the detractors of government-operated gambling operations. Even though Jackson certainly was a major gambler when it came to horse racing, his Jacksonian Revolution served to stop much lottery behavior. State after state abolished lotteries and prohibited private parties from selling tickets. By the time of the Civil War, which effectively marked the end of the first gambling wave, only three states permitted lotteries.

Riverboat gaming began in the early 1800s as commerce moved into the Mississippi Valley. Robert Fulton placed a steamboat on the river in 1812. Soon, cardsharps were in business, fleecing unsuspecting farmers and merchants who had to use the boats to get their products to market. In the 1830s and 1840s, reformers effectuated the closing of many gambling operations on boats and in river towns from Saint Louis to New Orleans.

The first wave also carried horse racing to the eastern half of the continent, although greater gambling activity was found in the South. Race horses had arrived in Virginia by 1620. Circular courses were laid out in New York as early as 1665 and were quickly imitated elsewhere. Wagering on horse races was, at first, an activity that took place among gentlemen and was considered more of a sporting matter than true gambling. Similarly, the "landed gentry" engaged in poker games, whereas general gambling among the working classes was prohibited.

Restrictions were imposed on gambling almost from the beginning of the colonial period. Plymouth Colony, for example, banned card playing as early as 1621—only a year after the arrival of the Pilgrims. Similar bans were applied to other popular games and to gaming at popular locations, such as taverns. Such gaming was seen as destructive to the Protestant work ethic and a contributor to idleness and debauchery. Nonetheless, simultaneously with such bans, society endorsed lotteries, horse racing, and games among the rich throughout this period. The initial flirtations in the United States with gambling ended with the Civil War. Horses were needed for wartime activities, and racing had come to be viewed as wasteful. During these years, Southern gentry faced the loss of not only its social position but also its land. There was no time for poker, and the scandals of earlier lottery years had destroyed public appetites for that pastime.

Following the Civil War, a second wave of gambling began as devastated state and local governments searched for funding. Again, they turned to the lottery. Horse racing also regained popularity, as did card games on the western frontier. A number of southern states turned to the lottery in the Reconstruction Era, but only one survived after 1878—the notorious Louisiana Lottery. Ticket sales were authorized by the Louisiana legislature, promoted by bribery, and run by a New York syndicate. The lottery thrived because it was the only one in the country, and it merchandised tickets through the mail. The Louisiana Lottery became the target of a national reform movement, and Congress subsequently passed a law in 1890 prohibiting the sale of lottery tickets through the mail. The state legislature shut down the lottery games two years later.

The gold rush and silver strikes in the West drew fortune seekers by the tens of thousands. Gamblers who had been stifled by eastern reformers now had an alternative location in which to ply their trade. Gambling in gold and silver camps became a major entertainment activity for prospectors, miners, and cowboys, with opulent gaming houses springing up in San Francisco, Denver, and Colorado Springs. As gambling dives permeated the mining boomtowns and camps of the West, laws were enacted to stop the activity. A lack of law enforcement personnel, however, ensured that most of the regulations would remain unenforced. Simply maintaining civil order was a major task for the police. At this time, gaming houses also emerged in the East as the first harbingers of organized crime began to recognize the possibilities of offering games of chance to the upper classes.

Many such gaming houses were tolerated until another series of reforms smashed the nation's second major era of legalized gambling. In the first decade of the twentieth century, Arizona and New Mexico Territories banned gambling in the hopes of winning support for statehood. As mining activity subsided, so did the demand for gambling. This trend bolstered the ability of lawmen to enforce gambling regulations. Nevada finally closed its casinos in 1910, and all but a very few of the states banned wagers on horse races. For the most part legal gambling lay dormant after this period for several years. In 1931, casinos were legalized once again in Nevada, and during the remaining years of the decade horse racing returned to 21 states. These states, facing major budget problems related to their Depression economies, charted a trend of expanding track wagering that continued through the 1940s. Other states began permitting charity bingo games in the 1950s, and Florida began to allow bets on jai alai games. Lotteries, however, were not poised to enjoy rehabilitated legal status until the New Hampshire legislature passed a sweepstakes law in 1963.

With the initiation of the New Hampshire lottery in 1964, a third wave of legalized gambling swept the nation. New York soon approved a lottery; New Jersey followed suit. In 1969, Canada amended its Criminal Code to allow lotteries in provinces and to authorize charitable gaming. Every province and Yukon Territory moved to establish lotteries in the 1970s, and a variety of charitable and governmental gaming schemes led half of the provinces to open full-fledged casinos. In the United States, 37 states and the District of Columbia eventually authorized lotteries, and even more states authorized bets on horse or dog races. In 1976, New Jersey voters approved casinos for Atlantic City. The first Atlantic City casino—Resorts International—opened its doors during Memorial Day weekend in 1978. Soon there were predictions that casino gambling was going to spread across the land just as the lotteries had. However, this did not happen, at least not for another decade.

The forces propelling a spread of lotteries across the continent and the forces pushing casino gambling into new jurisdictions were somewhat diverse, although in the future there may be a coalescing of the forces.

As voters looked at lottery issues in the 1970s and 1980s, they focused their attention upon economic concerns, specifically tax revenues for governments. They weighed advantages and disadvantages of having lotteries, and for the most part votes favored lotteries. Only one state—North Dakota—has defeated a lottery proposition on a statewide ballot. It did not happen because North Dakotans opposed gambling but for precisely the opposite reason. North Dakota had established a statewide network of blackjack casinos that were operated to benefit the charities of the state. The charity organizations feared the competition of a state lottery and led the campaign against lotteries.

From the mid-1960s through 1988, only one out of a dozen states approved casino gambling through a public referendum vote. Since the South Dakota vote in 1988, there have been successful votes in Colorado, Missouri, and Michigan for commercial casinos, but there have been many defeats as well (Ohio twice, Florida, and Arkansas). Most of the approvals of casinos have been by legislative action without popular votes. The scattered successes have made casino gaming as well as other forms of gambling an item that is near the top of the political agendas almost everywhere that gambling is not already legal.

Gambling has also taken on a new dimension as Indian reservations in the United States and Canada have opened bingo halls and casinos in nine provinces and 30 states. Of all the Canadian and U.S. jurisdictions, only Hawaii and Utah authorize no legal gambling. (Horse race wagering is permitted by Tennessee law, but there are at present no tracks in operation; hence 47 states and all the Canadian jurisdictions have some form of legalized gambling today.)

Riding the Crest of the Third Wave

Why does legalized gambling continue to spread? The most salient answer can be expressed in a single phrase: the economic imperative. There is a lot of money to be made in gambling; many people want in on the action, and governments want a share of the money, too. In addition to economic motivations, gambling also is spreading because there is a popular demand for gambling products. Actually, this factor is related to the economic imperative. If there were no demand for gambling, it would not be a lucrative business venture for anyone. The popular demand for gambling, however, does not push the issue to the top of political agendas and to success in legislative chambers or in referendum votes. Rather, it seems that the popular demand for gambling only eases the way for the economically motivated pushes of the cause. We will first take a look at the economic beneficiaries who are pushing for the legalization of more gambling.

Operators of gaming establishments can be especially well positioned if they can maneuver themselves into a monopoly position for even a brief period of time. Governments perceive that they can reap financial benefits from gaming as direct operators or as tax collectors. Other entrepreneurs benefit from just being near gambling establishments. These businesspeople can sell goods to establishments or gaming customers.

Although there is evidence to suggest that people are more willing to support legalization efforts than they were in the past, overwhelming public demand for legalization does not exist. In marketing terms, it might be appropriate to conclude that legalization is not being "pulled" by public demand. Rather, it appears that entrepreneurs are "pushing" the spread of gaming.

Game operators, whether legal or illegal, salivate when they recall the opening of the Resorts International Casino in Atlantic City on Memorial Day weekend in 1978. This was the only casino in Atlantic City then and indeed the only casino in the United States east of Nevada. Resorts International maintained a monopoly status for more than a year. People waited hours at the casino door while the fire marshal tried to monitor the surging crowds. But he was hardly successful. Gaming writer Ovid Demaris describes the action:

> Customers were jammed twenty deep at the tables, aisles and slot machines were jammed, the casino was blue with smoke. The noise level of the 900 slot machines, of gamblers exhorting their dice, and of music blaring from the cocktail lounge had reached a numbing crescendo, but no one wanted to leave. People with money clutched in their fists pushed and shoved and fought for a chance to get at a table. (Demaris 1986)

Before the first day of action ended, the casino had won over a million dollars from these "lucky" players. Within nine months, Resorts International paid for its entire $77 million capital investment (Smith 1986). Similar "feeding frenzies" of players greeted the opening of monopoly casinos for Montreal, Quebec, and Windsor and Niagara Falls, Ontario.

Such stories help foment entrepreneurial dreams in this industry. A common wishful thought is: "Oh, to just have a monopoly operation." Similar successes on Indian reservations encourage investors to enter contracts wherein they pay for all capital and operating expenses and allow the tribes to reap 60 percent of net profits for seven years. After that time the entire investment is transferred to the tribes. Hopes for extraordinary windfall profits caused operators who complain about the 6.25 percent gross win taxes in Nevada to eagerly apply for a monopoly license for a land-based casino in New Orleans that carried an 18.5 percent state tax levy along with a guarantee that the casino give the government at least $100 million a year.

The experience of many companies with gambling products over the past two decades has convinced the sectors of the economy with capital control that gambling represents a good investment. As banks, stock equity markets, and bond markets open to gambling investors, more entrepreneurs see the industry as a viable option. On Wall Street, gambling has become legitimate.

It has not been only the casino and games operators who have garnered major profits from gambling. Several companies have become very successful by supplying needed products to the industry. For instance, International Gaming Technology (IGT) pioneered the development of the video poker machine. With the spread of gaming in the 1980s and 1990s, this company has realized soaring profits. Its investors have seen stock prices double, split, and double again.

Similarly, Scientific Games has profited handsomely from the spread of lottery games into new jurisdictions. The company prints instant lottery tickets and manufactures other lottery supplies. The biggest company in its market, Scientific Games is well positioned to win contracts for its products when a new lottery is created. In 1984, the firm invested $2 million in a lottery campaign for California, but the company's efforts to win votes went beyond the mere investment of money. Scientific Games actually wrote the ballot proposition!

After the campaign was over, it was clear that only one company could meet the specifications set forth for suppliers in the ballot proposal: Scientific Games. In an effort to find rival companies, state officials extended the bidding period, but to no avail. Scientific Games won an initial contract worth $40 million to supply tickets during the first year of lottery operation.

In their effort to unilaterally "drive" the legalized gambling market, entrepreneurs have wielded a major force in the strategic equation. Just as manufacturers of other products push their merchandise by activating wholesalers and retailers, gambling interests mobilize politicians to obtain the legal support necessary. Political players may see legalization as beneficial to their personal careers, especially during times of economic stress. The 1980s and 1990s witnessed an array of economic crises in state and local governments. Jobs were lost to international competition and to falling prices in certain sectors of the economy, such as the oil industry. State tax bases were eroded. At the same time, a federal budget crisis led officials in Washington, D.C., to cut aid to state and local governments while demanding that states assume operational and financial control of both old and new programs. All this has occurred in tandem with general antitax sentiments on the part of the public. Voters are crying out, "Read our lips! We will pay no new taxes!"

Painless Tax

Stated simply, states need new revenues at a time when the public is unwilling to accept new tax measures. The standard federal option of permitting deficits to grow is not available to most states, which have constitutional provisions that demand balanced budgets. The option of drastically cutting state services is not politically feasible. Politicians who turn either to taxes or to major budget cuts generally find themselves on the defensive at reelection time. It is a dilemma with few appealing solutions, save for one: legalized gambling. With this alternative, government revenues can be enhanced, and public service programs can be maintained. Moreover, taxes do not have to be hiked—at least those levied directly upon voters. Governor Ann Richards of Texas put it succinctly: "It's a question of money. Either we get it from a lottery or we'll get it from a huge tax bill" (LaFleur 1991).

I will discuss the viability of raising revenue through gambling in a later section. It may be suggested that this is not an ideal solution to state and local fiscal crises, and it is understood that most politicians realize the limitations of relying too much on this revenue source, but it is a revenue source that has political acceptability. After all, a politician's major need is to buy time, and gambling helps by providing immediate help in resolving many of today's fiscal crises.

The appeals of gambling companies are made to politicians in many ways. Each month, Scientific Games purchases a full-page slick color advertisement on the back cover of *Gaming and Wagering Business Magazine*, the leading trade publication for the gaming industry. Throughout most of 1985, the advertisement featured a large map of the United States and a headline that read, WHAT IT COSTS YOUR STATE BY NOT JOINING THE LOTTERY MAJORITY. In the advertisement, each state without a lottery had a figure above it representing the amount of money lost by not instituting a lottery. The numbers used in the advertisement ranged from $14 million for Alaska to $480 million for Texas.

The advertisement apparently appealed to state officials. In truth, the numbers represented were quite conservative, as many states came to realize. But the ad was successful. Fifteen of the 28 states included have since established lotteries (Scientific Games 1985).

The Spread of Gambling

For many legalization efforts, the combination of entrepreneurial drive and sympathetic public officials is all that is needed for success. However, even where legislators and governors are free to make gaming decisions without voter endorsement, they appear reluctant to do so without some consideration of public attitude. As leaders have tested the waters of public opinion, a growing acceptance of gambling has been detected, specifically the notion that states should permit residents to freely participate in gambling activities.

The era of expanded legalized gambling has coincided with a trend toward increased permissiveness in society. There certainly is a connection between attitudes about lifestyle, sex, pornography—even abortion and occasional drug use—and attitudes toward gambling. The notion that government has no business in our bedrooms relates to the notion that government has no business telling us how to spend our leisure time and our own money as long as we are doing so without coercion or harm to others.

A snowballing effect occurs when numbers of jurisdictions endorse the legalization of particular forms of gambling. Figure 4.3 (see Chapter 4), a map showing the dates when states and provinces established lotteries, illustrates this. Similarly, the order in which midwestern states bordering the Mississippi River and its tributaries endorsed riverboat casino gaming provides a good example of the phenomenon. Jurisdictions imitate one another in hopes of preventing their neighbors from taking business away from them. Imitation also occurs when jurisdictional neighbors can observe gaming operations in a way that enables them to lose moral inhibitions regarding gambling. Such observance enables them to become familiar with regulatory frameworks and consequences.

The one time when a snowball did not get rolling was immediately after the Atlantic City casino legalization. Following that episode, neighboring jurisdictions were presented with a very negative picture of wide-open casino activity. The inability of the Atlantic City casinos to effectuate community renewal in terms of housing, jobs, and quality of life—accompanied by suggestions of organized crime involvement with political decision making regarding casinos and evidence of increased street crime—led neighboring officials to reject the promised benefits of casino gaming (Dombrink and Thompson 1990).

Throughout the 1980s, a number of jurisdictions rejected casinos while other locales succeeded in establishing lotteries. The negative consequences of lotteries and the negative aspects of limited casino gaming in mountain towns or on riverboats apparently have not been as easy to observe. The same public that appears to harbor apprehension about Las Vegas–style gaming seems to accept casinos if they are floated from local river docks or tucked unobtrusively away in mountain towns.

In sum, the times have ripened for the spread of gaming, and entrepreneurs appear to be at the ready to meet market demand with plenty of commercial ventures.

Government in the Gaming Enterprise

The gambling legalization crusade often receives acquiescence from a portion of the public that has come to believe that people win when they gamble. Gambling proponents and gambling entrepreneurs have a built-in advantage for their product. Customer service studies show time and again that people have a great propensity to complain when they experience a bad product or bad service, whereas if they experience a good product or good service, they tend to remain silent. On the average a person will tell 8 to 10 other people about bad products. Twenty percent will tell at least 20 other people. The person who has purchased a "lemon" of a car will spread the word; so will the person who has experienced a bad meal at a restaurant. Stories about good products, conversely, will be told to an average of 3 other people. It takes 12 good product stories to make up for the negative effects of word-of-mouth advertising about a single bad product situation.

This is the situation for almost all products. But there is one product about which losers stay strangely silent and about which it is the winners who eagerly spread the word. That product is gambling. Losers will not go around the office the next day and tell about their casino losses. They won't tell spouses, friends, or any others. Why not? It is embarrassing. They feel "stupid." Their friends might think that they are foolish to "throw away money" by gambling. However, everything is different if they win. They are heroes. People congratulate them on how "smart" they were to play that machine or that game. Spouses want to celebrate with them. They feel they are on top of the world. They enjoy a feeling of control. In a study of gambling in Latin America, I described the winners as experiencing a highly valued condition called machismo (Thompson 1991). The only way you can experience a feeling of machismo if you lose is to remain silent, as the macho never loses.

It is not too difficult to understand why some people want gambling opportunities to come to their communities. They want to win. A poor man on the streets of Detroit was asked about his opinion of the 1996 election that resulted in a favorable vote for casinos for his city. "Yes," he said, "it is about time that we in Detroit get a chance to win some money, too" ("Casinos Coming to Detroit" 1997). He truly felt that having a casino meant that the people of Detroit would be able to gamble and win. Why should he feel any different? He no doubt talks with people who have flown to Las Vegas or driven over to Windsor. What do they tell him? The losers tell him they had fun. The winners tell him they won money. No one tells him that they lost money. Word-of-mouth advertising has prepared people in the United States to be at least somewhat accepting of gambling.

Governments play a variety of roles that pertain to gambling. Five basic roles—from prohibition and toleration to regulation and actual management of gaming—are presented in the following sections.

Government Prohibition

Almost all governments at some time play the role of gambling prohibitor. Indeed, we can even find the following passage in the constitution of the state of Nevada, the sole jurisdiction in the United States that has established gaming as its primary industry: "No lottery shall be authorized by this State, nor shall the sale of lottery tickets be allowed" (Article IV, Section 24). Methods of enforcing gambling prohibition range from vigorous policing with special vice units to minimal concern—even de facto law enforcement toleration of illegal activity.

Legal prohibitions of gambling activity probably predate biblical times. In our own legal tradition they can be traced to the Middle Ages. Richard I of England prohibited gambling—except for royalty—in the twelfth century. Parliament passed the first law on gambling in 1388 (Rose 1986). The first English settlers in the North American colonies confronted a need to control gambling. In 1624, the Virginia House of Burgesses commanded that ministers should not spend their "tyme idelie by day or by night, playing dice, cards, or any unlawful game." In 1630, the Puritan Colony of Massachusetts Bay recognized that gambling was a problem for its population and ordered that "all persons whatsoever that have cards, dice, or tables in their houses shall make away with them before the next court under punishment of pain" (Berger and Bruning 1979).

Although gambling is a serious policy issue, prohibition efforts have at times entered the realm of the ridiculous. For instance, the Key West, Florida, city council passed a resolution making it illegal to bet on a turtle race, and Mirror Lake, New Hampshire, banned wagers on rat or mice fights. A North Dakota law once banned gambling while consuming pretzels and beer, and Corvallis, Oregon, determined that women could not gamble while having coffee. The town of Callicon, New York, stipulated that no gambling should take place in a barber's chair, and Lemon Springs, North Carolina, ruled that it was illegal to make wagers within four hours after eating onions or garlic.

Like the frivolous stipulations above, most jurisdictions have restricted only selected gaming activities. Only Utah and Hawaii have total bans on all gambling.

Government Toleration

Governments often play a second role—that of passive observer. In these cases, government sits on the sidelines and allows private social gambling without regulation or oversight. Under the common law of England—a body of court decisions that often were observed in the United States—gambling was permissible unless a legislative body had declared otherwise (Rose 1986).

Nonetheless, British authorities stopped the games when they became disorderly, and courts intervened if disputes arose between betting parties. In fact, considerable legal attention was devoted during the colonial period to lawsuits involving horse race gamblers. Early courts also were asked to assist gamblers in collection of money owed them by other gamblers, but in 1710 the English Parliament passed the Statute of Anne, which declared that gambling debts could not be collected through the courts. Since then, the issue of suing to recover winnings has been debated in many U.S. jurisdictions, but it was not until 1983 that Nevada elected to allow gambling collection through the courts (Rose 1986).

The role of silent observer remains an important one for government today. It was incorporated into the Indian Gaming Regulatory Act, passed by Congress in 1988. The law allows self-regulation by tribes on traditional Indian games, such as wagers on athletic contests. Another provision stipulates National Indian Gaming Commission regulation of bingo for two years, after which a tribe can be certified for self-regulation (if, of course, all has gone well during the preceding two years). Casino game regulation, however, was placed in the joint domain of states and tribes.

Most charity gaming in the United States remains self-regulated by operators, and the level of oversight for some forms of commercial gaming is limited to traditional law enforcement functions.

Minor Government Regulation

A third governmental role may involve legalized private gambling with minimal standards and regulatory procedures. For instance, operators may be required to have a permit and agree to certain rules, such as hours of operation and wager limits. Operators also may be required to file a report of their activities. Regulation of charitable bingo games and raffles often falls into this minimal level of activity—that is, when any regulation is required at all.

The regulation of slot machine gaming follows this pattern in some states where lotteries place the machines (called video lottery terminals, or VLTs) in private establishments. Computerized data systems account for the cash flow through the machines, but there usually is little additional oversight. VLT programs are advanced in the sense that they bring healthy revenues to governments and private entrepreneurs without the necessity of bureaucratic agencies to control them. The system of lottery ticket distribution is quite similar.

In Nevada, as detailed below, there is a well-developed system of government control over casinos. But because the number of regulators is relatively small, they focus nearly all their attention on the larger casinos of Las Vegas, Reno, Lake Tahoe, and Laughlin. Establishments in these towns have hundreds or even thousands of slot machines and scores of gaming tables. Regulators find themselves with little time for policing the nearly 2,000 restricted holders that operate 15 or fewer slot machines. Since these licensees pay fixed taxes on each machine, there is no need for government to track cash flow, and the state's main concern is that the machines are manufactured by companies that can assure properly functioning mechanisms.

Specialized Government Regulation

A fourth role of government is to administer detailed regulatory processes through special boards and commissions. These processes include the licensing of operators and employees, preceded by extensive background investigations; establishing the precise rules for each game played; careful ongoing monitoring of gaming activities with on-premise inspections by board or commission employees; detailed accounting of financial transactions involved in the gaming operations; and the collection of fees and specific taxes. North American governments that permit commercial casino gambling and wagering on horse and dog races typically follow this pattern of extensive regulation by specialized administrative units.

The philosophy of regulation can vary considerably in these situations. Nevada emphasizes control through internal casino management. The legislature has created a two-tiered structure with the full-time Gaming Control Board and the part-time Nevada Gaming Commission. The board conducts thorough background investigations on all license applicants and makes license recommendations to the commission. The commission makes the final decision on the application (Cabot and Rubenstein 1993).

The Nevada Gaming Commission does not maintain a staff. The Gaming Control Board staff, consisting of fewer than 100 field inspectors, is responsible for visits to over 2,000 gaming sites, including the major casinos plus all businesses offering slot machines only. A staff of board auditors monitors independent audits conducted for the casinos by accounting firms. This staff is large enough to conduct only a very few on-site spot audits. A tax division of the board collects gaming taxes and fees and transfers these to the state treasury. Except for application investigation fees, which are paid by the casinos, all regulatory costs incurred are financed out of the general state budget, as authorized by legislative appropriations.

The state also has provisions for a Gaming Policy Committee, which may offer advice to the legislature and to the commission regarding casino laws and regulations. However, this committee has rarely been called by the governor to meet (Gaming Control Board 1977).

New Jersey offers a contrasting model of casino regulation. A five-member Casino Control Commission, appointed by the governor, works beside the Division of Gaming Enforcement within the state attorney general's office. These two entities have large staffs and share functions. The division is responsible for investigating all license applications, reviewing casino operations with inspections and audits of books, and prosecuting regulatory violations in front of the commission. The division also makes license recommendations to the commission, which may conduct independent investigations before making final decisions. The commission is empowered to police casino operations. Its members are present in casinos at all times that gaming is being conducted. The commission also collects casino fees and taxes, assigns the costs of regulation to individual casinos, and collects these expenses as well (Lehne 1986). Either the commission or the division may initiate investigations into gaming conduct at any time.

Although Nevada requires licenses only for establishments, owners, and key employees as well as selected individuals in special cases, New Jersey requires them for each employee. The more intense, hands-on regulatory approach taken by New Jersey has come about because most New Jersey casinos began operations at about the same time (within three or four years of one another) within an atmosphere of suspicion and concern about organized crime. The contrasting approaches of the two states are reflected in regulation costs. In 1996, the New Jersey Commission and Division of Gaming Enforcement spent over $51 million to regulate 13 casinos in one city (Cabot 1996). Nevada's Gaming Control Board and Commission spent $18 million to regulate 351 unrestricted casinos (offering both slot machines and table games) and nearly 2,000 restricted casinos (15 or fewer slot machines) statewide. The Nevada board employed about 300 persons; New Jersey employed 700.

The costs of regulation are not borne entirely by the government agencies of these states. Many costs are shouldered by the casino establishments. It has been estimated that a major facility will incur costs of over $1 million in order to successfully apply for a casino license in Nevada. The regulatory process requires that many records be kept by the casinos. Circus Circus enterprises spends $1 million each year in record storage costs alone (Cabot 1996).

Horse racing operations also require close supervision and regulation. Almost all jurisdictions that allow such wagering have specialized racing commissions. These commissions approve applications of the "associations" that are created by track owners to organize betting. The commissioners also assign dates for races and collect license fees and revenues from betting pools. Commission staffs conduct financial audits and appoint stewards to oversee the integrity of the races. Horses are tested to assure that no illegal drugs influence the outcome of races (Day 1950).

Racing commissioners also rely upon other organizations to assist in track regulation. A National Association of State Racing Commissioners helps standardize rules among the states and exchanges information on racing participants. The American

Jockey Club is a private organization of horse owners and others who are interested in the breeding industry. The club publishes a detailed book, *Rules of Racing*, which is sanctioned by the commissions. The Jockey Club also manages what is called the *Stud Book*. This is a registry of all thoroughbreds eligible to run in horse races. The club and the track associations appoint stewards who, along with the state commission's stewards, monitor all races (Day 1950).

Government as Entrepreneur

A fifth role of government is that of entrepreneur. Governments own gambling operations and manage them as if they were private enterprises. The lotteries in 37 states and 10 provinces are all entrepreneurial government operations. Canadian provinces also run casinos. For instance, the Crystal Casino in Winnipeg is operated by the Manitoba Lottery Corporation, a branch of the Manitoba government's Ministry of Finance, and the Ontario Casino Corporation, entirely owned by the provincial government, owns and operates Casino Niagara and Casino Windsor. The Manitoba corporation runs bingo halls and a slot machine system throughout the province, as do several government corporations in other provinces. Nine provinces and a few states run networks of video lottery terminals through their lottery organizations.

The fact that gambling operations are actually run by governments has done much to allay public fears that games are dishonest or controlled by organized crime. Lotteries are considered a "clean," even "proper," means of collecting public revenues. Moreover, critics of gambling believe it is important to have direct public oversight for gambling to assure that operations meet public standards for propriety. As long as gambling operators themselves are public employees, this oversight control can remain strong.

Yet there are strong opponents to government-operated gambling. These detractors claim that government should not encourage gambling or, for that matter, any other commercial activity. As gaming operators, governments must eventually encourage participation in the activity, and there is potential for conflicts of interest and dishonesty. Cheating does occur in government casinos, and lottery operations have been compromised. Does government have the innate ability to close down its own tarnished revenue generators as it closes down dishonest private gambling enterprises? Probably not.

In 1979, the personnel conducting the drawing for the Pennsylvania lottery rigged the number on the daily game. A television commentator gained access to the Ping-Pong ball machine that was used for drawings. Along with others he weighted down balls so that only certain combinations of numbers could be drawn. The small group then circulated around the state and placed large bets on the possible combinations. One of the numbers was drawn. However, the group was discovered because several of their confederates did not use discretion when placing their bets. Word of the scheme got out, and government prosecutors gathered the evidence and successfully prosecuted several of the culprits. Several went to prison. All the members of the public who made losing bets the day of the scheme were cheated. They were cheated by government employees, by a government gambling operation. No money was refunded to the public, and the state of Pennsylvania did not miss a day in its daily drawings. The state acted as if nothing had happened, except that it did a better job of locking up the Ping-Pong ball machine in the future.

A major disadvantage of government-owned gambling operation is that the operations may require large initial capital investments. This is especially the case with casinos. Governments could find themselves at considerable risk by entering such ventures. Also, governments may be reluctant to invest the capital necessary to make operations viable. In the same light, governments that operate with civil service pay schedules may be hesitant to offer gaming executive salaries comparable to those earned by executives in the private sector. Hence, government may lose access to the best talent.

A final concern about government-sponsored gaming is the impact it has on law enforcement. Efforts to control illegal gambling can be weakened if citizens, police, prosecutors, and judges surrender to predispositions of government-generated "cleanliness." Indeed, defendants charged with illegal gaming may assert that their only crime is that they are engaged in competition with a government monopoly.

The issue of integrity in gaming enforcement is not confined to jurisdictions where the government "owns" the gaming operations. Independent oversight can also be compromised. Persons inside the gaming regulatory agencies can possibly favor certain gaming establishments in hopes of securing future employment. Casinos and race tracks do offer management salaries that are much larger than those offered by regulatory bodies. This "revolving-door" phenomenon of regulators joining gaming companies is not always a negative one, however. Over the course of the operations of the Nevada Gaming Board, board employees—for instance, inspectors and auditors—have been encouraged to join casino companies because the state wanted to be assured that the personnel within the gaming industry were very well acquainted with the specific and often complicated rules and regulations of gaming. Work with the regulatory board served as a training ground for the industry. Conversely, when a slot machine laboratory inspector used his position to learn about certain biases of certain machines and then became a gambler, this training ground exercise was certainly frowned upon. The inspector actually became a member of a gang of slot machine and keno game cheaters, and he was subsequently convicted of a felony and placed in the Black Book of persons banned from entry to all Nevada casinos (German 1997).

Independent regulation can also be compromised when owners of gaming establishments are large political contributors to gubernatorial and legislative campaigns. A general ban on such contributions by the industry could help assure that such compromises would not occur and that politicians would not expect contributions from gaming for assurances that negative regulations would not be passed. New Jersey bans contributions from the casinos to persons running for office. In Nevada, the casinos are certainly the largest political contributors to all campaigns. To be on the safe side, most of the casinos will make contributions to candidates of both major parties in the general election. The heaviest influence of political money from the industry is not in Nevada, however. Rather, it is in states that have yet to legalize certain forms of gambling or have yet to design all the regulations for that gambling. One "card club" in California made over a million dollars in contributions during three state legislative campaigns, ostensibly to preclude the legislature from passing a state regulatory law for card clubs. Whether or not that was the objective, the result was that the legislature had failed—as of early 1997—to pass such a measure.

Why Do People Gamble?

People have asked this question for centuries, and for centuries the answers were the same. People who gambled were deviants. By their activities they were violating the rules of civil society, the laws of the government, and the tenets of their religions. It was even commonly accepted that gamblers were possessed of criminal minds or were in some other way depraved or subject to evil spirits.

Although considerable scholarly attention is still given to the psychological and personality disorders of certain kinds of gamblers (usually pathological or compulsive), the notion that gambling is in and of itself deviant is now generally rejected. It is certainly rejected by those persons who study the industry today. Academicians who study gambling are now found in all parts of the university. The most prominent gaming scholars are now in departments of economics, as gambling is viewed to be a normal commercial activity. Other students of gaming are found throughout other departments in colleges of business. Political scientists (of which I am one) also give attention to the field, as do historians, sociologists, and a whole new (within the last generation) growing field of scholars who study recreation industries. The psychologists and the criminologists are still around, but they no longer dominate academic meetings that focus upon the subject of gambling.

Almost a parenthetical question is how gambling can be considered somehow abnormal or deviant when overwhelming numbers of adults engage in it. A 1974 study by the University of Michigan Survey Research Center revealed that 61 percent of the participants had gambled during the previous year. More than 80 percent indicated they approved of legalizing some form of gambling activity (Commission on the Review of the National Policy Toward Gambling 1976). By 1995, surveys indicated that the approval number was as high as 90 percent (Harrah's Entertainment, Inc. 1996; Mississippi State University Gambling Group 1995).

Recent studies show that the percentage of the population who had gambled in the previous year holds steady at just above 60 percent, but casino visits were increasing as more facilities were available. Over 24 percent had made a casino visit in a 12-month period before the survey (Mississippi State University Gambling Group 1995).

These gamblers come from all sectors of the population. They are male and female; rich and poor; Protestant, Catholic, and Jewish. They represent all races and educational levels. The gambling industry is expanding as more and more normal, responsible, rational human beings engage in it.

Since life is full of risks, the risks associated with gambling can also be viewed as elements of a "regular" existence. It has been so since the beginning of time, with every known society having gambling in one form or another. Many reasons can be given to explain why normal people gamble. Some of the reasons are rational; others are almost completely void of rationality.

Some people actually treat gambling as an investment. For them, gambling is a calculated technique for making money. These people are professional gamblers (Dombrink and Thompson 1990). The professional gambler seeks to discover ways to beat the odds—it is possible. Professionals at horse tracks carefully study the performance of horses and jockeys and examine the running times for various distances under various weather conditions at different times of the year. Armed with such information, these gamblers may actually gain an edge over the posted odds. Similarly, sports gamblers closely follow baseball, basketball, and football teams. They collect information regarding players' injuries, coaching styles, and performance trends in home or away games.

Professional poker players endeavor to cultivate betting and bluffing skills to their advantage. Proficiency with these skills, or a lack thereof, can indeed make "every hand a winner" or "every hand a loser," as Kenny Rogers sings in his popular song "The Gambler." Poker requires an intimate knowledge of card distribution and probability, but the true skill in poker comes in the ability to read other people. Professionals hone these skills through years of experience. Whereas the odds are fixed against every player in games like craps and roulette, players compete against one another in poker—a contest in which one player *has* to win.

Other professional gamblers are drawn to progressive jackpot games. Such jackpots are found with some casino slot machines or with government lottery games known as lotto. In lotto and at progressive slot machines, a portion of a player's loss is put into a jackpot each time the player loses. The jackpot thus grows until one player wins. When the jackpot reaches a certain amount, the odds actually begin to favor all the players. The odds of winning a million dollar jackpot, for instance, may be 2 million to 1. However, because of previous player losses, the jackpot may increase to $3 million while the odds remain at 2 million to 1. Logically and rationally, the chances for "good" bets have increased.

In one actual situation, an Australian group calculated that the moment the superlotto jackpot in Virginia exceeded $10 million, the odds favored the player. After the prize grew over $15 million, they made their move. Using computers they actually set about to purchase every possible combination of lottery numbers. However, they could only move so fast. By the time they had purchased only 8 million of 10 million available chances, the deadline for buying tickets arrived. Their chances of winning were 8 in 10.

As the odds were on their side, they did win. The prize was $23 million. Their real "luck" was that no other player also bought the winning combination. Had that been the case, their prize would have been divided, and their share would only have been $11.5 million. They were good calculating professionals. But their prize was not as good as it looked. Of course, they had to pay both federal and state income taxes, and the prize was paid out over a 20-year period. The prize actually represented the same return they could have received if they had purchased one of the better blue-chip stocks or mutual funds. The value of the prize equated to about an annual return of 13 percent on their investment. Good, but not phenomenal. The state of Virginia had no reason to complain about the activity of this group. However, many "regular" players did complain, so the state revised certain buying practices. Persons can no longer use computerized methods to purchase tickets.

Similarly, gangs of professional gamblers will sometimes virtually monopolize a casino floor, pulling handles on all the machines tied into the progressive jackpot. These teams will play the slots for hours—even days—until one of them wins the big jackpot.

Sometimes it may be economically rational to gamble even when the odds are stacked clearly against a player. Consider the value of $1 to a poor person. Can this dollar bill carry very much value at any specific time? A dollar cannot buy many groceries. It can't pay all the rent or purchase clothing or otherwise wield very much power to improve the quality of life in any discernible or lasting fashion. The loss of that dollar, therefore, would not be considered a major setback or even a noticeable event. But although a dollar means very little in these times, it still buys a poor person the chance to win $10,000 or $1 million or $100 million in a lottery. Any such prize would be a godsend for a poor person. Hence, some gambles, although not likely to bring the big prize, represent an exchange of something with little value for something else that potentially can be of a very high value. The specific odds in this case are quite irrelevant to the logic of placing the bet.

Although the poor usually lose in such games, lottery tickets give them dreams and hopes for a better existence. Some of these people may actually realize these dreams. Or they may win smaller prizes that can bring moments or short periods of great happiness.

Gordon Moody is a Methodist minister and founder of the Gordon House for problem gamblers in London. I had occasion to speak with him about the English lottery. Although I expected a critique of the government-sponsored game, Moody surprisingly referred to the lottery as "a bit of kindness" for the working-class poor. The lottery, he said, allowed poor people to dream of some-day having an automobile or a better apartment. "What other chance do they have?" Moody asked (Moody 1990).

For the middle class and the affluent, gambling can offer benefits not measurable in financial terms. Most gambling takes place in a social setting, usually outside the home, and therefore represents an opportunity to spend time with friends. This social benefit represents perhaps the greatest motivation for bingo players. Similarly, casino gaming is a popular recreation, taking place as it does in crowded, partylike settings, but even lotteries played in complete isolation can have social benefits. The drawing of a winning number is a shared experience. The very thought of the prize stimulates optimists to seek one another out to share dreams and plans. The game also contributes to community dialogue, which might otherwise be limited to the weather or last night's newscast. Indeed, a survey of California lottery players found that having fun was the reason half of them had purchased tickets.

Some players justify their gambling habits as a method of contributing to charity. Many bingo operations appeal to these kinds of sentiments, as do lotteries, which often market the game as an elemental financial component of some educational program, park project, or other noble cause.

The horse betting parlor is perhaps one of the most socially oriented institutions in the gambling world. For participants, the parlor becomes an attractive alternative to the monotony and boredom of their "regular" lives. In this escapist world, the gambler assumes new roles for brief moments or hours. No longer a parent, spouse, worker, or supervisor, he or she is stripped of outside social standing. New social standings are assigned to those players who win races or those who have valuable information on the next race. It is very much a temporary world—one that allows people to forget the conditions and problems of life (Rosecrance 1988).

Las Vegas operates on the notion that people need such an escape—a three- or seven-day vacation during which they can forget their tensions, regenerate their spirits, and forget business deals or other concerns. In gambling, the only deals that matter are the ones struck with cards or dice, and even though gambling can be very stimulating, it has a soothing effect on players. However, the excitement of the activity can be just as prevalent as the relaxation it brings, and the excitement of gambling is, in fact, usually given more emphasis in advertising. Gambling brings a psychological rush. It focuses the attention and makes the blood flow a little faster.

Gambling can also give some players a fleeting illusion of self-control. This is valuable to those whose lives are manipulated and programmed by forces beyond their influence. Whether the person is selecting a number for a lottery ticket or a number on a roulette wheel, the cognizance of making that choice independently is satisfying. The gambler can choose whether to play or not, how much to wager, which number to select, or which strategy to pursue.

Some players carry this illusion of control a step further. They feel they have a special mystique that allows them to beat the odds. Most of these personality types never contemplate the true mathematical odds, which do not favor them, and certainly the lotteries and casinos do not openly inform gamblers of their disadvantage. Still, for brief moments in the gambling world, delusions of self-control can offset the realities of a grimmer life, which more often than not is controlled by others.

My study of Latin American casinos revealed that male players use gambling as an arena for demonstrating machismo. Since Latin American society denies most men the perception that they are dominant or in charge, gambling becomes an outlet for assertiveness. When the gambler wins, he can strut to the admiration of others, who may start to place their own bets and demonstrate their own bravado (Thompson 1991). As indicated earlier, few people display behavior suggesting that they are losers.

Professor Felicia Florine Campbell (1974) suggests that gambling should be available to seniors in rest homes because so many of the elderly are trapped in boring, lonely routines dedicated almost entirely to physical preservation. She argues that the presence of slot machines would give residents something to look forward to or dream about, and gambling could increase the motivation of the elderly. She reports that in recent years, several large casinos catering to seniors have been established in Las Vegas, including Sam's Town, the Gold Coast, Arizona Charlie's, and the Santa Fe. These casinos provide buses to transport seniors to and from the gambling halls. A person walking through these establishments must keep an eye out for aged players in wheelchairs or with walkers or oxygen tanks. Indeed, even though slot machines do not exist in nursing homes, many seniors still do enjoy gambling excitement in casinos (Campbell 1974).

Critics of this marketing thrust toward elderly gamblers finger casino owners as crass profiteers who are taking advantage of senior citizens' desperation, boredom, and loneliness. Gambling, in fact, affects the psychological weaknesses of many kinds of

TABLE 1.1
Why People Gamble
(N = 937)

Reason	N	Percentage
To win money	473	50.5
For entertainment	313	33.4
For excitement	172	18.4
For curiosity	99	10.6
To socialize	89	9.5
For worthy causes	38	4.1
As a distraction	38	4.1
As a hobby	34	3.6

players—especially those who have little control over their wagering habits. These people can lose the ability to manage their finances while gambling and, in turn, the ability to support their families. In some cases they may turn to violent loan agents (loan sharks) or resort to criminal activities to fund their habit. This kind of activity can take them further and further down the road of self-destruction. At the extreme, some gamblers have even committed suicide.

Although there are many positive and even logical reasons for being a gambler, some compulsive players do lose sight of rationality. Estimates of the number of compulsive players in the gambling crowd range from 1 to 5 percent. Why do these people gamble so relentlessly? Explanations have drawn on Freudian personality analyses, learned behavior and reinforcement theory, and social experience models of behavior (see the section "Problem Gamblers" for a discussion of these explanations).

The prevalence of the various motivations so far described has been revealed in surveys. I participated in designing and analyzing a random telephone survey of 1,522 adults across the United States (Mississippi State University Gambling Group 1995). Of the respondents, 937 (or 61.6 percent) had made a wager during the previous 12 months. These respondents were asked to indicate why they gambled. They were given a list of reasons from which to chose, and they were permitted to choose one or several reasons. Over half indicated that "winning money" was a reason. The second most cited reason was "for entertainment." The answers are shown in Table 1.1.

Perhaps the survey points out an irony that does not bode well for gambling in the future. If most are playing in order to win, and in a collective sense winning is impossible, there may in the future be a player disillusionment that could translate into opposition to legalization.

Social and Religious Views of Gaming

Social Views

Three major surveys on gambling were conducted in 1974, 1982, and 1992. The Survey Research Center of the University of Michigan conducted the one in 1974 for a national commission on gambling policy. It found that 61 percent of the population had gambled during the previous year (Commission on the Review of the National Policy Toward Gambling 1976). Males were found to gamble more than females, whites more than nonwhites, highly educated players more than less-educated ones, and younger people more than older people. In addition, Catholics were identified as more likely to gamble than Protestants, Jews, Methodists, Baptists, and Fundamentalists.

A majority of the respondents favored bingo legalization (68 percent), horse betting (62 percent), and lotteries (61 percent). Fewer than half supported legalization of dog betting (49 percent), casinos (40 percent), and off-track betting (38 percent); fewer than one-third approved legalized sports betting (32 percent).

The second survey was commissioned by *Gaming Business Magazine* and conducted by the Gallup organization in August 1982 (Klein and Selesner 1982). During the eight intervening years between these two studies, casinos were authorized and opened in Atlantic City, and new lotteries were established in several states. In the second survey, a majority supported the legalization of most forms of gambling: bingo (74 percent), lotteries (72 percent), off-track betting (54 percent), and casinos in resort areas (51 percent). Only the legalization of betting on professional sporting events failed to win majority support (48 percent approving). In contrast to the 61 percent that indicated they gambled in the first survey, only 40 percent of the Gallup respondents said they had gambled during the previous year.

Another national poll sponsored by the Harrah's casino organization in 1992 found that 50 percent of the adult population had visited a casino at some time; 22 percent had made visits during the previous year. Respondents indicated entertainment as their primary motivation for gambling. Higher proportions of gamblers were found in the northeastern and western states than in the midwestern or southern states. Harrah's also pinpointed a solid majority of Americans (55 percent) who supported the view that gambling was "perfectly acceptable for anyone." Thirty-five percent indicated that gambling was "acceptable for others, but not for me." Only 10 percent said gambling should not be acceptable for anyone (Harrah's Entertainment, Inc. 1992).

Harrah's has continued to sponsor national surveys on gambling every year since 1992. In its most recent study, which covers gambling activity in 1995, Harrah's found that only 9 percent disapproved of all gambling for everyone. A Canadian survey taken at the same time found almost identical results. Sixty-one percent of the Canadian adults found gambling to be acceptable for everyone, whereas only 10 percent found it unacceptable for everyone (Harrah's Entertainment, Inc. 1996). Harrah's found that an equal proportion of males and females participated in casino gambling, that the median age of the casino gamblers responding to the telephone survey was 47, and that the median household income was $39,000.

I participated with a team from Mississippi State University in designing and executing a national telephone survey in early 1995. The results confirmed many of the Harrah's findings. Seventeen percent responded that "gambling is wrong," yet only 11 percent felt that casino gambling was "not acceptable for anyone." Even with this seemingly strong evidence in support of gambling, the respondents were quite hesitant about having casinos in or near their communities. Respondents were asked to indicate the desirability of various kinds of projects with some economic development potential for their communities. They clearly ranked prisons, chemical plants, and industrial waste sites as the least desirable facilities. Dog and horse tracks were the next "least" desirable facilities. Casinos and paper mills ranked equally at the next more desirable level. However, the casinos trailed the midgroup of military bases, then sports stadiums, and then hotels in desirability. The most desirable facilities in ascending order were golf courses, shopping malls, and discount stores (Mississippi State University Gambling Group 1995).

The results of the rankings were somewhat consistent with those found in a Las Vegas study of the desirability of casinos in neighborhoods as compared with other facilities. Casinos were considered more desirable than sewer plants, nuclear waste transportation routes, military bases, industrial areas, and railroads but less desirable than heavily traveled streets, schools, freeways, restaurants, parks, and shopping centers—in that order (Thompson et al., 1993).

Actual election returns indicate that voters are indeed becoming more permissive. Public lottery propositions now nearly always win approval, and support for other forms of gambling, although mixed, is increasing. Prior to 1988 (with the exception of a 1976 New Jersey vote), all campaigns for casinos failed, but since South Dakota approved limited casino gaming for the town of Deadwood in 1988, successful referendum campaigns for casinos have been waged in Colorado (1990), Missouri (1992 and 1994), and Michigan (1996). The Michigan vote was for three unlimited stakes land-based casinos within the city of Detroit. Arizona voters also approved a proposition in 1996 that mandated that the governor negotiate agreements so that more Indian reservations could have casinos. To be sure, the 1990s have also seen popular rejections of casino propositions. In 1994, voters said no to casinos in Florida, and they gave the same response to proponents of casinos in Ohio and Arkansas in 1996. In every election since 1990, Colorado voters have rejected propositions that would have expanded the number of towns allowed to have casinos in that state. (See Table 4.5 in Chapter 4.)

Public support for gaming is also evidenced in the increasing numbers of legislative endorsements of gambling. Casinos have been accepted by legislatures in Iowa (1989), Illinois (1990), Mississippi (1991), Louisiana (1992), and Indiana (1993). The provincial governments of Ontario, Quebec, Manitoba, Saskatchewan, and Nova Scotia have also approved casino gaming. Although these propositions have normally incorporated gaming limitations of some kind (numbers of games, the size of bets, numbers and locations of casinos), they do illustrate a new public willingness to embrace gambling.

As the uninitiated receive more exposure to gambling near their hometowns, they may cast off old inhibitions and sample the activity themselves. If they find gambling to be entertaining, positive attitudes and permissiveness may grow even more. The surveys cited above have found greater acceptance of gaming in regions where there is more of it, specifically the northeastern United States and the West.

Elections and legislative campaigns reveal more than just the popular view of gambling. Political maneuvering and lobbying are orchestrated by powerful interests with considerable financial resources. Many campaigns for casinos and lotteries are well supported by gaming industry companies, whereas opposition groups often tend to coalesce around church organizations and ad hoc civic groups that have limited funding.

Church interests spent $22,000 in an effort to defeat casinos in New Jersey in 1976, whereas casino supporters spent over $1.3 million to turn votes in their favor. A single company, Resorts International, contributed the largest share of funding—over $200,000. This helped the firm win the state's first casino licenses and windfall profits that exceeded $100 million before a second casino was licensed to compete with them. Likewise, Colorado casino supporters outspent their opponents nearly 75 to 1. Many of the proponents were able to cash in on their campaign investments by either winning licenses for casinos or selling land to casino developers (Dombrink and Thompson 1990).

The campaign for a California lottery was supported by a $2 million donation from a supply company that subsequently won a $40 million contract to furnish instant lottery tickets. This contribution certainly turned out to be a good business investment. Conversely, churches and civic organizations can achieve moral victories but are not likely to reap financial rewards if they are successful in halting gambling propositions. It certainly is not realistic for them to expect more plate donations, as their appeals for campaign money have probably exhausted their parishioners' and constituents' resources.

The greatest amount of casino money put into a referendum campaign was the $17 million the industry devoted to passage of the casino proposition in Florida in 1994. Indeed, this was the largest sum of money ever spent in a referendum campaign in the United States. It was also an unsuccessful campaign.

Money and the expectation of financial reward drive gambling movements. In the process, the public can find itself a pawn or even a passive partner. People may not want gambling, but they may discover that they desire additional tax burdens even less. Gambling, when presented in a positive light with unchallenged advertisements, can be sold as the lesser of two evils—consequently being positioned to win public approval, although this result does not always follow.

Religious Views

Patterns of public attitude toward gambling also have religious dimensions. The 1974 University of Michigan survey suggested that gambling was legal in some states and not in others because of religious dynamics (Commission on the Review of the National

Policy Toward Gambling 1976). Personal attitudes on gambling are no doubt formed to a certain degree by religious principles. Since the dawn of civilization and the most rudimentary emergence of religion, the pious have been concerned with gambling. Although the activity has been recognized dogmatically as a sin, religious organizations nevertheless tend to incorporate gambling into their agendas. Only a small part of the religious community advocates a wholesale condemnation of gambling, and most faiths take the view that the activity is not harmful with proper control and moderation.

There have been many rationales for religious censure of gambling. Some doctrines maintain that individuals should seek purity and perfection as a ticket to salvation and heaven. These religions view gambling as a sin that detours the participant from the path of cleanliness and righteousness. This view holds that gambling unearths wanton feelings, a desire for worldly goods, and inattentiveness to the work ethic. The religious may feel that gambling destroys a person's sense of responsibility or ability to care for and support loved ones. They assert that gambling diverts one's personal attentions to God and consumes time that could be spent in serious contemplation of prayer and ritual.

Religious doctrine also morally condemns gambling as a form of stealing. Gambling winners, so some church leaders argue, gain property from gambling losers without giving back something valuable in exchange. The gambler is viewed as disrespectful to the material domain of others and to the prerogatives of God. Some faiths may reason that personal property ownership does not actually exist because, in truth, all belongs to God. Mortals are thought to be only leasing pieces of a deity's estate— and one clause in that lease is that mortals be good stewards of the property. Gambling, these religions submit, is not a responsible method of housesitting in God's world. In such a moralistic context, a religion may view people who engage in wagering as literal thieves.

Church elders say that by participating in gambling, we trifle with God's plan for the universe. These doctrines assert that fortune is the sole prerogative of God. Gambling denigrates God's options and scoffs at his control over our destiny. Several variations of such religious themes arise in different religious organizations. We also can find discussions of gambling in the mythologies and rituals of many faiths. These passages depict battles between God and Satan as the chief determinants of the fate of gambling.

Still, a litany of religious organizations approves of forms of play that resemble the play in gambling. Historical records of some faiths portray leading figures turning to lotteries or dice rolling to determine the proper decision to make at a critical time. Certainly in the modern era, many faiths have utilized lottery forms (typically raffles and bingo games) as ways in which to make money to support their worthy ventures, and proceeds from these games are usually earmarked for more traditional church purposes.

Biblical References

A majority of Americans are tied through family and culture to faiths of Judeo-Christian origin. It may be instructive to examine biblical references of these faiths to gambling.

Although the Bible contains no explicit condemnations of gambling, even in the Ten Commandments, the following passage from Isaiah in the Old Testament (65:11–12) comes very close: "But you who forsake the Lord who set a table for fortune and fill cups of mixed wine for destiny, I will destine you to the sword, and all of you shall bow down to the slaughter."

In Proverbs (13:11), it is suggested that winnings from gambling activity are ephemeral: "Wealth hastily gotten will dwindle, but he who gathers little by little will increase it." Other scriptures suggest that gambling may be wrong because it represents covetousness or stealing, which is directly condemned (Exodus 20:15, 17).

Many biblical passages that refer to the use of lottery drawings defer judgment over the activities. Rather, they collectively make an impartial acknowledgment of the use of the gambling-like activities for various purposes. The Old Testament in several places presents the lottery as a mechanism to determine the desires of God. High priests used a lottery technique called Urim and Tummin to make decisions (Exodus 28:30; Leviticus 8:7–9). Sailors turned to the drawing of lots to determine who among them had sinned and caused inclement weather. In one familiar biblical story, the results pointed to Jonah, who was cast overboard (Jonah 1:7–8). Saul was chosen by drawing to be king (1 Samuel 10:20–21), and David was instructed in a drawing which way to go to take command of his troops (2 Samuel 2:1). Soldiers were selected for battle by lottery (Judges 20:9), and lotteries were used to divide lands, select the first residents of Jerusalem (Nehemiah 11:1), and select animals for sacrifice on the day of atonement (Leviticus 16:7–10).

The New Testament contains additional lottery references. For instance, a twelfth disciple (Mathais) was chosen to replace Judas by means of a drawing (Acts 1:21–26). Another notable story refers to the Roman Centurions who rolled dice for the robes of Christ at the crucifixion (Matthew 27:35). This is one of the rare cases where lottery-type gambling is presented in the Bible as a means for selfish gain, and in this context, the activity has to be considered very negative. In all other biblical references, lotteries are used for serious purposes rather than simply for recreational games.

Christian

With the mixed body of biblical evidence, some Judeo-Christian denominations categorically repudiate all gambling, whereas others adopt the opposite view—that gambling in and of itself is not sinful. These views are connected to two general schools of ethics: the teleological or worldly view and the deontological or universal view.

Teleological ethics seeks to examine a particular activity and asks whether the activity results in positive or negative results. This system of thought has parallels in the notions of positive law and subscribes to the notion that it is the prerogative of humans to understand when an activity is right or wrong, beneficial or harmful, and when to regulate it. In recent years, the term "situational ethics" has become attached to the teleological perspective. Certain fundamentalist groups term the teleological approach one of "secular humanism." Those who hold to this viewpoint regard some gambling as permissible and some as sinful, depending on its context.

The deontological or universal system of ethics maintains that gambling and other "sinful" activity is wrong at all times and under all conditions. This system has parallels in natural law, or the law that is thought to be God given, absolute, and eternal.

Churches need not be consistent on their treatment of sin. Religious doctrine, whatever its ultimate source, is interpreted and translated by many over the centuries. Consistency is difficult for the individual, no less entire groups, no matter how divinely inspired they believe their position to be. Catholic doctrine has a decidedly natural law and deontological orientation, but on the issue of gambling the Catholic Church falls very much into the teleological camp. This is not to suggest that Catholics fail to recognize problems in gambling behavior. L. M. Starkey writes in *Money, Mania, and Morals* (1964) that "Catholic moralists are agreed that gambling and betting may lead to grave abuse and sin, especially when they are prompted by mere gain. The gambler usually frequents bad company, wastes much valuable time, becomes adverse to work, is strongly tempted to be dishonest when luck is against him, and often brings financial ruin upon himself and those dependent upon him."

The argument is not complete without consideration of the issue of freedom. As *The New Catholic Encyclopedia* (1967) states, "A person is entitled to dispose of his own property as he wills so long as in doing so he does not render himself incapable of fulfilling duties incumbent upon him by reason of justice or charity. Gambling, therefore, though a luxury, is not considered sinful except when the indulgence in it is inconsistent with duty."

Catholic Church doctrine considers as sinful that person who gambles with someone else's money or with money needed for the support of others. The church also condemns gambling when it becomes compulsive or disruptive to family and social relationships. Moreover, the freedom to gamble implies a knowing freedom to enter into a fair and honest contract for play. Cheating at gambling is considered wrong, as are all dishonest games.

The church also judges gambling according to its consequences. When results are favorable, gambling may be viewed as worthy of promotion. An example of this is the limited-stakes bingo games that are conducted inside the church for purposes of raising funds for schools or hospitals.

When considering their position on gambling legalization, church leaders want to know if the activity places disadvantages on poor people, results in pathological behavior, or is monitored to ensure honesty. Since the status of these criteria varies from situation to situation, the church has supported some public referenda while opposing others.

Starkey offers a summary of the Catholic—teleological—approach to gambling in this 1962 statement from a Roman Catholic Bishop in England: "It is always a great sorrow to me that we have to use such undignified means of raising money as bingo and the pools. But let us make it clear that we shall use these methods—and even more undignified ones—so long as they are this side of honesty and so long as we need the money for our schools" (Starkey 1964, p. 101).

The Church of England and its offspring, the American Episcopal Church (essentially reformed Catholic organizations), both accept the general Catholic approach toward gambling.

Most Protestant denominations, as well as Baptists, Mormons, and Jehovah's Witnesses, categorically oppose gambling as

a sinful recreation. Gambling is wrong all the time. This deontological or absolute ethical perspective is reflected in many official
church statements. The Social Principles of the United Methodist
Church proclaim that

> Gambling is a menace to society, deadly to the best
> interests of moral, social, economic, and spiritual life,
> and destructive of good government. As an act of faith
> and love, Christians should abstain from gambling and
> should strive to minister to those victimized by the
> practice. Community standards and personal lifestyles
> should be such as would make unnecessary and unde-
> sirable the resort to commercial gambling, including
> public lotteries, as a recreation, as an escape, or as a
> means of producing public revenue or funds for sup-
> port of charities or government. (General Conference of
> the United Methodist Church 1984)

The Southern Baptist Convention is the largest non-Catholic
denomination in the United States. Their director of family and
moral concerns told the Commission on the Review of the National Policy Toward Gambling much the same story:

> In all its resolutions, the Southern Baptist Convention
> has rejected gambling. Obviously, some forms of gam-
> bling are more serious than others, but all forms have
> been consistently rejected in Southern Baptist statements
> and resolutions. The use of gambling profits for worthy
> activities has not led Southern Baptists to endorse gam-
> bling. The availability of gambling tempts both the
> reformed gambler and the potential gambler to destruc-
> tion. For the entire community, gambling is disruptive
> and harmful. Thus, concerned citizens should work for
> laws to control and eliminate gambling. (Bell 1976)

The Salvation Army opposes gambling, and the Church of
Jesus Christ of Latter-day Saints (Mormons) has been vehement in
maintaining its disapproval. In 1925, church president Heber J.
Grant proclaimed: "The Church has been and now is unalterably
opposed to gambling in any form whatever. [A]ll members of the
Church [are urged] to refrain from participation in any games of
chance or risky speculation" (Grant 1926).

An interesting side issue arose in the Mormon Church recently
over temple privileges. Mormon Church members must be in good

standing in order to enter temples, but Mormons who work in gambling establishments or in gambling-related jobs can be denied entry. When the church decided to build a temple in Las Vegas (about 10 percent of the Las Vegas population are Mormons), the number of members holding jobs in casinos prompted a review of policy. Church leaders decided that casino workers who did not personally gamble and did not overtly encourage others to do so could retain good standing status along with temple privileges as long as they met other church obligations.

Although many churches maintain their total opposition to gambling, they, like the Church of Jesus Christ of Latter-day Saints, show some willingness to adjust to the fact that gambling activity permeates society in many ways. In my 17 years of participation in a United Methodist congregation in Las Vegas, I have never heard a condemnation of gambling from the pulpit. The only time that gambling has been the subject of a formal speech in the church building, I have been the one giving the speech, and my approach has been closer to the teleological Catholic approach than the traditional Methodist approach. Moreover, whenever the congregation wishes to have a special dinner that cannot be handled by the kitchen facilities of the church building, the dinner is held in a casino's banquet facilities. Although no casino chips appear in the offering plate, many members of the congregation derive their livelihood from work in the gambling industry.

I had an opportunity to be in New Orleans in 1993 and attended a press conference organized by then governor Edwin Edwards. Edwards was soliciting public support for the legalization of a casino for downtown New Orleans. He was boasting that the casino would bring 25,000 jobs to the community. He was also trying to neutralize opposition coming from an African American alliance of Baptist and fundamentalist ministers—persons who held fast to the deontological position on gambling. Edwards gave the stage to one of the ministers. The pastor of an inner-city church began his talk with a rousing condemnation of gambling. Over and over he said, "Gambling is disgraceful, I hate gambling." Then he finally paused and said, "I am tired of having to fight gambling, but I am more tired of picking up dying children who I find on the streets because of drugs or violence, because they could not get jobs, because their parents could not get jobs. If this casino means jobs, and if it means that I will not have to pick up any more dying children, I won't hate gambling any the less, but I can't oppose this casino."

Jewish

Religious principles in the Jewish faith are interpreted and applied through tenets derived from Jewish scripture and other religious works, such as the Torah. Rabbis, or religious scholars, are trained to interpret the religious law, much as Supreme Court judges are trained to interpret constitutional law.

Jewish law has changed and grown over time and is subject to a variety of interpretations, so rabbinical scholars have offered many interpretations of gambling throughout history. Today, there is no singular Jewish view of gambling, but there is a trend toward the teleological orientation. Jews certainly do not universally condemn gambling, but the constant state of disagreement that exists in Jewish intellectual circles ensures a plethora of opinions. One legal interpretation, for example, disqualified two types of gamblers—dice players and pigeon racers—from standing as witnesses in court. A rabbi maintained that these gamblers were committing theft by accepting winnings, but another scholar disputed this, arguing that only the habitual gamblers should be disqualified, and the disqualification should derive not from the indictment of gamblers as thieves but rather because the activity does not further the "betterment of society" (Jacobs 1973).

Another rabbi said it is permissible to participate in gambling when the "stakes are placed on the table" but never in games where players incur debt. Jewish moralists have endorsed lotteries as acceptable so long as lottery winners realize their good fortunes are a blessing from God. Other Jewish communities, however, disdain the "get-rich-quick" attitude connected with lottery playing and prohibit participation, even while admitting that ancient Jewish law doesn't forbid gambling. These thinkers view gambling as a route to financial ruin and family deterioration (Jacobs 1973).

Political groups within the Jewish faith have issued aggressive denunciations of gambling. A resolution of the Central Conference of American Rabbis called upon its members to discourage their congregations from using gambling for fund-raising. The group said the use of lotteries, off-track betting, or any other form of gambling promoted by government agencies to raise revenues is deplorable and called upon fellow Jews "to provide counsel for compulsive gamblers and their families" (*Resolution of Central Conference of American Rabbis* 1986).

The United Synagogue of America has vigorously opposed the legalization of bingo games for charitable purposes. They have held that raising money for religious purposes is in and of itself a religious activity that must not be defiled by gambling. In 1960, a Brooklyn, New York, congregation was expelled from the association of synagogues for allowing bingo games to be used for religious fund-raising (Starkey 1964).

These contemporary views seem to belie Jewish history. Gambling has long been part of Jewish tradition and culture and is often tied to religious celebrations. On the holiest Jewish holiday of Yom Kippur, one story relates, Aaron took two goats to the temple. There, one of them was selected by lottery to be sacrificed to atone for the sins of the Jewish people. The other goat was sent off to the wilderness. Then there is the ritual of Urim and Tummin referred to earlier. The ritual was used by high priests to help them make decisions. In this practice, two small stones were wrapped with papers on which different decisions to a question were recorded. One of the stones would then be randomly drawn from the priest's breastplate.

About 2,500 years ago, a Persian king arranged to massacre the Jewish people and selected the day for the attack with a roll of dice. However, the day chosen turned out to be a bad day for such a campaign, and the Jewish people escaped. The dice apparently had favored them, and a Jewish holiday known as Purim was established to celebrate the lucky day with merrymaking and gambling. Hanukkah, too, is seen as a lucky day because of its connection to the story of Jewish survival with the assistance of a single oil lamp. A theme of Hanukkah is that faith can bring much from little. Thus, the lamp celebration is held on Hanukkah, which is also known as "the New Year's Day for gamblers" (Linn 1986).

Notwithstanding the many indulgences in gambling on these holidays, Jewish law and Jewish authorities still frown on the practice. Throughout history Jewish leaders have regarded the professional gambler as an outcast—"he is a thief and plays no part in the betterment of society" (Jacobs 1973). The gambler is "untrustworthy" and "wastes time in idleness." It has been thought that time spent gambling is lost from study and productivity (Werblowsky and Wigoder 1966).

At times these scholars have even interpreted disasters such as storms and pestilence as punishment for gambling. Accordingly, gambling has been banned, save for the above-mentioned holidays. Even then, gambling gets a nod of approval only if players do not participate for selfish gain. Winning players are expected to donate moneys to charity (Linn 1986).

Islamic

In the year 610, a story goes, the Prophet Muhammad was approached by an angel who revealed to him the Word of God. The Word of God was transcribed as the Koran, Islam's most holy book. Muhammad spent the next 22 years of his life traveling and teaching the Word. The Word prescribed the methods of living a holy life, and Muhammad directed his own actions accordingly. His life and the Koran serve as benchmarks for a faith now followed by nearly a billion people in North Africa, the Middle East, and Asia.

The Koran and Islam take a very negative view of gambling. The following passages are found in the Koran:

> They will ask you about wine and maysir [a gambling game]: In both is a great sin as well as some uses for people. The sin is greater than their usefulness. (Sura 2:219)
>
> Only would Satan sow hatred and strife among you, by wine and games of chance, and turn you aside from the remembrance of God, and from prayer; will ye not, therefore, abstain from them? (Sura 5:90–93)

Islam regards gambling as "unjustified enrichment" and the process of "receiving a monetary advantage without giving a countervalue." Evidence presented by gamblers is not admissible in an Islamic court, and anyone in the faith who receives gambling proceeds is obligated to donate them to the poor. Gambling is generally placed in the category of amusement, and Islamic jurists have ruled that "every amusement is worthless frivolity if it distracts from obedience to God" (Rosenthal 1975). If a person allowed the "time for prayer to pass without praying, because he is engrossed in the game, it indicates disrespect for his duties" (Rosenthal 1975).

There are a few exceptions in the Islamic religion to the prohibition on gambling. Wagering is permitted for horse racing because such betting was historically an incentive for military training. By participating in racing, the faithful Islamic maintained not only his fitness but the readiness of his steed so that both could answer when called to fight infidels in the holy wars. Similarly, betting was permitted on shooting contests, and prizes could be given for winners of competitions involving Islamic law and religion. Such prizes, even if given in the context of wagering, provided additional incentives for the adherents of Islam to be worthy and faithful (Schacht 1964).

Hindu

The philosophy and ethics practiced by Hindus dominate much of India and the subcontinent of South Asia—a region populated by a billion people. Hinduism is the oldest living religion and is quite dynamic, growing more with the new teachings of Hindu masters and gurus. Hindus worship a litany of gods, often in the form of physical statues or idols, and acknowledge them for various purposes. The religion has no single founder, no central organization, and no leader. It also has no single book of doctrine. Rather, a series of books conveys interpretations of what the Hindu gods demand and collectively espouses a few central precepts. Moral beliefs are referred to as the dharma of Hinduism.

One basic Hindu conviction is that people must renounce the world and withdraw in order to obtain liberation. Different people can choose different paths to reach liberation. Hinduism is a religion that espouses that liberation and death can lead to rebirth in a higher class or social status. Eventually, the faith holds, righteous believers can ascend to a godlike status and achieve Nirvana. However, those who are bad or who lead worldly lives without seeking liberation are punished with reincarnation in lower social class or life-form—even that of an animal.

The dharma of Hinduism as expressed in Hindu books contains many references to gambling. The mythology of the faith discusses the gambling play of Hindu gods that, when speaking to Hindu mortals, admonish against gambling. In the early Vedic era, epic poems were recorded in the *Rig Veda*. One was called the "Hymn of the Gambler" or "The Gamester's Lament." In it, the god Savitr warns against gambling (Bashman 1967):

> She did not scold me, or lose her temper
> She was kind to my friends and me
> But because of a throw two high by one
> I have rejected my loving wife.
>
> Her mother hates me; my wife repels me
> A man in trouble finds no one to pity him
> They say, "I've no more use for a gambler
> than for a worn-out horse put up for sale."
>
> The dice are armed with hooks and piercing,
> they are deceptive, hot and burning, like children
> they give and take again, they strike back at their
> conquerors. They are sweetened with honey through
> the magic they work on the gambler.

> The gambler grieves when he sees a woman,
> another man's wife, in their pleasant home.
> In the morning he yokes the chestnut horses [dice]
> In the evening he falls by the hearth, a beggar.
>
> Don't play with dice, but plough your furrow!
> Delight in your property, prize it highly!
> Look to your cattle and look to your wife,
> you gambler! Thus noble Savitr tells me.

Since knowledge was regarded as one of the paths toward liberation, Hindu students received special treatment in the law. They were also warned not to gamble and indoctrinated with the belief that those who do gamble will die young and "go to Hell"—an uncomfortable purgatory-like existence—while awaiting rebirth in a more miserable condition (Hopkins 1924). Hinduism lifts this prohibition for adults but disallows cheating. Adults are allowed to enter the historic gambling halls of kings, who were warned, but allowed, to gamble. The Laws of Manu advise kings that gambling is one of the most "pernicious" of the royal vices (*Encyclopedia of Religion* 1928). The divine Krishna added that gambling was the worst "desire-born" vice.

In the Vedic era, repentant gamblers sought out heavenly nymphs who themselves gambled and begged forgiveness (Hopkins 1924).

Under Hindu law, gamblers are disqualified as legal witnesses and owing to their "depravity" are considered "thieves and assassins"—people in whom "no truth can be found." Hindu law books indicate that gambling is among the most serious of vices and renders a person impure. Furthermore, it is taught that "the wealth obtained by gambling is tainted" (*Encyclopedia of Religion* 1928).

Buddhist

Siddhartha Gautama was born into a rich Nepalese family in 568 B.C. and led a young life of relative leisure. However, when he was 29 years old, he experienced a series of visions that led to events that eventually brought the Buddhist religion to more than a billion people in South Asia and China. Gautama's three images—an old man, a sick man, and a dead man—convinced him that the world was full of suffering. He also saw a vision of a wandering holy man and became convinced that he, too, would have to wander in order to find the path leading out of suffering.

Gautama cast off his life of leisure and left his family in search of truth. At first he was convinced he would have to live an existence of poverty and self-denial. His initial lack of success led to despair and meditation, but in time Gautama came to know the enlightenment for which he quested. With this enlightenment he became the Buddha—the one filled with truth—and began to preach to others about the Middle Path. This path lay between total self-denial, with its rejection of the world, and a noncontemplative worldly life. For five decades the Buddha traveled through Nepal and India attracting followers, establishing temples, and instructing people about the Middle Path.

Buddha taught that the world was burdened with suffering as a result of desire. If we desire and are not satisfied, he said, we know the suffering of frustration, but if we do achieve our wants and are satisfied, we shall only begin to desire more and will become preoccupied with fears that others will take our achievements away. We suffer in cycles that persist from birth to death and then again through new births and new deaths. These cycles can only be broken with enlightenment. A person who has reached enlightenment, or the level of a Buddha, can ascend to a state of Nirvana, which is a condition of utter happiness and peace. With death, then, such a person arrives in a heavenlike resting place.

Buddha and others who reached enlightenment gave many instructions about the Middle Path. The Buddha first had to achieve an existence of perfect virtue. The ten "perfections" of the Buddhas included generosity, self-sacrifice, morality, renunciation, wisdom, energy, forbearance, truthfulness, resoluteness, loving kindness, and equanimity (Spiro 1982). These perfections were obtained through a rejection of worldly passions and an embracing of good deeds.

The instructions for the Middle Path required attention to the Noble Eightfold Path: knowledge of the truth, intentions to resist evil, saying nothing to harm others, respecting life and morality, holding a job that doesn't hurt others, freeing the mind of evil, controlling feelings and thought, and practicing proper forms of concentration ("Buddhism" 1978).

The path to enlightenment could be blocked by frivolous and sinful actions. Participation in gambling activity only served to lead one away from the Middle Path. Since gambling heightens passions and desires, it is to be avoided. In one account of Buddha's instructions, the Parabhava Sutta, the addictions to dice, strong drink, and women are listed among the "means whereby men are brought to loss." In the Tevijja Sutta, monks, who closely followed Buddha, were warned that spectacles, games, contests using animals, and dice are addictive distractions that destroy virtue (*Encyclopedia of Religion* 1928).

Buddhist laymen are instructed to avoid six things that are said to contribute to loss of virtue: liquor, feasts, bad companions, laziness, "walking in the streets at untimely hours," and gambling (Morgan 1956).

Buddhism, like Hinduism, observes many gods, but Buddhist gods have a functional purpose of steering devout followers in the right direction. These gods are people who have achieved enlightenment during their time on earth, and unlike the gods of Hindu mythology, they continue to lead their lives as models for others to emulate. Part of this model behavior includes abstinence from gambling.

Shinto

The Shinto religion of Japan emerged after hundreds of years of contact with Buddhism. In many senses Shinto beliefs and practices are amalgamations of Buddhism and other Eastern systems of religious thought, including Confucianism. Many of the gods worshipped in Shinto temples are also Buddhist gods. Shintoism was different in that it nearly became a state-sanctioned religion when it took on very nationalistic characteristics in the 1800s. This occurred partly because the emperor of Japan was considered a descendant of the Sun God. Also, unlike Buddhism, in Shintoism gods were considered entities that could help the Japanese achieve worldly goods and desires. Nevertheless, many Buddhist precepts remain embedded in Shintoism, and gambling is condemned by the religion as an activity that diverts one from the path to virtue and righteousness.

Pros and Cons of Legalized Gambling

Legal campaigns to win approval for various forms of gambling are usually argued around three basic issues: economics, crime, and compulsive behavior. Moral issues such as those outlined in the preceding section do not generally dominate contemporary discussions of gambling, although they were very important at one time as a roadblock to legalization. On the other side of the ledger, gaming proponents may advance the "freedom" issue, saying that adults should have the "freedom" to engage in any kind of activity they desire with their own money, given that the activity doesn't hurt other people. However, this "freedom" issue is not a moving force in campaigns for legalization of gambling.

The most compelling issue advanced by proponents of legalized gambling involves economics. Gambling advocates invariably present the argument that gaming activity will generate new funds for public treasuries that can be spent on myriad worthy causes and that will also create jobs and general economic growth in the community. They stress that gambling taxes are politically more acceptable than other forms of taxation because they are paid voluntarily by the gamblers themselves.

Gambling proponents seek to minimize concerns about crime by emphasizing that gambling is best controlled when it is legal. Legalization, they say, drives criminals from such enterprises.

Often, gaming advocates exploit law enforcement resources as a political issue. They suggest that people will gamble whether it is legal or not, thereby taxing precious police enforcement resources needed for the more urgent problems of murder, rape, robbery, and arson. This argument basically holds, too, that laws prohibiting gambling are basically unenforceable.

Gambling supporters also insist that problems related to compulsive gambling affect only a very small portion of the population and that these people can be kept away from gambling institutions and treated for their behavior.

Opponents of legalized gambling are always ready to dispute these points. They counter that gambling taxes are not truly voluntary and that job creation and predictions of economic growth are only illusory.

Moreover, opponents see legal gambling as a catalyst for many kinds of criminal activity rather than a tool that will help free police resources to fight serious crime. This side of the debate views gambling as a personally destructive activity that leads many to pathological behavior when they lose control over their wagering addiction. Gambling opponents prophesy a decay of social responsibility in communities that sanction gambling.

Economics

There is considerable debate over gambling's economic impact on society. The debate, however, is not centered on the question of whether or not a lot of money is involved in the gambling industry, for the answer to that is clear. More than $550 billion is wagered each year in legal games in the United States. Gamblers lose over $44 billion each year or, put another way, gambling enterprises win over $44 billion annually. This amount represents 7.3 percent of the personal income of the nation. This volume of money dwarfs the $8 billion spent in the recorded music industry each year and the $5 billion paid by moviegoers and video renters each year. Clearly, gambling is the number one entertainment industry in terms of cash flow and profit.

Many gambling proceeds do find their way into public treasuries. With tax benefits at the top of the proponents' justification lists for legalization, a closer examination of gambling taxes is warranted.

An effective tax should, first and foremost, generate money for the public welfare. Do gambling taxes churn up sizable revenues for deposit in government accounts? The aggregate direct tax revenue from gaming nationally is approximately $20 billion a year. The Evans Group (1996) reported that casino activity "added an estimated $5.9 billion to federal tax receipts in 1995." This includes income taxes on corporate profits as well as wages. Gaming taxes and state and local income and property taxes levied on casino properties and wages of their employees yielded another $3 billion. State lottery proceeds retained by state and local governments totaled $11.1 billion in 1995.

Certainly this is a lot of dollar power for public programs. Does this money go a long way toward satisfying the fiscal needs of the federal government and state and local governments? In sum, state tax revenues amount to between $350 and $400 billion a year, which suggests that gaming revenues accounted for somewhat less than 4 percent of the total state taxes. As a revenue generator, gambling ranked sixth behind general sales taxes, individual income taxes, corporate taxes, gasoline taxes, and license fees. Gambling revenues did, however, exceed those of death taxes, severance taxes, property taxes, and tobacco and alcohol taxes (Council of State Governments 1996).

The importance of gambling as a revenue source can also be assessed by examining situations in individual states. In Nevada, the nearly $500 million brought in through direct casino win taxes amount to 42 percent of the state's tax revenues. (Other taxes relating to gaming and tourism—for instance, sales taxes paid by visitors—bring the estimated figure to over 50 percent.) However, in New Jersey, casino taxes provide less than 3 percent of the funds for state coffers. When New Jersey adds its lottery revenue and horse race tax revenues to this, the percentage of state revenue from gambling climbs to almost 6 percent.

Mississippi, perhaps the most successful of the newer casino gaming states, received $189 million in casino taxes in 1995. This represents over 7 percent of the state tax base. Although Illinois raised more money through casino taxes (the gambling tax rate is 20 percent of the casino win compared to an 8 percent tax in Mississippi), the $286 million raised represented just over 2 percent of the state tax receipts.

None of the remaining states receives higher than 7 percent of its tax revenues from gaming. Lotteries, for instance, yielded a maximum of 4.7 percent of the total for Maryland, and the average was closer to 2.1 percent. In many states, lottery taxes yielded less than 1 percent of the revenues. Horse racing revenues also represented small portions of state treasuries. In New Hampshire, taxes on horse racing produced just over 3 percent of the state total; only in four additional states did horse racing buttress the state's wallet by as much as 1 percent (Council of State Governments 1996; Mikesell and Zorn 1986).

Although such revenue totals may be minor ones in terms of the overall spending equation, proceeds from gaming taxes in some areas are earmarked for specific purposes, such as parks, education, or tax relief for seniors. In these cases, of course, the proportion of revenues contributed by gambling levies is much greater. However, state policymakers have time and time again refused to increase spending on specific projects or programs when gambling revenues are earmarked for such activities. Instead, the tendency is to reduce general fund contributions to the project by the sum of gambling revenue produced. In effect, then, nearly all gambling taxes must be considered as mere components of a state's amalgamated funds and not principal funding resources for projects or services.

As such, gambling taxes make a real difference only in Nevada. Gaming revenues there are potential funding powerhouses for individual charities and for small organizations or governments. Bingo games have been effective in raising funds for a variety of charities, private schools, and hospitals, and Nevada Indian reservations have pooled quite large sums of money through gambling. Indeed, almost all Nevada tribes that permit gambling have discovered these operations to be the strongest reservation employers and the leading source of funding. This is a function of the small population of most reservations.

A second criterion for assessing the worthiness of a tax is its reliability. Governments can plan ahead for anticipated sums of revenue from reliable levies that have shown themselves to provide stable yields year after year. Generally, Nevada casino tax revenues have demonstrated solid reliability and have consistently grown between the 1950s and the 1990s. Still, it is not unheard of for budget authorities to miscalculate estimated tax yields, giving rise to occasional fiscal crises. Such was the case in the early 1980s when casino taxes leveled off. It was also true in the mid-1990s when increasing tax yields did not make up for additional costs imposed upon the state's infrastructure by a growing tourism industry, notably water system costs and transportation system costs, and for increased costs of education necessitated by population increases.

For many years, lotteries appeared to be excellent revenue sources for the states that permitted them. From the inception of lottery programs and into the 1980s, double-digit revenue growth occurred in many locations. However, these revenue gains did not last, and some states have experienced revenue declines. Clotfelter and Cook's in-depth study (1989) of lotteries found that collectively lotteries have the greatest volatility when compared to other tax systems but that the volatility is not that much greater than sales taxes, income taxes, or other state revenue sources.

A passive lottery game was instituted in Illinois in 1974, and an instant game followed the next year. Sales of lottery products increased from $129 million to $163 million in the second year. Encouraged, the Illinois legislature wrote budgets that anticipated additional revenue growth, but at the same time the novelty of playing the lottery began to wear off, and for the next three years sales fell 60 percent. A similar situation seems to be occurring in California, where 1992 lottery sales declined 17 percent from the previous year. The California scramble is now on to adjust marketing strategies in an attempt to rebuild sales.

Another measure of an effective tax relates to the efficiency of revenue collection. Gambling taxes pose a problem here, because some operators have been successful in hiding revenues. This, however, is not a major difficulty. Most gaming enterprises do pay the required amount of taxes owed—especially government-run lotteries.

The administrative costs of collecting casino taxes vary considerably between the two biggest casino states. Of course, not all casino regulation is oriented toward tax collection, but regulation is necessary to keep the industry operating properly. New Jersey spends approximately $80 million annually for casino regulation. This amount is charged back to the casinos and should be subtracted from the aggregate 1995 casino revenues of $296 million. In other words, regulatory and collection costs amount to 27 percent of the statewide revenue generated. New Jersey pays 27 cents for each revenue dollar it brings in from a casino. Nevada's system exhibits greater efficiency. The state spends about $25 million in administration to collect $500 million in revenues—only 5 percent of the total, or 5 cents on the dollar.

Pari-mutuel systems usually operate on a share basis. Out of the pool of money wagered by the betting public, 85 percent may be returned to the bettors. The remainder is split between track operators, horse racing associations and horse owners (including prizes for race winners), and the state government. These three groups may each get 5 percent in a typical split. Operators pay the costs of regulation and collection. The efficiency of this system is comparable to that of the New Jersey casinos.

In general, the efficiency of gambling sources as revenue generators leaves something to be desired. Collection and administration costs range from a low of 18 cents on the dollar in Maryland to more than a dollar in Colorado, Montana, and Kansas. Canadian governments typically spend 43 cents. For instance, in fiscal 1989, U.S. lotteries spent about $2.1 billion to raise and collect $7.3 billion for various government treasuries—a 23.1 percent chunk of the revenues.

The taxation issue raised most vociferously in lottery debates is that of equity. If the purpose of lotteries is to raise money for government, it is prudent to ask whether that revenue is being drawn from the people who can most afford to pay for government services. The answer: probably not. It appears that the lottery represents a very regressive tax.

Many lottery studies suggest that the game appeals to certain segments of the population more than others. One study found that 65 percent of lottery tickets were purchased by 10 percent of the population. For example, ticket purchasers in California were more likely than not to be less educated or hold low-paying jobs (Mangalmurti and Cooke 1991).

Since the poor account for a greater share of lottery ticket purchases, taxes on those purchases are considered regressive. Economist Daniel Suits found that in Massachusetts, people with annual incomes below $5,000 drew 1.9 percent of the state's individual income while purchasing 8.9 percent of the lottery tickets. Connecticut citizens earning under $10,000 a year commanded an 8 percent share of state income and a 20 percent share of lottery sales. In a tax index developed by Suits, lotteries in such states appeared to be the most regressive form of taxation (Mangalmurti and Cooke 1991).

Other scholars have found similar results. John Mikesell and Kurt Zorn concluded that "lotteries place a greater relative burden on low-income families, because low-income groups spend a higher percentage of their income on lottery tickets than do high-income groups. The spending pattern has been found frequently" (Mikesell and Zorn 1986).

One reason explaining the higher incidence of play among poor citizens is the method in which lotteries are marketed. Much advertising portrays the game as a plausible, easy, even recommended way of escaping the rut of poverty. Such merchandising ploys send the message that success can be achieved painlessly, without hard work or perseverance (Mangalmurti and Cooke 1991).

State lottery bureaucrats know the poor are vulnerable to these kinds of appeals and install more lottery sales outlets in poor neighborhoods. One Delaware study found that lottery sales stations were almost nonexistent in the high-income areas outside of Wilmington, with one ticket-dispensing machine for every 17,714 persons, whereas in working-class neighborhoods machines were available for every 5,032 residents, and in lower-income areas there was a machine for every 1,981 people (Mangalmurti and Cooke 1991).

Similarly, a 1984 study in Maryland discovered one lottery outlet for every 1,850 residents in Baltimore, a city with an average household income of $16,800. In contrast, Montgomery County, where families averaged $34,000 annually, contained a lottery station for every 5,800 residents (Karcher 1989). Another study found similar distribution inequities in and around Detroit.

There is considerable debate over whether casino taxes share the same regressive qualities of lottery taxes. Industry studies show that casino players in the United States have median household incomes of $39,000 compared with a U.S. population median household income of $31,000. Moreover, in excess of half of the Las Vegas gamblers come to the casino city on air flights, and most stay at hotels now averaging room rates of over $75 a night. Poor people cannot travel in this manner, at least not often. The case can be made that the typical casino gambler in Las Vegas can afford his or her occasional visit to the casinos. This may not be the case in all casino locations in the United States and Canada. I participated in studies of casino gambling at Indian facilities in Wisconsin and on riverboats in Illinois. Almost all of the patrons at these casinos arrived by automobile or by bus tours. Very few stayed overnight at or near the casino location. In Wisconsin, average household incomes were below $30,000. In Illinois, the average incomes were between $40,000 and $45,000. However, the average decreased for those players who lived closer to the casinos and players who came to the casinos more often (Thompson and Gazel 1996; Thompson, Gazel, and Rickman 1995).

Legalized gambling is offered as a remedy for unemployment. The claim that gambling is a producer of jobs is confined largely to casino operations. George Sternlieb and James Hughes observed that "the promise of increased employment played the largest part in winning endorsement for casino gambling [in New Jersey]" (1983). Likewise, the battle cry of casino advocates in Chicago is "Jobs! Jobs! Jobs!" A proposed $2 billion casino complex there has been touted as the route to 57,000 new jobs. An additional 25,000 new positions were projected for a New Orleans casino project.

These are not just promises, either; casinos have succeeded in hiring many, many people. The Evans Group found that casinos employed 337,000 people in the United States in 1995, resulting in payrolls in excess of $9 billion (The Evans Group 1996; Harrah's Entertainment, Inc. 1996). The gaming industry in Las Vegas typically employs two persons for each new room constructed for a casino hotel.

However, although the industry points with pride at the results of job creation, there is debate over whether or not there are net job gains as a result of casinos. For some communities the answer has to be yes. For others, there may be considerable doubts about the bottom-line results.

Certainly more jobs will be created by casino projects that attract tourists because the gamblers will need additional services. Jobs may also be generated through construction activity, but this economic shot in the arm may later be revealed as transitory. If construction materials, labor, and casino workers are imported, the promise of additional jobs and lasting economic gain will have turned out to be a pipe dream. Moreover, construction company profits may or may not remain in the community following completion of the project, and construction materials may not even be supplied locally. In such scenarios, communities run the risk of boom-bust cycles that can temporarily disrupt the social calm and later leave a bitter aftertaste.

Job-related questions other than those related to quantity must be considered when deciding which stand to take on gambling propositions. What kinds of jobs? Will they be skilled, lucrative positions or minimum wage entry-level positions? Are the local unemployed eligible? How stable will these positions be?

An assessment of these concerns in Atlantic City points to mixed results. New casinos there did provide more than 40,000 jobs, but most of them were awarded to applicants who lived outside the economically depressed city. In fact, the unemployment picture in Atlantic City proper did not change materially after the casinos arrived. Evidence also showed that the hotels in most cases did not produce highly motivated work atmospheres because the jobs paid on the low end of the scale.

There were some upsides to the situation. Young, unskilled applicants were able to move into many of the new positions quickly, and some skilled jobs were created. These higher-responsibility slots were the kinds that demanded applicants with high integrity.

In the mid-1990s, Las Vegas has emerged as perhaps the best example in the United States of *job-fare*, the term being used to describe the change from welfare-recipient status to worker status for the previously unemployable. Many casinos seek workers from the pool of unemployed, particularly among minority groups, including new (legal) immigrants. The casinos train the workers on the most basic skills needed for the jobs. Indeed, a major casino even provided English-language lessons for its new workers.

Although many of the casino jobs can be criticized in part because they are lower-income jobs, many are unionized jobs, and most carry full benefit packages, including family health care.

A possible downside is still connected to the proliferation of gaming sites across the country. Suppose casinos are overbuilt in certain locations, and the availability of facilities exceeds the demand for gambling. These new casinos could fall flat. Even in Las Vegas and Atlantic City, some big casinos have failed while the general gambling scene has remained stable or actually grown. Other than bankruptcy lawyers, there are few winners when a casino goes under. General layoffs can be very devastating for new gaming communities and particularly for newly employed persons who looked at casino employment as perhaps their last best hope of joining the workforce.

The proponents and the opponents can debate the particulars of the economic benefits and costs of gambling on and on and on. So much tax revenue, but is it enough? Is it regressive taxation? So many jobs. But are they good jobs? Do they really constitute new jobs or just replacement jobs for people laid off elsewhere? The microarguments are without end, without closure. There is, however, a model that can be used to assess whether the bottom-line results of adding gambling—for instance, a casino—to a community are positive or negative for that community. The model involves a very simple analysis of two factors in the gambling equation: (1) Where does the money come from? (2) Where does the money go? The model can be represented by a graphic display of a bathtub.

Water comes into a bathtub, and water runs out of a bathtub. If the water comes in at a higher rate than it leaves the tub, the water level rises; if the water comes in at a slower rate than it leaves, the water level is lowered. A local or regional economy attracts moneys. A local or regional economy discards moneys. Moneys come and moneys go. If as a result of the presence of a casino more money comes into an economy than leaves the economy, there is a positive monetary effect because of the casinos. The level of wealth in the economy rises. However, if more money leaves than comes in, then there is a negative impact from the presence of casino gambling.

Moneys come into casino economies because of gambling. Players lose moneys to the casino games. Also, players attracted to a location because it has a casino will spend money on food, lodging, transportation, and other items. Casino projects also attract construction money. The moneys coming into the casino economy circulate and recirculate at rates that are called multipliers.

Moneys leave casino economies for several reasons. Moneys brought to the casino by local residents actually is leaving other sectors of the local economy, so it must be subtracted from the positive side (the water into the tub). Other moneys leave the casino economy—special taxes on casino play go off to capital cities (state capitals and Washington, D.C.), never to be seen again (or, in truth, only a small portion of the money will be seen again in a few local services, such as salaries for gaming regulators on the site of the casino). It is unlikely that a central government will give added general services to a local area just because the area is providing an extra share of taxes as a result of the presence of casinos. Casinos need many supplies, a large part of which are purchased from sources outside of the area of the casino economy. This is money lost. So too are profits that go to casino owners who live outside of the economic area of the casino. Some casino owners may reinvest moneys in the local economy, but few have incentives for doing so, especially if they are allowed to have only one property of a certain size.

Casino economies also lose moneys as a result of the costs of government services that are not directly offset by casino contributions: extra police protection outside the casino, better roads to the casino, traffic control in the casino area. Also, the casino may attract or motivate criminal activity, resulting in police and judicial system costs as well as costs of victimization and insurance premiums for those living near the casino. Additionally, the presence of casinos will likely be associated with some increases in pathological gambling behaviors, and these carry costs for society—for the economy of a casino area. These factors will be dealt with in a separate discussion (*see* "Problem Gamblers" in this chapter).

All the factors indicated above vary from casino (or gambling) location to casino location. The specific type of casino regulation in a jurisdiction can affect the variations. Casino owners may have to be state residents; they may have to give preference to local suppliers; taxes can be high or low. Casinos can be required to pay for extra police officers or give moneys to help programs for problem gamblers. To understand the bottom-line effects of a casino we must also know the real (often unstated) reason for the casino's existence. If the casino exists to block the local resident from going elsewhere to gamble, it may be successful without attracting outside players. If the measure of success is job production, however, a large portion of the players will have to be visitors. How many will depend on other variables, such as where profits end up and what the tax rates are.

The Las Vegas Bathtub Model

The Las Vegas economy has witnessed phenomenal growth in the past few years. This has occurred even in the face of competition from around the nation and the world as more and more locations have casinos and casino gambling products. The Las Vegas economy is strong because the overwhelming amount of gambling money (as much as 90 percent) brought to the casinos comes from visitors. Visitors also stay in Las Vegas an average of four days, spending much money outside of the casino areas. Las Vegas has money leakages. However, state taxes are very low, and much of the profits remain as owners are local, or if they are not, they see great advantages in reinvesting profits in expanded facilities in Las Vegas. The costs of crime and compulsive gambling associated with gambling are probably major; however, many of these costs are transferred to other economies, as most problem players return to homes located in other economic areas. Las Vegas is not a manufacturing or an agricultural region, so most of the purchases (except for gambling supplies) result in leakages to other economies. Las Vegas does have several gambling locations—bars, 7-11 stores, grocery stores—that represent very faulty bathtubs, bathtubs with great leakages.

Other U.S. Jurisdictions

Atlantic City's casino bathtub functions appropriately, as most of the gamblers are from outside the local area. However, players are mostly "day trippers" who do not spend moneys outside the casinos. Most purchases—as in Las Vegas—result in leakages for the economy. Like Las Vegas, state gaming taxes are reasonably low; other taxes, however, are high.

Most other U.S. jurisdictions do not have efficiently functioning bathtubs, because most offer gambling products for the most part to local players. Indian casinos may help local economies because they do not pay gambling excise taxes or federal income taxes on gambling wins, being wholly owned by tribal governments who keep profits (which are, in effect, tribal taxes) in the local economies.

Using Some Real Numbers with the Model

In 1995, I participated in gathering data on the economic impacts of casino gambling in the state of Illinois (Thompson and Gazel 1996). Illinois has licensed ten riverboat operations in nine locations of the state. The locations were picked because they were on navigable waters and also because the locations had suffered economic declines. We interviewed 785 players at five of the nine locations.

We also gathered information about the general revenue production of the casinos and also the spending patterns of the casinos—wages, supplies, taxes, and residual profits. The casinos were owned by corporations, most of which were based outside the state and none of which were based in the particular casino communities.

The focus of our attention was the local areas within 35 miles of the casino sites. The data were analyzed collectively, that is, for all the local areas together.

Our survey indicated that 61.3 percent of the players were locals; they lived within 35 miles of the casinos. In 1995, the casinos generated revenues of just over $1.3 billion for the local areas. The categories of revenue are shown in Table 1.2.

The local players were responsible for 57.9 percent of this revenue. However, from our survey we determined that 30 percent

TABLE 1.2
Sources of Casino-Generated Revenues

Gambling revenues	$1,097,249,969
Other in-casino revenue (food, gifts, etc.)	$108,154,990
Tips	$46,688,966
Nonlocal expenses out of casino (transportation, lodging, food, shopping)	$52,071,445
Total	$1,304,165,370

TABLE 1.3
Expenditures of Casino Revenues

Wages	$301,800,000
Tips	$46,688,966
Payroll tax	$19,315,200
Free services to players	$20,823,279
Taxes—state gaming and local	$273,559,656
Purchases	$225,901,240
Total casino costs	$841,399,374
Precorporate tax profits	$364,005,585
Illinois corporate tax	($18,200,279)
Federal corporate tax	($117,573,804)
Retained profits	$228,231,502

of these local gamblers would have gambled in another casino location if a casino had not been available close to their home. Therefore, in a sense their gambling revenue represented an influx of money to the area, that is, the casino blocked money that would otherwise leave the area. We considered a part of the local gambling money to be nonlocal money, in other words, visitor revenue. Conversely, we considered that 22 percent of the visitors' spending was really local moneys, because many of the nonlocal gamblers indicated that they would have come to the area and spent money (lodging, food, etc.) even if there were no casino in the area.

We examined the expenditures of the casinos' revenues, as shown in Table 1.3.

Our research indicated that 90 percent of the workers lived within 35 miles of the casinos and that 60 percent of the supplies were purchased from vendors within the area. However, most of the taxes left the area. The local government kept only one-fourth

TABLE 1.4
Monetary Impact on Local Economy

Positive impacts:	
Wages and tips	$207,452,856
Employee benefits	$32,594,400
Local purchasing	$133,971,414
Local retained profits	$11,411,575
Local retained taxes	$122,827,154
Nonlocals' spending	
Outside casino	$52,071,445
Subtotal positive inflows	$560,328,844
As recirculated money (× multipliers)	$1,301,930,264
Negative impacts:	
Spending from local residents	$528,493,069
Spending from nonlocals coming anyway	$124,662,787
Subtotal negative impacts	$653,155,856
As recirculated moneys (× multipliers)	$1,541,582,438
Total negative impact of casino gaming for local areas	$239,652,174

of the gaming tax along with property taxes. We did assume that the local area would recapture 20 percent of the full state tax amount through normal services as well as services involved with regulating the gaming. Most of the casinos were owned by out-of-state corporations. The Illinois owners did not reside within the local areas. We assumed that only 5 percent of the retained profits remained in the local area, as the casinos were not allowed to reinvest in expanded gaming facilities.

To assess the net economic impacts of the casinos on the local areas, we examined the positive inflows of moneys and then the negative outflows. As we calculated each number we also multiplied it by a factor provided by the U.S. Department of Commerce (or an estimated number based on Commerce numbers). These factors, called multipliers, represent the times a dollar coming into a community will recirculate before it leaves the economy. In terms of the negative outflows, the multipliers indicate how many times the money would have been respent had it not left the economy directly.

Before we calculated the multipliers (which differed for each category), we found the following positive additions of money to the local economy because of the presence of casinos (see Table 1.4).

The mayors and local politicians rejoice when the casinos move to their towns. They see new jobs, and soon they see new tax revenues they did not see before. The casino companies keep pointing out these positive benefits; however, the positives that are easily observable may only hide an unwelcome truth just below the surface. If most of the gamblers are locals, as they are with Illinois riverboat casinos, the local economy gets hurt. In the case of Illinois, although the casinos generate $1.3 billion for the local economy, they also result in an exiting of much more money. In fact, the information gathered for our study suggests that for every dollar the casinos bring into the local Illinois casino communities, $1.18 leaves the economy.

Crime

Opponents of gambling, on the one hand, make almost shrill statements about how organized crime infiltrates communities when they legalize gambling. The opponents also suggest that various forms of street crimes—robbery, auto theft, prostitution—come with gambling, as do embezzlement, forgery, and various forms of larceny caused by desperate problem gamblers.

On the other hand, proponents of gambling contend that the evidence of any connections between crime and gambling is rather weak. They contend that the stories of "mob" involvement with gambling are a part of the past but not the present, and that even then the involvement was more exaggerated than real. Most cases of increased street crime are passed off as resulting from increased volumes of people in casino communities. Proponents show that all entertainment communities (e.g., Las Vegas, Orlando, Anaheim) witness increases in crime as more tourists come to the locations. Moreover, proponents of legalized gambling even argue that because gambling may lead to job growth in gambling communities, crime may actually go down. They suggest that employed people are less inclined to be drawn to criminal activities than are people without jobs and that by legalizing gambling, society can fight the effects of illegal gambling.

Before looking at findings in other studies, some examinations of the opportunities for crime in gambling establishments should be reviewed. Criminologists have identified opportunity as a factor in explaining much criminal activity. For instance, Leslie Wilkins indicated in a 1964 study that the number of vehicle thefts was related to the number of vehicles in use in a society. The existence of targets facilitates criminal activity. Wilkins's work was substantiated with some qualifications by Patricia Mayhew (1990), who also found relationships between numbers of bicycles and bicycle thefts. Walter C. Reckless explained greater amounts of crime among urban rather than rural populations in terms of opportunity: "The urban population is more exposed to property and materialism than the rural population. It is exposed to a much larger volume of secondary contacts, which accustom it to all kinds of threats, nuisances, and pressures in the crowded streets, stores, offices, factories, movies, and conveyances" (Reckless 1961, p. 65). Criminologist Marshall B. Clinard concurs: "[V]iolators in rural areas would be much less apt to turn to property offenses as their outlet than violators in urban areas, who are confronted with much greater property opportunities and with a more permeating criminal sophistication" (quoted in Reckless 1961, p. 66).

Of course, when the notorious bank robber Willie Sutton was asked why he robbed banks, he simply replied, "That's where the money is!" It should be expected that criminal activity also surrounds the premises of casinos, as "that's where the money is," too! If opportunity is a driving force for crime, the presence of gambling activity may constitute a magnet for crime.

Several types of crime might be associated with the presence of gambling, particularly gambling concentrated in one site, such as casino gambling. The crimes could include inside activity concerning gambling facility owners, business associates, and employees; could be tied to the playing of the games; and could involve patrons.

In the first type, organized crime elements might try to draw profits off the gaming enterprise through schemes of hidden ownership or through insiders who steal from the casino winnings. Management might steal from the profit pools to avoid taxes or to cheat their partners. Organized crime figures might become suppliers for goods and services, extracting unreasonable costs for their products. Crime families have been the providers of junket tours for players, and in New Jersey for various sources of labor, for instance, in the construction trades. Organized crime also may become involved in providing loans to desperate players, and the existence of the casinos may facilitate laundering of money for cartels that traffic in illegal activities such as prostitution and the drug trade.

Another set of crimes attend the actual games that are played. Wherever a game is offered with a money prize, someone will try to manipulate the games through cheating schemes. Some casino cheating involves marked cards, crooked dice, and uneven roulette wheels. Schemes may involve teams of players or individual players and casino employees. In some cases the casino organization may attempt to cheat players.

The greatest concern for crime and casino involves activities of casino patrons. The casinos present criminals with opportunities. Players who win money or carry money to casinos may be easy marks for robberies—forceful as well as those by pickpockets. Hotel rooms in casino properties are also targets. But it's not just casino patrons who suffer from criminal attacks. In the late 1970s, a 12-year-old boy was murdered in Kalamazoo, Michigan, by a teenaged neighbor. The teenager had been at a local bingo game the night before when the 12-year-old's mother had won the big jackpot. The teenager was searching the house for the money when the victim discovered him.

Gamblers are also targets for prostitutes and other persons selling illicit goods such as drugs. Desperate players are also drawn to crimes in order to secure money for play or to pay gambling debts. Their crimes involve robberies and other larcenies as well as such white-collar crimes as embezzlements and forgeries.

Casino employees and executives in some cases also commit criminal activity by evading taxes, particularly in the area of income from tips.

The issue of crime and gambling has been well studied. Well before the recent spread of casino gambling across the United States, Virgil Peterson, director of the Chicago Crime Commission, issued a scathing attack on gambling. In his *Gambling: Should It Be Legalized?* (1951), he asserted that "legalized gambling has always been attractive to the criminal and racketeering elements" (p. 120). He also said that "criminals, gangsters, and swindlers have been the proprietors of gambling establishments" (p. 137); that "many people find it necessary to steal or embezzle to continue gambling activity" (pp. 120–121); and that "the kidnapper, the armed robber, the burglar, and the thief engage" in crime to secure money for play (p. 123).

In a 1965 article that seemed prophetic considering events in New Jersey just a dozen years later, Peterson wrote, "The underworld inevitably gains a foothold under any licensing system. If state authorities establish the vast policing system rigid supervision requires, the underworld merely provides itself with fronts who obtain the licenses, with actual ownership remaining in its own hands; and it receives a major share of the profits" (Peterson 1965, p. 677; see also Dombrink 1981; Skolnick 1978).

Other stories of the relationships between organized crime and gambling are plentiful. While Peterson was gathering information for his book, the Senate Committee on Organized Crime was holding hearings under the leadership of Estes Kefauver in 1950 and 1951. The committee was very specific in identifying gambling as a major activity of organized crime:

> Gambling profits are the principal support of big time racketeering and gangsterism. These profits provide the financial resources whereby ordinary criminals are converted into big-time racketeers, political bosses, pseudo-businessmen, and alleged philanthropists. Player[s] are not only suckers because they are gambling against hopeless odds, but they also provide the moneys which enable underworld characters to undermine our institutions. The legalization of gambling would not terminate the widespread predatory activities of criminal gangs and syndicates. The history of legalized gambling in Nevada and in other parts of the country gives no assurance that mobsters and racketeers can be converted into responsible businessmen through the simple process of obtaining state and local licenses for their gambling enterprises. Gambling, moreover, historically has been associated with cheating and corruption. The committee has not seen any workable proposal for controlled gambling which would eliminate the gangsters or corruption. (U.S. Senate Special Committee to Investigate Organized Crime in Interstate Commerce 1951, pp. 2–3)

In 1963, Ovid Demaris and Ed Reid wrote *The Green Felt Jungle*, a shocking account of the mob in Las Vegas. Demaris continued the saga with his *Boardwalk Jungle* (1986), an early account of casinos in New Jersey. His story was built upon Gigi Mahon's *The Company That Bought the Boardwalk* (1980), a journalistic account of crime involvement in Atlantic City's first casino. The 1980s were noted as the decade when corporations took over ownership of the casinos of Atlantic City and Las Vegas. David Johnston found that many of the old ways of business remained with the new type of owners, in his *Temples of Chance—How America, Inc. Bought Out Murder, Inc. to Win Control of the Casino Business* (Johnston 1992; see also Thompson 1994, pp. 46–53).

New Jersey authorities certainly hoped things wouldn't turn out that way when gambling was approved in 1976. When Governor Brendan Byrne signed the new licensing and regulation law, he declared in no uncertain terms: "Organized crime is not welcome.

I warn them: keep your filthy hands out of Atlantic City." But, alas, Byrne's words flew to the wind (Demaris 1986; Pollock 1987).

From its initial involvement in casino licensing, New Jersey compromised its ability to control organized crime. The state attorney general's office investigated the first applicant, Resorts International, and concluded that the company was financed by underworld bosses and had a record of bribery and skimming in its Bahamas casino. The attorney general asked that the license be denied, but New Jersey's Casino Control Commission overruled the recommendation. The commission reasoned that such an action would represent a severe economic setback for Atlantic City, whose leaders were eager to start reaping the benefits of the new industry (Sternlieb and Hughes 1983).

It wasn't only wise-guy casino operators who created problems: Organized crime was found to be pervasive all over Atlantic City in junket operations, credit scams, slot machine cheating, laundering schemes for narcotics money, labor unions, and ancillary industries. The stench of crime even led investigators to the offices of the mayor and a U.S. senator.

The Federal Bureau of Investigation, suspecting that things were going awry, cast their net of attention over Atlantic City. In 1979, the FBI began a sting operation called ABSCAM, short for Abdul Scam (Demaris 1986; Pollock 1987). Agents posed as Arab sheiks, representing the fictitious Abdul Enterprises. The agents offered bribes to U.S. Senator Harrison Williams, six congressmen, and New Jersey politicians, including gaming regulators, along with a request for favorable consideration for a casino license. As the money traded hands, assurances were given that the license would be forthcoming. A literal who's who of notables in the state's licensing offices was named on secret tape recordings. Senator Williams was convicted of bribery, and Casino Control Commission chairman Joseph Lordi and vice chairman Kenneth MacDonald resigned (Demaris 1986). Following a separate investigation, Atlantic City mayor Michael J. Matthews was convicted and sentenced to a 15-year sentence for accepting bribes and payoffs from the Nicodemo (Little Nicky) Scarfo crime organization (Demaris 1986).

In the process, federal attorneys painted a dismal portrait of the early years of New Jersey casino gaming. Attorney Robert Del Tufo said:

> We have two governors in New Jersey. The one administration is that elected by the people. The other administration is that designated by the leaders of

organized crime. [It] is a government that lives off blood money and drug money and rules from the alleys and back rooms and the shadowy places you and I never go. No party—and no candidate—can lay legitimate claim to the first government of New Jersey until it deals with the second. (Demaris 1986)

The New Jersey State Police superintendent found that illegal sports betting increased substantially after casinos opened in Atlantic City. Crime families from Massachusetts, Pennsylvania, and New York conducted their operations in and around the casinos. One special FBI agent claimed that up to ten Mafia "families" were involved in "unions, junkets, and other ancillary businesses" connected with the city's casino scene (Demaris 1986).

Gambling-related crime is not confined to "mob" organizations. It also reaches the street levels as individuals are given opportunities to "get rich quick" that do not involve pulling on slot machine handles or rolling dice.

University of Illinois Professor John Warren Kindt writes that "the criminal justice system will incur not only increased costs, but the types of crimes will change to redress new forms of [gamblers'] misconduct. Bad debts and increased insurance fraud are projected to increase significantly" (Kindt 1995; Florida Department of Law Enforcement 1994; see also Kindt 1994).

In September 1995, L. Scott Harshbarger, Massachusetts state attorney general, commented to the U.S. House Judiciary Committee that he had been cautioned by "almost every attorney general who has faced the issue of casino gambling" that there was "a range of public safety, regulatory and social issues that are never addressed before the introduction of gambling." Harshbarger further commented:

One of the noted consequences of casino gambling has been the marked rise in street crime. Across the nation, police departments in cities that have casino gambling have recorded surges in arrests due to casino-related crime. In many cases, towns that had a decreasing crime rate or a low crime rate have seen a sharp and steady growth of crime once gambling has taken root. Organized crime is a second danger that accompanies casino gambling. While proponents might argue that organized crime's connection with casinos stopped with Bugsy Siegel in Las Vegas, the facts do not bear that out. In 1994 in Louisiana, 17 individuals associated with the Marcello, Genovese, and Gambino crime families were indicted for RICO violations for profit skimming through video poker machines that had recently been legalized. (quoted in *Gambling under Attack* 1996, p. 785)

More solid data have come from analyses of criminal statistics. George Sternlieb and James Hughes's 1983 study of Atlantic City revealed that crime increased rapidly in the community after the introduction of casinos in 1978. Activity of pickpockets increased 80-fold and larceny over five times; robberies tripled, as did assaults (p. 192). Simon Hakim and Andrew J. Buck found that the levels of all types of crime were higher in the years after casinos began operations. The "greatest post-casino crime increase was observed for violent crimes and auto thefts and the least for burglaries." As one moved farther from Atlantic City in spatial distance, rates of crime leveled off (Hakim and Buck 1989). Friedman, Hakim, and Weinblatt, however, found that increases in crime extended outward at least 30 miles to suburban areas and to areas along highways that extended toward New York and Philadelphia (Friedman, Hakim, and Weinblatt 1989).

Similar studies have pointed out high crime rates in Las Vegas. In the early 1980s, the governor of the state of Nevada expressed outrage when a publicized critic of gambling said that one in eight Las Vegas women aged 15 to 39 was a prostitute. The governor had good reason to be irate. The critic was wrong— only one in nine of the women was a prostitute. At the beginning of the 1980s, Las Vegas could also boast that it had the nation's highest crime rate. Other studies showed high crime rates in Mississippi gambling communities (Hancock County, Mississippi 1994).

Similarly, a study of Windsor, Ontario, found some crime rates increasing after a casino opened in May 1994. Overall, previous decreases in rates of crime citywide seemed to come to an end, whereas rates in areas around the casino increased measurably. The downtown area near the casino found more assaults, assaults upon police officers, and "other violent crimes." Particularly noticeable were increases in general thefts, motor vehicle thefts, liquor offenses, and driving offenses (Windsor [Ontario] Police Department 1995).

My study of crime rates in all Wisconsin counties before and after the introduction of Indian casinos found statistically significant associations between certain crimes and the proximity of casino facilities. Notably, there were higher incidents of burglaries, drug use, and driving while intoxicated in casino counties and counties adjacent to those counties. It was estimated that the additional crimes, not in evidence in the other counties, cost the state over $50 million a year in criminal justice system costs—arrests, trials, and sentences (Thompson, Gazel, and Rickman 1996a).

Not all the evidence points in the same direction. I have also talked with many players at casinos in rural areas and find that they are places to which many seniors go precisely because they are considered safe places for entertainment. They are well guarded both inside and outside.

Several riverboat communities in Iowa, Illinois, and Mississippi saw decreases in crime rates following the establishment of casinos. Moreover, Albanese (1985) and Chiricos (1994) demonstrated that higher incidents of crime in Atlantic City were due in large part to increases in visitor traffic. If numbers of tourist visitors were included in permanent census figures, crime rates would be stable or might even be less than they were before casinos came to Atlantic City. A study by Ronald George Ochrym and Clifton Park compared gaming communities with other tourist destinations that did not have casinos. They found that rates of crime were quite similar. Although crime statistics did soar following the introduction of casinos in Atlantic City, so, too, did crime in Orlando, Florida, following the opening of Disney World. If the casinos themselves were responsible for more crime, gaming proponents suggest that Mickey Mouse also must cause crime (Ochrym and Park 1990).

Casino proponent Jeremy D. Margolis, a former assistant U.S. attorney, discounts the crime factors as well. He commented to the House Judiciary Committee:

> People often ask whether the presence of gaming in their community would cause an increase in street crime. The facts are these: Las Vegas, Nevada, the city that is synonymous with casinos, is among the safest cities in America. Those who cite crime as a reason to oppose legalized gaming tend to ignore the Las Vegas example and instead tend to focus on a misleading interpretation of crime statistics in America's other major gaming venue, Atlantic City. Those who raise the specter of an Atlantic City teeming with crime bred by casinos serving as a blueprint for a crime wave in any community that legalizes gaming obviously misunderstand the statistical realities in Atlantic City. (quoted in *Gambling under Attack* 1996, p. 785)

Advocates of legalizing gambling suggest that there is a certain quantity of illegal gambling existing in any society and that the process of legalization will serve to eliminate the illegal gaming and channel all gambling activity into a properly regulated and taxed enterprise. As with the other evidence, the research here is also mixed. Nevada certainly had a large amount of illegal gambling before "wide-open" casino gambling was legalized in 1931. Since 1931, there has been very little evidence of illegal casino gambling games in Nevada. Illegal operators simply obtained licenses from the state government.

Similarly, David Dixon found that illegal bookmaking was effectively replaced by legal betting when Great Britain passed legislation permitting betting shops in 1960 (Dixon 1990). However, opposite results have been found elsewhere. An examination of casinos in the Netherlands by coauthors William Thompson and J. Kent Pinney found that legalization in 1975 seemed only to promote an expansion of illegal casinos that had operated before laws were passed for government-operated casinos (Thompson and Pinney 1990). Clearly, the illegal operators were not permitted to win licenses. The government also placed many restrictions on its own casinos—they had to be located (at first) outside cities; they could not advertise, give complimentary services, or operate around the clock. Illegal casinos found new places to advertise—at the doors of the legal casinos when they closed at 2 A.M. Similarly, David Dixon found that when Australia established its government-operated betting parlors, illegal sports and race betting underwent a major expansion (Dixon 1988; 1990).

In general, Robert Wagman explained that the efforts to get rid of the illegal operators may actually have achieved an opposite effect (Wagman 1986). Actually, some law enforcement officials are now saying that indications are that the lottery may actually be helping the illegal game. Players are being introduced to the numbers concept in the state-run game; then they switch to the illegal game when they realize they can get a better deal. Then, too, the legal state game has solved the perennial problem faced by the illegal games of finding a commonly accepted and widely available three-digit number to pay off on. Most of the illegal street games now simply use the state's pick-3 number (Wagman 1986).

The strong revenue possibilities that gaming ventures offer may lead some proponents of these ventures to make large financial contributions to the political process. There are references above to the large sums that have been given to certain referenda campaigns for legalization of forms of gambling. Most of this money is given openly and within the boundaries of the law, if not of the moral standards of society. Sometimes money that is directed to legislative lobbying or to specific individual politicians crosses the line of legality or at least the lines of propriety.

The gaming industry has been a major lobbying force in terms of financial contributions at the national level and even more so at the state level. Casinos put more than $4.4 million into federal elections during 1995 and 1996. More than $2.6 million was given in "soft" money to the Democratic and Republican Parties (National Coalition Against Legalized Gambling 1996). The goal of the donations was certainly to stop efforts at establishing national taxation of gambling revenues and having federal regulation. Such goals were also pursued by the card-rooms of California in the state legislature. Over the past six years, the card-rooms have spent millions to defeat state regulations of their industry. Tribes in California have also made contributions for the specific purpose of helping persons win office who would favor their casinos. In the 1994 California gubernatorial election, the Indian tribes contributed more than $1.5 million to the Democratic candidate for governor. They gave $740,000 to a campaign for office of attorney general (Dunstan 1997, pp. x-1–x-3).

The situation has been worse elsewhere. In Missouri the Speaker of the House was charged with criminal violations for taking money from casino interests. He resigned from office. In Louisiana the FBI has investigated improper contributions to members of licensing agencies. Seventeen legislators in South Carolina were convicted of accepting bribes from racing interests to legalize their gambling operations. Six members of the Arizona legislature pleaded guilty for accepting bribes to legalize casinos (Dunstan 1997, p. x-4).

Problem Gamblers

Although many are willing to debate the suggestion that gambling offers positive social redemptions, few would disagree that, as a habit, it can be a very destructive force in individual lives. People get hooked on gambling, almost as they do on drugs or alcohol. They lose fortunes. Some may borrow and steal to support their habit, and, sadly, some have lost all hope and committed suicide.

The issue of compulsive gambling arises whenever legalized gambling becomes a political issue. Horrible examples of obsessive gambling and self-destruction are exposed in antigaming advertisements. However, although these may help illustrate a problem area, they do not always illuminate. More fundamental considerations are at work in problem gamblers than the symptoms of their compulsion. Why do people become addicted to this risky activity? How do they evolve to this level? Which games draw them in, and where do they play? How many potential gamblers are there, and what can be done to treat them?

In 1974, the Commission on the Review of the National Policy Toward Gambling conducted a survey (published in 1976) that indicated that 61 percent of the adult population in the United States had participated in gambling that year. This suggested that the United States contained some 100 million gamblers. It is most likely that an overwhelming percentage of these people did not have a serious problem with gambling, or any problem at all, because most individuals who take gambling risks are aware of the financial perils that await them. Most gamblers, in fact, behave in a rational manner when they play. They have decided they are willing to risk losses in exchange for the thrill of the diversion. Some have even learned the odds well enough to gain a level of wagering skill that earns them money. Even though most gamblers may be playing in order to "win money," as a survey reported above suggests, these same players are knowledgeable about the fact that most gamblers do lose money.

Others, however, have been known to take leave of their reason upon entering the fantasy world of popping lights, ringing bells, and clinking coins. Some of these personality types, caught in an atmosphere of inflated hope, may seek out individuals with similar character traits and gambling habits. The most obsessive and compulsive of the gamblers may become so entranced as to lose awareness of the very people and activity that surrounds them. At this point the lines that demarcate pure wishfulness and true probability vanish, and they begin to live the game instead of the reality. Durand Jacobs finds that compulsive gamblers enter into dissociative states with trances, memory blackouts, and even out-of-body experiences (1989).

Traditionally, people with dominant gambling habits were viewed as morally deprived. This overly simple view of problem gambling was first challenged by Sigmund Freud and his colleagues. Freud analyzed the writings of Fyodor Dostoyevsky, author of *The Gambler*, which was thought to be autobiographical, and reasoned that Dostoyevsky's frantic behavior had risen from a desire for self-punishment. Later studies along these same lines concluded that certain kinds of gamblers derived a masochistic pleasure from losing (Freud 1928).

The psychological theories built upon the work of Freud are generally not considered helpful in the explanation of most episodes of compulsive gambling. Instead, today's students of the subject concentrate upon three other approaches: (1) physiological explanations, (2) sociological theories, and (3) behavioral theories.

Many believe that there is a chemical basis, or physiological underpinning, for gambling addictions (Blaszczynski et al. 1986 Carlton and Goldstein 1987; Roy et al. 1988). Although there may be no evidence that gambling introduces chemicals into the body, as do other addictive-type activities (drug use, alcoholism), several scholars have found that the pathological gambler has certain chemicals in his or her neurological system that are not found in other people. One study also found that the pathological gamblers had significantly lower levels of certain endorphins in their systems (Blaszczynski et al. 1986). There is also a chemical component to the depressive states associated with excessive gambling.

Sociologists see gambling as part of the process of role identification and role behavior and of social class orientation (Bloch 1951; D'Angelo 1983; Devereux 1949; Herman 1967; Rosecrance 1985, 1988; Scott 1968; Zola 1963). Men gamble more often than women because gambling can be associated with the male role of acquiring financial resources for the family while the female remains at home and converts these resources into items to satisfy family needs. Many reference groups of male gamblers also attract other members of the gender to the games. Gamblers also become communities that provide a range of socially supportive opportunities for the player. Gambling communities can become alternative locations for playing out life roles for people who find it difficult to cope in other (or the larger) society (Rosecrance 1985, 1988).

People may also be drawn to gambling because games are played in places where "normal" business contacts can be made. Certainly Las Vegas is not one of the nation's leading business convention centers because businesses *want* their employees to gamble. However, the conventions put the employees in a gambling atmosphere. Sociological scholars may also find wide variations in gambling behaviors among age groups, religious groups, and national identity groups. Many of the sociological dimensions of the gambling problem are presented in the well-noted work *The Chase*, by Henry Lesieur (1984).

Several students of gambling have found explanations for compulsive activity in the theories of behavioral conditioning made very popular by B. F. Skinner (Dickerson 1984; Skinner 1974). (The ideas go back to Greek classical writers and to early English theorists such as Jeremy Bentham.) People gravitate toward activities that bring pleasure, and they avoid activities that bring pain. The schedule of rewards associated with an activity may determine how much a person participates in the activity. Frequent gamblers have defined the anticipation of a gambling win as a very pleasurable experience. However, to get the pleasure, the person must actually be in a place where a gamble can be made, and he or she must be able to make the gamble. To be sure, there is pain, very serious pain, that accompanies gambling losses. However, the compulsive gamblers are able to project that pain off into a distant future, neglecting it, as they seek an opportunity for pleasure that is immediately available. Although basically sociological-cognitive in its approach, Lesieur's categorization of the pathological gambler's career as a "chase" (1984) makes use of this pleasure-pain principle while recognizing other drives to gamble as well.

Theorists and scholars argue about which theory has the most merit, but most students of the subject see both merits and limits within each line of explanation. Some have developed approaches that incorporate aspects of all these theories as well as other ideas. The explanatory notions developed by Henry Lesieur (1984), Robert Custer (Custer and Milt 1985), and Sharon Stein (1989) fall into this category. Although disputes may rage on among the small community of scholars dealing with the problem of explaining compulsive gambling, the community has found a modicum of agreement around some basic concepts that help define or identify the compulsive gambler. The concepts have also led to creation of several survey instruments that can identify individuals as compulsive gamblers and also help in making estimates about the numbers of compulsive gamblers within various communities.

Richard Rosenthal (1989) has identified four categories of descriptive syndromes about which there is a degree of consensus. First, the compulsive gambler is involved in a progression of behavior. The phenomenon is dynamic and ongoing. The compulsive gambler bets more and more and more—more often and with more money—as time moves on (the idea of the "chase" as described by Lesieur [1984]). Second, the compulsive gambler cannot accept losing. When he or she loses, the gambler takes it as a personal defeat that must be quickly rectified by winning bets that can make up for the losses. Losses generate guilt feelings, and they are concealed from other people. Third, the compulsive gambler is preoccupied with gambling at all times. When not gambling, the gambler is reliving old gambling experiences and craves future gambling opportunities. Fourth, the compulsive gambler exhibits a disregard for the consequences of gambling. He or she borrows when consciously knowing that repayment is unlikely, lies to those nearby, is drawn into such criminal behaviors as check forgery and embezzlement, and neglects family obligations. Rosenthal also lists what he calls ancillary factors and predisposing factors that enable the compulsive gambler. However, the major enabling factor is not mentioned in his work: the presence of a gambling activity—the availability (more or less immediately or conveniently present) of an opportunity to gamble.

In 1980, the American Psychiatric Association (APA) endorsed a medical model of pathological gambling symptoms and defined the problem as a disorder of impulse control. Since that time the APA has developed a list of criteria that can be used to assess if a person is a pathological or compulsive gambler. These were included in the APA's 1987 *Diagnostic and Statistical Manual of Mental Disorders* (DSM). The list includes:

1. Frequent preoccupation with gambling or with securing money in order to gamble.
2. The need to gamble with more and more money in order to achieve a needed level of excitement.
3. Becoming restless or irritable when not gambling.
4. Gambling in order to escape from personal problems.
5. Chasing losses by coming back to gamble again in order to get even.
6. Denial of losing after having done so.
7. Borrowing money from others to support gambling.
8. Committing illegal acts to get money to gamble.
9. Jeopardizing family relations, friendships, and job to continue gambling.

If a person indicates that he or she has several of the characteristics in this survey and other similar ones (e.g., the South Oaks Gambling Screen, the Gamblers Anonymous survey), the person is deemed to be a potential pathological gambler.

Most treatment programs set up for problem gamblers have accepted this medical definition, suggesting that pathological gambling is often a permanent, irreversible condition. The best cure, it has been determined, is abstinence—total, complete, and permanent. A return to the activity at any level is likely to bring on the full problem once more. Just as the alcoholic must control himself by never again imbibing a single drink, the addicted gambler who seeks a remedy must never place another bet.

Gamblers Anonymous is a program that utilizes group therapy and personal support to assist problem gamblers and encourage them to stay away from the action. In 1972, a local chapter of the organization in Ohio requested that a nearby Veterans Administration Medical Center start an inpatient program for compulsive gamblers. This was the first such program in the United States (Rosecrance 1988). Other groups bound together that same year to form the National Council on Compulsive Gambling, an organization that advocates support programs based upon the above-mentioned medical conditions. The group has successfully lobbied state governments to win funding for its programs. Maryland, New York, New Jersey, Connecticut, and Iowa, among other states, finance these programs from gambling tax revenues.

The American Psychiatric Association model and Gamblers Anonymous treatment methods, however, are not universally accepted. Sociologist John Rosecrance has suggested that psychiatrists and clinicians defined the criterion for pinpointing compulsive players by studying and treating mostly those problem gamblers who were profoundly affected. Rosecrance asserted that these were individuals who had completely surrendered their will and would have been viewed as unusual even by other gamblers with financially debilitating, albeit less serious, habits.

Rosecrance could claim intimate familiarity with the phenomenon he studied. He spent his adult years as a race enthusiast, betting heavily, and often more than he could afford. He won and he lost, and he generally made the betting parlor his alternative social existence. As a scholar and observer of this scene, Rosecrance was acquainted with many other habitual gamblers—people who might have been called compulsive by others. Rosecrance realized they were not truly compulsive—they pursued their recreation with both feet firmly grounded, even when the betting became irrational or they lost, and they would engage each other with psychological coping mechanisms. Although they were detached from the outside world, these players, unlike the severely strung-out gambling loner, never completely lost sight of their desperate circumstances while keeping their own company (Rosecrance 1988).

Rosecrance felt that losing huge amounts of money was the chief reason that some addicted gamblers become despondent. People tend to become emotionally and mentally unbalanced as they lose money, but the distress of a losing gambler never manifests in exactly the same way. Some are quite capable of quitting early; some may quit a bit later; some who stay the course are lucky enough to begin winning again. These players may also be capable of stopping before losing their good fortune again.

Rosecrance concluded that there are many types of problem gamblers and said their treatment should take into account the social setting and their reasons for seeking such an alternative setting. The solution to the problem of obsession, he suggested, need not be total abstinence. Rosecrance advocated more gradual withdrawals, counseling to help habitual gamblers learn to play with less money, and counseling to assist in the understanding of personal problems involving spouses, children, or jobs. These kinds of difficulties, he reasoned, lay at the heart of the gambler's flight from the responsibilities of life. The better a gambler is at learning to take control of his or her life, the more likely it is that he or she will evolve from a desperate to a responsible gambler.

How many pathological gamblers are there, and how many are prone to enter this condition? It is important to know the extent of problem gambling in any society. But we should realize that there are a host of other habit-forming activities that damage peoples' health and lives and are not subject to control. Millions of people enjoy alcohol, coffee, tobacco, sugar, and fatty foods. These things are ingested legally and voluntarily. Some people cannot control their intake and may suffer harm—even death—from car accidents, obesity, or lung cancer. Just because some individuals cannot control their indulgences, should society ban these items across the board? Other people enjoy the same products in moderation. So, too, do millions of people enjoy gambling without falling to ruin. The weaknesses of a few do not justify the punishment of many.

Policymakers must decide the severity of a problem before banning a product or earmarking public funding for treatment programs. Also, sensitivity to the scope of the problem can help them institute proper controls within the gaming industries. Of course, if a potential problem looks especially ominous, it is best to err on the side of caution and deny legalization of gambling.

As a mass-marketed phenomenon, gambling today would pose a potentially serious problem for society if a large number of people were evaluated as probable addicts. If it is thought that few are inclined in this direction, the potential for difficulty is naturally much smaller. At any rate, some people are bound to be affected. Knowing the probable extent of the problem would allow policymakers to determine the amount of financial burden that should be levied on gambling operators to finance treatment of the afflicted. If a large number of players were seen to be cultivating unhealthy gambling patterns, perhaps additional restrictions on players, gambling operations, and gambling advertising would be justified. For instance, people could be required to identify themselves when purchasing lottery tickets, or tickets could be tracked in the same way that certain prescription drugs are tracked. With such methods we could help assure that gamblers do not exceed their means or do not gamble with others' resources.

If, on the one hand, a problem-prone population is large enough, we could establish self-choice or family-choice mechanisms for exclusion from the ability to purchase gambling products. Or we could restrict credit gambling by requiring that people gamble only with funds they physically bring into a gaming establishment. We could restrict the distribution of alcoholic beverages. A most important approach would be to make efforts to keep our children away from gambling activity.

If, on the other hand, the problem-prone population is determined to be fairly small, we should closely and carefully consider whether to deprive the population at large of the ability to partake of recreational gambling. Personal freedom and choice are cherished values in our society, and Americans should care about preserving them.

How big is the potential for large-scale problem gambling? This is an important question for policymakers. Estimations of the numbers of compulsive or potentially compulsive gamblers vary widely—from less than 1 percent to more than 7 percent. The earliest estimates from Gamblers Anonymous suggested that there were between 6 and 9 million pathological gamblers in the United States. Dr. Robert Custer calculated that 2 percent of adult males were compulsive gamblers and that one-tenth of that proportion of females were compulsives (Custer 1980).

The first comprehensive national survey on compulsive gambling was conducted for the Commission on the Review of the National Policy Toward Gambling by the Survey Research Center of the University of Michigan in 1974. Researchers concluded that 0.77 percent of the adult population consisted of probable pathological gamblers. However, the rate in Nevada, the only state with legal casinos at the time, was 2.5 percent. These results suggested to the researchers that just over 1 million people were compulsives, whereas nearly 4 million would be if gambling were widely accessible to the full population (Commission on the Review of the National Policy Toward Gambling 1976). The survey basically asked people if they were compulsive gamblers. Later surveys utilized the DSM criteria listed previously or other such surveys, most notably the South Oaks Gambling Screen, to determine prevalence rates. The surveys ask if a person has gambled and had the problems listed within the last 12 months or at any time in his or her life. The results gained from surveys in various states and provinces range from under 1 percent for current pathological gambling to over 12 percent for having the problems at some time in their life. One survey of a Native American community in North Dakota, however, found that 14.5 percent of the adults were "lifetime" pathological gamblers.

What are the costs that such an incidence of pathological gambling imposes upon society? Several voices have offered opinions about the societal costs of problem gambling. Ladouceur, Boisvert, Pepia, Loranger, and Sylvain looked at personal debts, loss of productivity, illegal activity, and medical costs (Ladouceur et al. 1994). They indeed showed that problem gamblers had these losses and cause these losses, but they did not attempt to offer a bottom-line cost figure for the total societal effects of either one gambler or all the gamblers. Lesieur and Puig (1987) examined several illegal behaviors in general and insurance frauds in specific. They indicated a monumental cost for society from this fraudulent activity—one-third of insurance fraud is assigned to gamblers—but they did not break the figures down for individual gamblers, and they did not consider other costs. Kindt (1994) reported the social costs of individual compulsive gamblers without showing how the figures were calculated.

I participated in a survey of 98 Gamblers Anonymous members in Wisconsin in order to find precise costs. We assigned conservative numbers for each factor we surveyed. We found that on average, members of Gamblers Anonymous lost 7.5 hours from work each month as a result of gambling when they were suffering from problems. Gamblers also suffered from unemployment attributable to gambling, being unemployed for an average of 1.9 months each and spending an average of 1.3 months on unemployment compensation on an annualized basis.

The 98 had average debts of $38,664 when they went into treatment. Over one-fifth (22.9 percent) had sought the protection of bankruptcy from their creditors. The social cost of this lost debt amounted to $8,909 per member surveyed. On average, members stole $5,738. They were involved in 20 civil cases (other than bankruptcy) and 14 criminal cases. The average cost of therapy per gambler was $2,625. Additionally, a number of the gamblers had accepted various welfare moneys as a result of gambling. The

TABLE 1.5
A Summary of the Annual Societal Costs of One Compulsive Gambler

Employment Costs	
Lost work hours	$1,328
Unemployment compensation	$214
Lost productivity/unemployment	$1,398
Total employment costs	$2,940
Bad Debts	$1,487
Civil Court Costs	
Bankruptcy court	$334
Other civil court	$514
Total civil court costs	$848
Criminal Justice Costs	
Cost of thefts	$1,733
Cost of arrests	$48
Cost of trials	$369
Cost of probation	$186
Cost of incarceration	$1,162
Total criminal justice costs	$3,498
Therapy	$361
Welfare Costs	
Aid to dependent children	$233
Food stamps	$101
Total welfare costs	$334
Total annual social costs, each compulsive gambler	$9,469

survey information indicated that the typical member of Gamblers Anonymous had been a troubled gambler for three years before going into treatment. Therefore, we annualized the social costs of the gambling by dividing each average factor by three. As a result we found that the annual cost to society for one compulsive gambler was $9,469. The cost breakdown is shown in Table 1.5.

In addition to these quantifiable costs, we found that the problem gambler imposed other social costs. Of the 30 gamblers who were divorced or separated, 70 percent said gambling caused the breakup of their marriage. Almost one-fourth of these gamblers (24 percent) reported that they had actually attempted suicide, a proportion many times that found in the general population.

If the social costs we identified—approximately $10,000 ($9,469 plus a factor for divorce and attempted suicide)—were applied to the general population, the result would be a very large number.

Assuming that there are 200 million adults in the United States and Canada, a 1 percent incidence of pathological gambling would yield a social cost of $20 billion per year. This was a first attempt to study the costs of gambling in a precise manner. The bottom-line numbers can be offered only as a suggestion as to what the social costs might be. More studies are certainly necessary in this area (Thompson, Gazel, and Rickman 1996b).

The debate over the numbers will continue, but even with the lower estimates, proponents of gambling should not let the matter rest. Their argument that the entire population should not be punished by being denied the freedom to gamble because of the indiscretions of a few has some merit. However, it is not only gamblers who are hurt by irresponsible players. Lesieur and Custer write: "We would estimate that between 10 and 15 persons are directly affected by the typical pathological gambler, including spouse, children, parents, and other close relatives, fellow gamblers, people borrowed from and stolen from, employers and employees" (1984). Gambling proponents should be able to assert that the form of gambling that is proposed will contain safeguards to minimize the effects of compulsive behaviors on communities and also that treatment programs—whether based on the medical model or some other behavioral modification model, as recommended by Rosecrance's research—are available for those who will suffer from the presence of gambling in the community.

References

Abt, Vicki, James Smith, and Eugene Christiansen. 1985. *The Business of Risk: Commercial Gambling in Mainstream America*. Lawrence: University Press of Kansas.

Albanese, Jay S. 1985. "The Effect of Casino Gambling on Crime." *Federal Probation* 49, no. 2 (June): 39–44.

American Psychiatric Association. 1987. *Diagnostic and Statistical Manual of Mental Disorders*. 3d ed. Washington, DC: American Psychiatric Association.

Anderson, Kurt. 1994. "Las Vegas: The New All-American City." *Time* (10 January): 43–51.

Bashman, A. L. 1967. *The Wonder That Was India*. Calcutta: Rupa Company.

Bell, Raymond. 1976. "Moral Views on Gambling Promulgated by Major American Religious Bodies." In *Gambling in America: Appendix 1*, edited by the Commission on the Review of the National Policy Toward Gambling. Washington, DC: Government Printing Office.

Berger, A. J., and Nancy Bruning. 1979. *Lady Luck's Companion*. New York: Harper and Row.

Blanche, Ernest E. 1950. "Lotteries Yesterday, Today, and Tomorrow." *Annals of the American Academy of Political and Social Science* 269 (May): 71–76.

Blaszczynski, A. P., S. W. Winter, and N. McConaghy. 1986. "Plasma Endorphin Levels in Pathological Gambling." *Journal of Gambling Behavior* 5, no. 2: 1–14.

Bloch, Herbert. 1951. "The Sociology of Gambling." *American Journal of Sociology* 5, no. 57: 216.

"Buddhism." 1978. Pp. 555–557 in *World Book Encyclopedia*. Vol. 2. Chicago: World Book.

Burns, Ken. 1997. "Thomas Jefferson" (television special). Public Broadcasting Service.

Cabot, Anthony N. 1996. *Casino Gaming: Policy, Economics, and Regulation*. Las Vegas: International Gaming Institute, University of Nevada–Las Vegas.

Cabot, Anthony N., and Marc H. Rubenstein. 1993. "Nevada." Pp. 96–103 in *International Casino Law*, edited by Anthony N. Cabot, William N. Thompson, and Andrew Tottenham. 2d ed. Reno: Institute for the Study of Gambling, University of Nevada.

Campbell, Felicia. 1974. "The Gambling Mystique: A Positive View." Paper presented to the First Annual Conference on Gambling, 10 June, Las Vegas, Nevada.

Carlton, P. L., and L. Goldstein. 1987. "Physiological Determinants of Pathological Gambling." In *The Handbook of Pathological Gambling*, edited by T. Gaski. Springfield, IL: Charles C. Thomas.

"Casinos Coming to Detroit." 1997. CNN News, 7 November.

Cassiello, Nicholas, Jr. 1993. "New Jersey." Pp. 113–129 in *International Casino Law*, edited by Anthony N. Cabot, William N. Thompson, and Andrew Tottenham. 2d ed. Reno: Institute for the Study of Gambling, University of Nevada.

Chafetz, Henry. 1960. *Play the Devil: A History of Gambling in the United States from 1492 to 1955*. New York: Potter Publishers.

Chiricos, Ted. 1994. "Casinos and Crime: An Assessment of the Evidence." Unpublished manuscript.

Christiansen, Eugene Martin. 1996. "The United States Gross Annual Wager." *International Gaming and Wagering Business* (August): 55–92.

Clotfelter, Charles T., and Philip J. Cook. 1989. *Selling Hope: State Lotteries in America*. Cambridge, MA: Harvard University Press.

Cloward, Richard A., and Lloyd E. Ohlin. 1960. *Delinquency and Opportunity*. New York: The Free Press of Glencoe.

Commission on the Review of the National Policy Toward Gambling. 1976. *Gambling in America: Appendix 2: Survey of American Gambling Attitudes and Behavior*. Washington, DC: Government Printing Office.

Corporation of the President of The Church of Jesus Christ of Latter-day Saints. 1988. *Position of the Church*. Salt Lake City, UT: Corporation of the President of the Church.

Council of State Governments. 1996. *Book of the States 1995–6*. Lexington, KY: Council of State Governments.

Custer, Robert L. 1980. *The Profile of Pathological Gamblers*. Washington, DC: National Foundation for the Study and Treatment of Pathological Gambling.

Custer, Robert L., and Harry Milt. 1985. *When Luck Runs Out*. New York: Facts on File.

D'Angelo, Raymond N. 1983. *The Social Organization of Sports Gambling: A Study on Conventionality and Deviance*. Ph.D. diss., Department of Sociology, Bryn Mawr University.

Day, John. 1950. "Horse Racing and the Pari-Mutuel." *Annals of the American Academy of Political and Social Science* 269 (May): 57–58.

Demaris, Ovid. 1986. *How Greed, Corruption, and the Mafia Turned Atlantic City into the Boardwalk Jungle*. New York: Bantam Books.

Demaris, Ovid, and Ed Reid. 1963. *The Green Felt Jungle*. New York: Trident Press.

Devereux, E. C. 1949. *Gambling and Social Structure*. Ph.D. diss., Department of Sociology, Harvard University.

Dickerson, Mark. 1984. *Compulsive Gamblers*. London: Longman.

Dixon, David. 1990. *From Prohibition to Regulation: Bookmaking, Anti-Gambling and the Law*. Oxford: Clarendon Press.

———. 1988. "Responses to Illegal Betting in Britain and Australia." Pp. 247–279 in *Gambling Research: Proceedings of the Seventh International Conference on Gambling and Risk Taking*, Vol. 1, edited by William R. Eadington. Reno: University of Nevada, Bureau of Business and Economic Research.

Dombrink, John Dennis. 1981. *Outlaw Businessmen: Organized Crime and the Legalization of Casino Gambling*. Ph.D. diss., University of California–Berkeley.

Dombrink, John, and William N. Thompson. 1990. *The Last Resort: Success and Failure in Campaigns for Casinos*. Reno: University of Nevada Press.

Dunstan, Roger. 1997. *Gambling in California*. Sacramento: California Research Bureau.

Encyclopedia of Religion. 1928. Vol. 5. New York: Scribner.

The Evans Group. 1996. *A Study of the Economic Impact of the Gaming Industry through 2005*. Evanston, IL: Evans Group.

Florida Department of Law Enforcement. 1994. *The Question of Casinos in Florida: Increased Crime: Is It Worth the Gamble?* Tallahassee: State of Florida.

Freud, Sigmund. 1928. "Dostoyevsky and Parricide." P. 21 in *Complete Psychological Works of Freud*, edited by James Strachey. London: Hogarth Press.

Friedman, Joseph, Simon Hakim, and J. Weinblatt. 1989. "Casino Gambling as a 'Growth Pole' Strategy and Its Effect on Crime." *Journal of Regional Science* 29, no 4: 615–623.

"Gambling—The Newest Growth Industry." 1978. *Business Week* (26 June): 110–111.

Gambling under Attack. 1996. Washington, DC: Congressional Quarterly. (Also published in *CQ Researcher* 6, no. 33 [6 September].)

Gaming Control Board (Nevada). 1977. *Gaming, Nevada Style*. Carson City: Nevada State Printing Office.

The Gaming Research Group. 1995. *The 1995 United States Survey of Gaming and Gambling*. State University: Mississippi State University, Social Science Research Center.

General Conference of the United Methodist Church. 1984. *Social Principles of the United Methodist Church*. Nashville, TN: General Board of Church and Society, United Methodist Church.

German, Jeff. 1997. "Leaked Gaming Tapes Spark State Rift." *Las Vegas Sun* (25 February): 1A, 4A.

Grant, Heber J. 1926. *Improvement Era*. Salt Lake City, UT: Church of Jesus Christ of Latter-day Saints.

Hakim, Simon, and Andrew J. Buck. 1989. "Do Casinos Enhance Crime." *Journal of Criminal Justice* 17: 409–416.

Hancock County, Mississippi. 1994. *Crime Statistics*. Hancock County, MS.

Harrah's Entertainment, Inc. 1996. *Harrah's Survey of Casino Entertainment*. Memphis, TN: Harrah's.

———. 1992. *Harrah's Survey of Casino Entertainment*. Memphis, TN: Harrah's.

Haskins, Jim. 1979. *Gambling: Who Really Wins?* New York: Franklin Watts.

Herman, Robert D. 1976. *Gamblers and Gambling: Motives, Institutions and Controls*. Lexington, MA: D. C. Heath.

———. 1967. *Gambling*. New York: Harper and Row.

Hopkins, E. Washburn. 1924. *Ethics of India*. Port Washington, NY: Kennikat Press.

Indian Gaming Regulatory Act of 1988. 1988. U.S. Public Law 100-497. 25 October.

Jacobs, Durand. 1989. "A General Theory of Addictions: Rationale for and Evidence Supporting a New Approach for Understanding and Treating Addictive Behaviors." Pp. 35–64 in *Compulsive Gambling: Theory, Research, and Practice,* edited by Howard J. Shaffer, Sharon A. Stein, Blase Gambino, and Thomas N. Cummings. Lexington, MA: D. C. Heath (Lexington Books).

Jacobs, Louis. 1973. *What Does Judaism Say About?* New York: Quadrangle.

Johnston, David, 1992. *Temples of Chance—How America, Inc. Bought Out Murder, Inc. to Win Control of the Casino Business.* New York: Doubleday.

Karcher, Alan. 1989. *Lotteries* New Brunswick, NJ: Transaction Publishers.

Kindt, John Warren. 1995. "U.S. National Security and the Strategic Economic Base: The Business/Economic Impacts of the Legalization of Gambling Activities." *Saint Louis University Law Journal* 39, no. 2 (winter): 567–584.

———. 1994. "Increased Crime and Legalized Gambling Operations: The Impact on the Socio-Economics of Business and Government." *Criminal Law Bulletin* 43: 538–539.

Klein, Howard J., and Gary Selesner. 1982. "Results of the First Gallup Organization Study of Legalized Gambling." *Gaming Business Magazine* (November): 5–7, 48–49.

Ladouceur, Robert, et al. 1994. "Social Cost of Pathological Gambling." *Journal of Gaming Studies* 10, no. 4 (winter): 399–409.

LaFleur, Terri. 1991. "A Lottery Grows in Texas: Lone Star Lottery on '92 Ballot." *Gaming and Wagering Business* (September–October): 59.

Lehne, Richard. 1986. *Casino Policy.* New Brunswick, NJ: Rutgers University Press.

Lesieur, Henry R. 1984. *The Chase: Career of the Compulsive Gambler.* Cambridge, MA: Schenkman.

Lesieur, Henry, and S. B. Blume. 1987. "The South Oaks Gambling Screen." *American Journal of Psychiatry* 144: 1184–1188.

Lesieur, Henry, and Robert L. Custer. 1984. "Pathological Gambling: Roots, Phases, and Treatment." *Annals of the American Academy of Political and Social Science* 474 (July): 147–148.

Lesieur, Henry, and K. Puig. 1987. "Insurance Problems and Compulsive Gambling." *Journal of Gambling Behavior* 3.

Linn, Louis. 1986. "Jews and Pathological Gambling." Pp. 337–358 in *Addiction in the Jewish Community,* edited by Stephen Jay Levy. New York: Commission on Synagogue Relations.

Mahon, Gigi. 1980. *The Company That Bought the Boardwalk.* New York: Random House.

Mangalmurti, Sandeep, and Robert Allan Cooke. 1991. *State Lotteries: Seducing the Less Fortunate?* Heartland Policy Study, no. 35. Chicago: The Heartland Institute.

Mayhew, Patricia. 1990. "Opportunity and Vehicle Crime." In *Policy and Theory in Criminal Justice,* edited by Don Gottfredson and Ronald V. Clarke. Aldershot, UK: Avebury.

McQueen, Patricia A. 1996. "North American Gaming at a Glance." *International Gaming and Wagering Business* (September).

Mikesell, John L., and C. Kurt Zorn. 1986. "State Lotteries as Fiscal Savior or Fiscal Fraud." *Public Administration Review* 46 (July–August): 311–320.

Mississippi State University Gambling Group. 1995. National Gambling Survey. Starkville, MS: MSU Social Sciences Research Center.

Moody, Gordon. 1990. Interview by author. London, England, 20 August.

Morgan, Kenneth. 1956. *The Path of the Buddha.* New York: The Ronald Press.

National Coalition Against Legalized Gambling. 1996. *Newsletter* (winter).

The New Catholic Encyclopedia. 1967. New York: McGraw-Hill.

Newman, David, ed. 1962. Esquire's *Book of Gambling.* New York: Harper and Row.

Ochrym, Ronald George, and Clifton Park. 1990. "Street Crime, Tourism, and Casinos: An Empirical Comparison." *Journal of Gambling Studies* 6 (summer): 127–138.

The Old West: The Gamblers. 1978. Alexandria, VA: Time-Life Books.

Peterson, Virgil W. 1965. "A Look at Legalized Gambling." *Christian Century* 82 (May 26): 677.

———. 1951. *Gambling: Should It Be Legalized?* Springfield, IL: Charles C. Thomas.

Pollock, Michael. *Hostage to Fortune.* 1987. Princeton, NJ: Center for the Analysis of Public Issues.

Reckless, Walter C. 1961. *The Crime Problem.* 3d ed. New York: Appleton-Century Crofts.

Resolution of Central Conference of American Rabbis. 1986. 97th Annual Convention, Snowmass, CO.

Rose, I. Nelson. 1986. *Gambling and the Law.* Hollywood, CA: Gambling Times Press.

———. 1979–1980. "The Legalization and Control of Casino Gambling." *Fordham Law Journal* 8, no. 2: 245–300.

Rosecrance, John. 1988. *Gambling without Guilt*. Pacific Grove, CA: Brooks/Cole.

———. 1985. *The Degenerates of Lake Tahoe*. New York: Peter Lang.

Rosenthal, Franz. 1975. *Gambling in Islam*. Leiden: Brill.

Rosenthal, Richard J. 1989. "Pathological Gambling and Problem Gambling: Problems of Definition and Diagnosis." Pp. 101–126 in *Compulsive Gambling: Theory, Research, and Practice*, edited by Howard J. Shaffer, Sharon A. Stein, Blase Gambino, and Thomas N. Cummings. Lexington, MA: D. C. Heath (Lexington Books).

———. 1986. "The Pathological Gambler's System for Self Deception." *Journal of Gambling Behavior* 2: 108–120.

Roy, A. et al. 1988. "Pathological Gambling: A Psychobiological Study." *Archives of General Psychiatry* 45: 369–373.

Scarne, John. 1961. *Scarne's Complete Guide to Gambling*. New York: Simon and Schuster.

Schacht, Joseph. 1964. *An Introduction to Islamic Law*. Oxford: Clarendon Press.

Scientific Games. 1985. Advertisement. *Gaming and Wagering Business Magazine* (June): back cover.

Scott, Marvin B. 1968. *The Racing Game*. Chicago: Aldine Press.

Shaffer, Howard J., Sharon A. Stein, Blase Gambino, and Thomas N. Cummings, eds. 1989. *Compulsive Gambling: Theory, Research, and Practice*. Lexington, MA: Lexington Books.

Skinner, B. F. 1974. *About Behaviorism*. New York: Alfred A. Knopf.

Skolnick, Jerome. 1978. *House of Cards*. Boston: Little, Brown.

Smith, James F. 1986. "Las Vegas East? Atlantic City Ten Years after the Referendum." *Nevada Public Affairs Review*, Special Issue, no. 2: 50–55.

Spiro, Melford E. 1982. *Buddhism and Society*. Berkeley: University of California Press.

Starkey, L. M. 1964. *Money, Mania, and Morals*. New York: Abington Press.

Stein, Sharon A. 1989. "A Developmental Approach to Understanding Compulsive Gambling Behavior." Pp. 65–88 in *Compulsive Gambling: Theory, Research, and Practice*, edited by Howard J. Shaffer, Sharon A. Stein, Blase Gambino, and Thomas N. Cummings. Lexington, MA: D. C. Heath (Lexington Books).

Sternlieb, George, and James W. Hughes. 1983. *The Atlantic City Gamble*. Cambridge, MA: Harvard University Press.

Taber, Julian, John L. Collachi, and Edward J. Lynn. 1986. "Pathological Gambling: Possibilities for Treatment in Northern Nevada." *Nevada Public Affairs Review*, Special Issue, no. 2: 39–41.

Thompson, William N. 1994. "The States Bet on Legalized Gambling." Pp. 390–401 in *The 1994 World Book Yearbook*. Chicago: World Book.

———. 1991. "Machismo: Manifestations of a Cultural Value in the Latin American Casino." *Journal of Gambling Studies* 7 (summer): 143–164.

———. 1988. "Criminal Enterprise in American and European Casinos: A Comparative Analysis." Paper presented to the Western Society of Criminology, 25 February, Monterey, CA.

Thompson, William N., and Ricardo Gazel. 1996. *The Economics of Casino Gambling in Illinois*. Chicago: The Better Government Association.

Thompson, William N., Ricardo Gazel, and Dan Rickman. 1996a. *Crime and Casinos: What's the Connection*. Mequon: Wisconsin Policy Research Institute.

———. 1996b. *The Social Costs of Gambling in Wisconsin*. Milwaukee: Wisconsin Policy Research Institute.

———. 1995. *The Economic Impact of Native American Gaming in Wisconsin*. Milwaukee: Wisconsin Policy Research Institute.

Thompson, William N., and J. Kent Pinney. 1990. "The Mismarketing of Dutch Casinos." *Journal of Gambling Studies* 6 (fall): 205–221.

Thompson, William N., R. Keith Schwer, Richard Hoyt, and Dolores Bronson. 1993. "Not in My Backyard: Las Vegas Residents Protest Casinos." *Journal of Gambling Studies*: 47–62.

U.S. Senate Special Committee to Investigate Organized Crime in Interstate Commerce. 1951. *Report [Kefauver Report]*. Washington, DC: Government Printing Office.

Wagman, Robert. 1986. *Instant Millionaires*. Washington, DC: Woodbine House.

Walker, Michael. 1992. *The Psychology of Gambling*. Oxford: Pergamon Press.

Wayne, Pelton R. 1980. "Laughable Gaming Laws." *Gambling Times* (January): 26–27.

Welles, C. 1989. "America's Gambling Fever." *Business Week* (24 April): 112–115.

Werblowsky, R. J. Z., and G. Wigoder, eds. 1966. *Encyclopedia of the Jewish Religion*. New York: Holt, Rinehart and Winston.

Wilkins, Leslie. 1964. *Social Deviance*. London: Tavistock Publications.

Windsor (Ontario) Police Department. 1995. *Crime and Casino Gambling: A Report*.

Wynne, H., G. Smith, and R. Volberg. 1995. *Pathological Gambling in Alberta*. Edmonton: Alberta Gaming Commission.

Zola, Irving K. 1963. "Observations on Gambling in a Lower-Class Setting." *Social Problems* 10: 360.

Chronology 2

B efore European settlers came to American soil, many native nations engaged in ritualistic gambling games.

The European societies that sponsored exploration and settlement of the Western Hemisphere also had a variety of gambling games. Florence was the first European state to have a lottery; it started in 1530. Lotteries came to France in 1533, and England chartered its first government lottery in 1566.

The institution of gambling was well established in North America and throughout the world by the time Capt. John Smith brought his colonists to Jamestown in 1607. Almost immediately, Smith was back in London seeking financial help to keep his settlement going. Soon John Smith's Virginia Company was given permission to raise funds through the sale of lottery tickets. The chronology below records critical events in the history of North American gambling from Smith's landing through the 1990s.

1612   A lottery is organized in London to support Virginia Colony in North America. Four drawings are held between 1612 and 1615. Ticket purchasers are told they are honoring both "God and Country." Thus are the seeds for

1612
cont.

modern lottery advertising sown by the founders of the first permanent European settlement on the continent.

1620

Twenty mares are shipped from England to Virginia Colony, and horse racing with private wagering becomes a regular activity for the settlers.

1621

The first restrictions on gambling are established in Plymouth Colony. Opposition to forms of card playing and gambling are also instituted in early Massachusetts Bay Colony. Although the lottery activity in London may have saved Virginia Colony, gambling activity is quickly seen as a dangerous vice when taken up by the new settlers, at least in New England. Soon, prohibitions on many gambling activities are found throughout the Northeast. The need for these prohibitions serves as an indication that gambling activity is quite widespread among the new Americans from the first days of colonization.

1665

A permanent oval horse racing course is laid out on the Hempstead Plain on Long Island, New York Colony. This marks the commercial beginnings of a facet of the gambling industry in North America. Racing before this time consisted of match races over long, straight courses, with betting between individuals only. The new track activity is so successful that soon large oval courses can be found in a majority of the colonies.

1682

The Quaker government of Pennsylvania Colony passes antigambling legislation. However, the futility of prohibition is witnessed here and elsewhere by continued gambling. Pennsylvania's leading citizen, Benjamin Franklin, is a frequent lottery player throughout his adult life in Philadelphia.

1728

Three Arabian horses are shipped to England from the Middle East. From these three horses a stock of racing horses is developed. Today, almost every thoroughbred racing horse can trace its lineage to one of the three horses.

1765

The British Parliament passes the Stamp Act, which provides for the taxation of playing cards. The Act is one of the first of the "Obnoxious Acts" considered responsible for the eventual rebellion in America. That the British target playing cards as a potential source of tax revenues is an indication of how much Americans love card games. A good portion of the card decks found in the colonies at the time were manufactured by America's leading printer, Benjamin Franklin.

1776   Thomas Jefferson gambles as he composes the Declaration of Independence. John Rosecrance's 1988 *Gambling without Guilt* describes entries in Jefferson's diary from June 1776 that detail his and his wife's wins and losses at backgammon and lotto. Following independence, the first wave of legalized gambling manifests itself as lotteries fund war activities. In 1777, the Continental Congress initiates a lottery game. Massachusetts, New York, and Rhode Island legislative bodies follow suit.

1790s   Lotteries become a major economic tool for financing civic projects. Lottery funds help build the new capital city on the Potomac. Many colleges, including Harvard, Yale, Columbia, Rutgers, and Dartmouth, use lottery moneys to construct buildings. Other schools and even churches do the same. From 1790 to 1830, 21 state governments issue licenses for nearly 200 lottery schemes.

1810   Former president Thomas Jefferson says he never gambles on lotteries, and he issues a letter very critical of lotteries and gambling.

1812   The first steamboat operates on the Mississippi River, inaugurating an era of riverboat gambling in the West. The boat is Robert Fulton's *New Orleans*. The boat sinks but is replaced by a larger *New Orleans* in 1815. The new boat has passenger accommodations and spacious areas where cardsharps seek to fleece money from farmers and traders.

1815   New Orleans licenses casino gaming enterprises in the city. New Orleans was already wide open to gambling when it became part of the United States with the 1803 Louisiana Purchase. Legislation and licensing are seen

1815 cont.	as a means to control the widespread gambling and generate moneys for municipal improvements.
1820	The number of western riverboats with gaming grows to 69.
1826	Jefferson supports the use of lotteries as a means for persons to dispose of their property in a respectable manner so that they can pay their bills. He calls lotteries a tax "laid on the willing only."
1827	John Davis opens the first complete casino in the United States in New Orleans, at the corner of Orleans and Bourbon Streets. The high-class establishment caters to aristocratic tastes and includes entertainment and the best dining available. Although open only until 1835, it serves as a model for modern Las Vegas– and Atlantic City–type casinos.
1832	The high point of early lottery play, with 420 lottery games in eight states. However, scandals and mismanagement plague most of the games.
1833	The Jacksonian Era ushers in a mood of general governmental reform. This affects gambling, as reformers call for a cessation of all such activity. Pennsylvania and Maryland are the first to prohibit lotteries, and most other states follow suit. Between 1833 and 1840, 12 states ban lotteries. By the time of the Civil War all legal lotteries have halted. This marks the end of the first major wave of legal gambling in the United States.
1835	New Orleans declares casinos to be illegal. High-class aristocratic gaming halls such as John Davis's close, but lower-class gambling dens continue to operate illegally. The antigambling reform movement moves up the Mississippi River. A vigilante committee torches the gambling dens of Vicksburg, Mississippi, and lynches five gamblers.
1836	The first stakes horse race in North America is held in Quebec. In a stakes race, the horses run for a prize, a part of which is put forth by the owners of the horses.

1848 The gold strike in California marks a new trend: mining camp gambling halls. Eastern reform and western opportunity define the redistribution of gambling sin activity in the 1840s and, 100 years later, the 1940s. While opportunity brings prospectors west, reform pushes gamblers in the same direction, with gamblers drawn by the opportunity to strike gold in the halls themselves. San Francisco, the major headquarters for obtaining provisions, becomes a central venue for gambling activity. Much of the San Francisco gaming is concentrated in the Chinese quarter of the city. Reformers win approval of various antigambling laws, but these remain ineffectual as mining continues to attract fortune hunters.

1860 Riverboat gambling reaches its apex, with 557 boats operating on the eve of the Civil War. *The Old West: The Gamblers*, published in 1978 by Time-Life Books, suggests that there were as many as 2,000 gamblers running games, and it is estimated that 99 percent of them cheated players.

1864 The Travers Stakes horse race was run for the first time at Saratoga, New York. It was the first stakes race in the United States. Originally it became part of the triple crown of racing. However, that honor was later lost, and the Triple Crown races became the Preakness, the Belmont Stakes, and the Kentucky Derby.

1865 The totalizator is invented in France. It is a calculator that permits horse race bets to be pooled and odds calculated (or recalculated) as bets are being made. The device allows for the creation of the pari-mutuel system of betting. This facilitates a means of taxing horse race betting and also of collecting funds for race purses (prizes to winning horses). The totalizator was not used in North American tracks until 1933, but today the pari-mutuel system is in place at every major track in North America.

1867 The inaugural running of the Belmont Stakes takes place in Belmont, New York.

1868   Gambling gets a second wind as the Louisiana lottery begins a three-decade reign of abuse and corruption. Initially started to bring needed revenues to a war-torn bankrupt state, the lottery is soon overcome by New York entrepreneurs who sustain it by regularly bribing state officials. The lottery enjoys great success as tickets are sold through the mail across the continent.

1873   The inaugural running of the Preakness stakes takes place at the Pimlico race track in Baltimore, Maryland.

1875   The first Kentucky Derby is run on 17 May at Churchill Downs in Louisville. It is won by Aristides.

1877   Congress actually adjourns so that members can attend horse racing events at the Pimlico track in Baltimore.

1887   Charles Fey invents the slot machine in San Francisco. This first machine accepts and pays nickels. Soon similar devices are found throughout the city, and since patents on the concept of a gambling machine are not granted by the government at this time, the door is opened for imitation by other manufacturers. To dodge authorities who declare the machines illegal, manufacturers and operators begin to award merchandise or indirect cash payments to winners. One century after its invention, slot machine gaming will become the number-one form of gambling in North American casinos.

1890   Congress bans the sale of lottery tickets through the mail. This significantly affects the Louisiana Lottery, which was the target of the law. Two years later the Louisiana Lottery is voted out of existence. These actions represent the beginning of the end of the second wave of legalized gambling in the United States.

1891   The Broadmoor Casino Resort opens in Colorado Springs, Colorado. This casino brings a new elegance to western gaming. The building is 244 feet long and sits beside a lake. As many as 15,000 players visit the establishment each day. However, the casino fails to make money from gambling because people gamble among themselves rather than playing "house-banked games" that involve players making wagers against the casino, with the casino always having odds in its favor. The casino is destroyed by fire in 1897.

The first organized regulation of horse race courses begins with licensing of jockeys and trainers by a private board of control in New York State. The growth in popularity of race betting requires the establishment of integrity in racing, as many bettors were driven away by the fear that races were fixed. Now regulators assure that jockeys, managers, and owners have "clean" backgrounds. Regulators are empowered to ban those caught cheating from racing activities. Track activity is now monitored by neutral parties.

1892   The antigambling movement takes hold in Canada as Parliament bans almost all forms of gambling by means of revisions to the Criminal Code.

1894   The Jockey Club of New York is established. It helps to develop national standards for horse racing.

1900   The total prohibition on gambling in Canada begins its century of unraveling as an amendment to the Criminal Code permits small raffles.

1906   Kentucky becomes the first state to establish a government-run state racing commission. At the same time, other states begin to ban horse racing. Tennessee closes its tracks in 1906; California closes its tracks in 1909; and New York closes its tracks in 1911.

1907   The Arizona and New Mexico territorial governments outlaw all gambling in their quest for statehood.

1910   The era of antigambling reform seems nearly complete in the United States. Nevada closes its casinos, and legalized gambling in the United States, with the exception of a few horse race tracks, is dormant.

1910 cont.	In Canada the Criminal Code is again amended, this time to allow betting at racing tracks.
1922	The Canadian Criminal Code adds a provision banning the use of dice in any gambling activity. This ban continues today, as the charitable and government-operated casinos of Canada do not have dice games. However, some casinos have simulated dice games by placing dice configurations within roulette wheels or on slot machine reels.
1925	Limited gaming activity is permitted at fairs in Canada.
1931	The state of Nevada legalizes wide-open casino gambling. At first, gaming is confined to small saloons and taverns and is regulated by counties. Casino taxes consist of set fees on each table or machine game. The taxes are shared between local and state governments.
1933	At Arlington Park, Illinois, the totalizator is used at a U.S. horse race track for the first time. The totalizator machine allows the track to effectively implement the pari-mutuel system of betting invented in France in 1865. This system permits all bets to be pooled. The track ceases to bet against the players and instead receives a fixed fee or percentage of the betting pool for redistributing the bets from losers to winners. Soon legal horse race betting returns to several Depression-bankrupt (or near bankrupt) states as a revenue mechanism.
1935	New horse race betting legislation is approved in Illinois, Louisiana, Florida, New Hampshire, West Virginia, Ohio, Michigan, Massachusetts, Rhode Island, and Delaware.
1938	California legalizes horse race betting.
1940	New York legalizes horse race betting.
1941	The Las Vegas Strip begins its legacy as the world's primary casino gaming location. The El Rancho Vegas is the first casino on the Strip and is soon

joined by the Last Frontier and the Desert Inn. These new-style casinos offer hotel accommodations and recreational amenities to tourists.

1945   The state government of Nevada begins to license casinos for the first time. In addition to set fees on each game, the casinos begin to pay a tax on the amount of money they win from players. Nevada casino activity increases as World War II ends, but operators of illegal gaming establishments throughout the country face a new wave of reform. Reform is triggered with the end of World War II as public resources and public concern turns to domestic problems. Gamblers shift operations to Las Vegas.

1946   Gangster Benjamin (Bugsy) Siegel, financed by organized crime kingpin Meyer Lansky, opens the Flamingo Casino on the Las Vegas Strip. The casino features a showroom with Hollywood entertainment.

1947   Siegel's murder in June sensationalizes the Strip and firms up Las Vegas's reputation as a risky, naughty place where Main Street Americans can rub shoulders with notorious mobsters.

Idaho legislature passes a slot machine law that permits licensing and taxing of machines. A few years later the voters decide to once again outlaw machines.

1950   The U.S. Senate investigates organized crime and gambling casinos. Tennessee senator Estes Kefauver leads a committee that fingers Las Vegas as a "den of evil" controlled by "the Mob." Ironically, although some voices on his committee call for a closure of casinos in Las Vegas, an opposite effect is realized. Gaming in Las Vegas is strengthened. The investigations serve mainly to hurry the closure of illegal establishments in other jurisdictions. This hastens the exodus of operators to Las Vegas, where they help build the industry. Further irony is found in the federal government activities of 1950. While the Senate committee is seeking a crackdown on casinos within the United States, Congress authorizes the expenditure of U.S. taxpayer funds to open a casino in

1950 cont.	Travemunde, Germany, under the provisions of the Marshall Fund for business recovery in Western Europe after World War II.
1955	Nevada creates the Gaming Control Board under the direction of the State Treasury Commission. A process of professionalizing gaming regulation begins as an effort to convince federal authorities that the state can run honest, crime-free casinos.
1959	The Nevada Gaming Commission is created to oversee the decisions of the Gaming Control Board. Gaming regulation is removed from the State Treasury Commission.
1963	The third wave of legalized gambling in the United States begins with the New Hampshire lottery. This new sweepstakes is the first government lottery since the closing of the Louisiana lottery. The state sells its first lottery ticket in 1964. It is a $3 ticket for a semi-annual game patterned after the Irish Sweepstakes. However, the game does not do as well as the state officials had hoped. Public interest wanes as a result of the high ticket price and the lengthy wait for lottery results.
1966	Billionaire Howard Hughes moves to Las Vegas and begins to purchase Nevada casinos from owners with suspicious connections to organized crime. This helps to improve the city's image. Hughes has a flamboyant image but also a reputation as an entrepreneur with integrity. Federal authorities, most notably Attorney General Robert Kennedy, continue to focus attention on organized crime in Nevada.
1967	New York begins a lottery, but it fails to meet state officials' budget expectations. Like the New Hampshire games, the lottery's monthly draw game proves to be too slow. Few other jurisdictions take notice of the lottery.
1968	The federal government initiates actions to prohibit Howard Hughes from purchasing any more Las Vegas casinos (specifically the Landmark) on anti-

trust grounds. Hughes is angered and allegedly initiates a plan to win federal approval by bribing presidential candidates Richard Nixon and Hubert Humphrey. Kennedy family confidant Larry O'Brien is on Hughes's staff at the time. Four years later it is suggested that Nixon ordered a break-in of O'Brien's office at the Watergate Building in Washington, D.C., to find out what information O'Brien has about the 1968 bribe. O'Brien at that time is National Democratic Party chairman.

1969   Nevada permits ownership of casinos by public corporations. This action is prompted by the industry's need to maintain and upgrade facilities and a continuing need to improve the state's image. After purchasing the Landmark, Howard Hughes stops purchasing casinos under further federal antitrust actions, and his disintegration into a complete recluse precludes him from improving his properties. In 1970, he leaves Las Vegas.

New Jersey authorizes a lottery. In 1970, the state begins sales of weekly lottery tickets using mass-marketing techniques. The New Jersey operation is successful from the beginning, and other states realize that large revenues can be had from gaming if ticket prices are low and games occur regularly. Lotteries begin to spread quickly.

The Canadian Criminal Code is amended to permit lottery schemes to be operated by governments and charitable organizations. Soon many of the provinces have lotteries, and the door is opened for the charities and governments to offer casino games.

1970   The Yukon Territory permits the Klondike Visitors' Association to conduct casino games from mid-spring through the summer at Diamond Tooth Gerties in Dawson City. This is the first legal casino in Canada.

Loto Quebec, an agency of the Quebec provincial government, initiates the first lottery gaming in Canada.

1974   Massachusetts becomes the first North American jurisdiction to introduce an instant lottery game. This becomes the most popular lottery game of the decade, and all other lotteries begin to sell instant games.

Maryland authorizes the creation of an interest-only lottery program like one used in England. The player buys a no-interest bond and may cash it in at full purchase price at any time. However, as long as the player holds the bond, he or she is illegible to win lottery prizes, which are awarded in lieu of interest payments. The system is never implemented.

The Western Canada Lottery Corporation initiates the first intergovernmental lottery in North America. The provinces of Manitoba, Saskatchewan, Alberta, and British Columbia operate these games together. British Columbia later drops out of the joint operation in order to have its own lottery games.

1975   New Jersey starts the first "numbers game" with players selecting their own three-digit numbers. The game is offered with hopes that it will drive the popular illegal numbers games out of business. Other lotteries adopt the numbers game as well, often adding a four-digit number game. There is little evidence that illegal games will stop.

1975–1976   The Commission on the Review of the National Policy Toward Gambling issues a report affirming the notion that gambling activity—its legalization and control—is a matter for the jurisdictions of state governments. However, the commission concludes that casinos should be located in remote areas far removed from metropolitan populations. The commission is authorized by the 1970 Organized Crime Control Act.

1976   New Jersey voters authorize casino gambling for Atlantic City by a margin of 56 percent to 44 percent. The successful 1976 campaign follows an unsuccessful campaign for casinos in 1974. The campaign is well financed by the Resorts International Casino organization of the Bahamas. Minor opposition by religious officials is unorganized.

The Atlantic Lottery Corporation is formed by action of the provinces of Newfoundland, Prince Edward Island, New Brunswick, and Nova Scotia. Lotteries are begun in these four provinces, thereby bringing the games into all Canadian provinces.

1977   New Jersey creates a regulatory structure for casino gaming that includes an independent Casino Control Commission, and a Division of Gaming Enforcement is within the state attorney general's office.

1978   Casino gaming begins in Atlantic City with the opening of Resorts International on Memorial Day weekend. Crowds jam the single casino, which realizes windfall profits from a monopoly status that lasts 14 months.

High-stakes bingo games begin on the Seminole Indian reservation in Hollywood, Florida, signaling a new period of Indian gambling. In subsequent federal court litigation the Native Americans retain the right to conduct games that are unregulated by the state.

The Province of Ontario initiates the world's first lotto game, called Lottario. The game requires players to select six numbers, and all play is entered into an on-line computer network. A jackpot prize is given to any player who picks all six numbers. If there is no winner, more prize money is added to the next drawing.

Jackpots in U.S. lotto games have grown to exceed $100 million. Soon afterward Quebec introduces its own on-line lotto game. Many states and provinces rush to imitate the lotto games, which quickly lead all other types of lottery games in sales.

1985   The Canadian national government agrees to place responsibility for the administration of all gambling laws with the provinces in exchange for a $100 million payment to offset the costs of the Calgary Winter Olympics of 1988. The Criminal Code is revised in accordance with the agreement. Nevertheless, the national ban on dice games remains, as does a national stipulation that slot (and video) machine

1985
cont.

gaming must be operated by governmental agencies and that there can be no betting on single sports events.

1985–1986

The President's Commission on Organized Crime fails to issue a report on gambling, as it now considers gambling to be, for the most part, a legitimate industry.

1987

The U.S. Supreme Court upholds the rights of Indian tribes to offer unregulated gambling enterprises as long as operations do not violate state criminal policy. The *Cabazon* v. *California* case determines that any regulation of noncriminal matters must come from the federal government or be specifically authorized by Congress.

1988

The Indian Gaming Regulatory Act is passed by Congress in response to the Cabazon decision. The act provides for federal and tribal regulation of bingo games and for mutually negotiated Indian–state government schemes for the regulation of casinos on reservations.

The voters of South Dakota authorize limited ($5) stakes casino games of blackjack, poker, and slot machines in casinos in the historic town of Deadwood.

1989

The South Dakota legislature passes enabling laws, and gaming begins in Deadwood. The gaming is regulated by the South Dakota Commission on Gaming. A state lottery also begins operation of video lottery terminals throughout South Dakota.

The Iowa state legislature approves riverboat casino gaming with limited ($5) stakes betting on navigable waters in the state.

Oregon starts the first sports game-based lottery in the United States. Prizes are given to players who select four out of four winners of football or basketball games. Point-spread handicaps are utilized. Proceeds of the gambling are assigned to support college athletics in Oregon.

The Manitoba Lottery Foundation, a government-owned entity, opens the first year-round permanent casino facility in Canada. The Crystal Casino is located in the classic Fort Garry Hotel in Winnipeg.

The jackpot prize in the Pennsylvania lotto game exceeds $115 million. It is won, and shared, by several lucky ticket holders.

1990   Riverboat casinos begin operation in Iowa. Riverboat casinos are also approved by the Illinois state legislature.

The voters of Colorado approve limited casino gaming for the historic mountain towns of Black Hawk, Cripple Creek, and Central City. Ohio voters refuse to authorize casino gaming.

1991   Riverboat casinos are approved by the Mississippi legislature. It is determined that the boats may be permanently docked. Casino boats begin operation in Illinois, and limited-stakes casinos start in Colorado.

Oregon and Colorado introduce Keno as a lottery game.

1992   The Atlantic Provinces—New Brunswick, Prince Edward Island, Nova Scotia, and Newfoundland—authorize video lottery terminals for locations throughout their territories.

The Louisiana legislature approves riverboat casinos and one land-based casino in New Orleans. Missouri voters also approve riverboat casinos.

Colorado voters refuse to expand casinos to additional towns.

Congress prohibits the spread of sports betting beyond four states currently authorizing it: Nevada, Oregon, Montana, and Delaware. New Jersey is given one year to approve sports betting for an Atlantic City casino, but the state declines to do so.

1993   The Ontario government approves a casino for the city of Windsor. The casino is to be government

1993,
cont.

owned but privately operated. The provincial government selects a consortium of Las Vegas casino companies, including Caesar's Palace, Circus Circus, and the Hilton, to operate the casino. The province of Quebec opens a government-owned and operated casino in Montreal at the site of the French Pavilion of the Montreal World's Fair. Quebec also approves gaming sites at Charlevoix and Hull. The Nova Scotia government removes video gaming machines from all locations that are accessible to young people.

The Indiana legislature approves boat casinos. Five boats are authorized for Lake Michigan ports, five for ports on the Ohio River, and one for an interior lake.

1994

Florida voters defeat a proposal for "limited" casino gambling. The proposal would have authorized about 50 major casinos for many locations around the state. Colorado voters again defeat efforts to expand casino gambling.

Riverboat casinos begin operation in Louisiana and Missouri.

The government of the province of Nova Scotia authorizes casino gambling.

1995

A temporary casino opens in New Orleans. It is operated by a group that includes Harrah's Casinos and the Jazzville Corporation. Riverboat gaming begins in Indiana.

Slot machine gaming is authorized for race tracks in Iowa on a local government option basis.

Provincially owned casinos open in Halifax and Sydney, Nova Scotia, and also in Regina, Saskatchewan.

1996

The New Orleans casino project closes and declares bankruptcy.

The U.S. Supreme Court rules part of the Indian Gaming Regulatory Act of 1988 unconstitutional. The Court determines that the act's provision allowing tribes to sue states over compact negotiations violates the Eleventh Amendment.

Congress passes a law setting up a nine-person commission to study the social and economic impacts of gambling on society in the United States.

In November, the voters of several states speak out on gambling, but they send quite mixed messages. Michigan voters approve a law that authorizes three major casinos for the city of Detroit. Ohio and Arkansas voters defeat casinos, West Virginia approves machine gaming for race tracks, and Nebraska voters say no to track machines. Colorado voters also say no to new casino towns. Washington State voters defeat slot machines for Indian casinos, but Arizona voters mandate the governor to sign compacts for new Indian casinos.

Two historical casinos on the Las Vegas Strip—the Hacienda and the Sands—are imploded to make way for newer and bigger gambling halls. Three new casinos open in Las Vegas: the Monte Carlo, the Orleans, and the Stratosphere. The Stratosphere boasts of having the tallest freestanding tower on the North American continent.

Casino Niagara opens in Niagara Falls, Ontario, in December. It is owned and operated by the Ontario Casino Corporation, a government corporation. The Ontario government also permits an Indian casino to open on the Rama Reserve near Orilla.

1997   Major casino expansion takes place in Las Vegas. This includes the opening of the New York, New York resort casino and expansions of the Rio, Harrah's, Caesars, and Luxor.

Major new casino projects begin in Atlantic City and in Mississippi. The Harrah's New Orleans project is given new life, and reopening is planned.

The National Gambling Study Commission begins operations.

Biographical Sketches 3

Gambling has at some point been embraced in every society, and some may feel these activities are directed by forces above and beyond the control of mortals. This would be an erroneous belief.

A gambling industry today responds to social forces, to be sure. But these responses have catalysts. The catalytic forces are manifest in individuals who see opportunities to be exploited or who perhaps see an emerging phenomenon that requires controls. It has been this way through the ages as players, entrepreneurs, and government leaders responded in different ways to a universal activity. This section is not comprehensive but rather presents representative profiles of persons in North America who have demonstrated an impact on the gaming industry. Indeed, with the rapid growth that has been witnessed, new industry giants may spring up to map the direction of gambling in the future.

The first section includes individuals who have been inducted into *International Gaming and Wagering Business*'s Gambling Hall of Fame since its inception in 1989. The second section lists leading entrepreneurs who have guided the development of the industry, and the third group consists of top players in the history of gambling.

Gambling Hall of Fame

Leonard H. Ainsworth

Len Ainsworth founded the Australian company Aristocrat Leisure Industries, one of the world's largest manufacturers of slot machines. Ainsworth began making slot machines in Sydney in 1953. Today, his company distributes machines in every country in which they are legal. He controls 70 percent of the Australian market and is number two among all companies in the world market. In 1994, he sold the company to his sons.

John Ascuaga

John Ascuaga began working in gaming resorts in Idaho after he had graduated from Washington State University. He had been born in Caldwell, Idaho, in 1926. When Idaho enforced the outlawing of slot machines in 1953, Ascuaga moved to Nevada. He worked with Richard Graves, an entrepreneur who had owned Idaho resorts. Ascuaga managed Graves's properties in both Carson City and Sparks, Nevada. In 1960, Ascuaga purchased the Sparks Nugget—now called Ascuaga's Nugget. Ascuaga developed the property into one of the leading privately owned casino hotel resorts in Nevada. John Ascuaga has also been a leading citizen, sponsoring a college education fund for top high school students in the state of Nevada.

William Bennett

Bill Bennett, who was born in 1925 in Glendale, Arizona, came to Las Vegas in 1966 as executive vice-president of Del Webb's Mint Hotel and Casino. In 1974, he purchased the Circus Circus property in partnership with Bill Pennington. The two entrepreneurs developed the Circus Circus Enterprises into the best "return on investment" gaming properties in the world. Their flagship casino, the Luxor, and the 4,000-room Excalibur are located in Las Vegas. The company also owns casinos in Laughlin and Reno, Nevada.

Benny Binion

Benny Binion, born in Texas in 1904, ran poker games and numbers in his native state until relocating to Las Vegas in 1946. He quickly became a legend in his new hometown by developing the

Horseshoe Casino, a property that catered to high-rolling professional gamblers. Binion accepted bets without limits. He founded the World Championship of Poker, held each year at the Horseshoe Casino. The "cowboy gambler" died in 1989.

Sam Boyd

Sam Boyd came to Las Vegas in 1941 after running bingo parlors in Hawaii. He was born in Oklahoma in 1910 and worked in the local Las Vegas casinos for several years before developing a number of properties, including the Union Plaza, California Hotel, and Sam's Town. Boyd became one of gaming's most successful entrepreneurs before his death in 1992.

William S. Boyd

After practicing law for 15 years, William S. Boyd joined his father, Sam, in the 1970s to launch a group of casinos under the family name. Today, he serves as the chief executive officer and chairman for operations in Las Vegas and Clark Counties and also has planned new ventures for Louisiana.

Donald L. Carano

Donald Carano is the chief executive officer of the El Dorado Hotel and Casino, Reno, and a major partner with Circus Circus Enterprises in the Silver Legacy, the first megaresort property in Reno. Born in Reno in the early 1930s, Carano worked his way through law school at the University of San Francisco by driving a truck. Donald returned home to start a law practice that focused upon land development. He purchased lands that would become the locations of his casinos, and in 1974 he opened the El Dorado. He has also been a partner in the Pioneer Hotel Casino and the Boomtown Casino of Verdi, Nevada. In 1985, he sold his interest in Boomtown in order to have the capital to become a partner in the Ferrari-Carano Winery of Sonoma, California. On 28 July 1995, he opened the doors of the Silver Legacy, the premier gaming property of northern Nevada.

Burton Cohen

Burton Cohen served as a major figure in the Las Vegas casino industry for nearly 30 years. In 1966, he moved to Las Vegas from

Florida, where he had been an attorney for nearly 20 years. He began his gaming career as an executive with the Frontier Hotel. He then became the general manager of the Circus Circus Casino, followed by a stint as the vice-president of the Flamingo Hilton and positions with Caesars Palace and the Summa Corporation, where he became the chief executive of the Desert Inn. His contributions to the well-being of the casino industry included a term as president of the Nevada Gaming Association, the leading lobby group for casinos prior to the establishment of the American Gaming Association.

James Morris Crosby

A businessman and developer, James Morris Crosby was instrumental in the remake of Atlantic City as the gambling mecca of the eastern United States. He was born in 1927 in Great Neck, New York, and received a degree in economics at Georgetown University in 1948. In the 1950s, he participated in a stock takeover of the Mary Carter Paint Company. To diversify, the company purchased a land development operation in the Bahamas in the early 1960s. Soon after this the company purchased a primary Paradise Island resort and persuaded the Bahamian government to grant the company a casino concession. From this base, Crosby was able to influence New Jersey politicians and voters on casino legalization. His company, now called Resorts International, opened the first Atlantic City casino in 1978. James Crosby was in the process of developing Atlantic City's most glamorous casino— the Taj Mahal—when he died unexpectedly in 1986 following lung surgery.

Paul Endy Jr.

Paul Endy Jr. is the chairman of the board of Paul-Son Gaming Corporation, a leading gambling supply company. Endy followed in the footsteps of his father, Paul Sr., who manufactured equipment for California card-rooms in the 1940s and 1950s. In 1963, Paul Jr. started Paul-Son and focused his marketing efforts on Las Vegas casinos. *Forbes Magazine* (5 December 1994) wrote that "Paul-Son is to gambling casinos what makers of pans were to gold miners." Today, Paul-Son is the largest maker of roulette wheels, craps tables, dice, and player's chips in the United States. Paul-Son also makes playing cards. In 1974, the company opened offices in Reno and in 1978 opened operations in Atlantic City. Paul-Son became a publicly traded company in March 1994.

Jackie Gaughan

A Las Vegas casino entrepreneur, Jackie Gaughan was born and raised in Omaha, Nebraska. He is credited with much of the development that has resulted in downtown Las Vegas's making a major contribution to the modern casino scene. His properties include the Union Plaza and the El Cortez.

Henry Gluck

Henry Gluck came to the United States in 1936 from his native land of Germany. He attended Wharton School of Finance and eventually advanced to the vice-presidency of Monogram Industries. He retired at the age of 43. In the early 1970s, Gluck returned to the corporate scene as the chairman of Caesars World. He succeeded in resuscitating the slipping Caesars Palace and restoring it as an industry giant.

Harvey Gross

Entering the casino business with six stools and slot machines at a Lake Tahoe gambling house in 1944, Harvey Gross's property has grown into Resort Hotel and Casino, a leader in the northern Nevada gaming industry. Today, the property boasts 88,000 square feet of gaming space and a 740-room hotel. With Gross's leadership, Tahoe has become a vital casino resort destination. Harvey Gross died in 1983.

William F. Harrah

Bill Harrah, who was born in California in 1911, brought his Golden State bingo hall experience to Reno in the late 1930s. Over four decades he built the Harrah's gambling empire around the concept of servicing the small player. Harrah was the first casino operator to utilize tour buses to transport players between his properties in central and northern California and the casinos he operated in Reno and Lake Tahoe. His was among the first gaming companies to be publicly traded on national stock exchanges. Harrah died in 1978.

Barron Hilton

The second son of Conrad Hilton was born in 1927. After several independent business ventures, he joined the Hilton Hotel Corporation in the 1950s. He made his mark with the company by guiding it into the gambling business. Soon after Nevada permitted public corporations to own casinos, Hilton acquired the Las Vegas International Hotel and Casino, at that time the largest hotel in the world. Hilton also purchased the Flamingo Casino on the Las Vegas Strip as well as gaming properties in Reno and Laughlin, Nevada. The Hilton Corporation's profits from its Nevada gaming properties exceed its profits from all its other U.S. properties combined. Barron Hilton has considerable interests outside gaming as well. He was the founding owner of the Los Angeles Chargers (now the San Diego Chargers).

Bud Jones

Bud Jones is the president and principal owner of the Bud Jones Company, a major supplier of casino equipment based in Las Vegas. He has over 40 years experience with the gaming industry. Since 1973 his company has been distinguished for producing a secure casino chip designed to stop counterfeiting.

Kirk Kerkorian

Kirk Kerkorian, like Howard Hughes, was an airline executive before developing an attraction to casino ventures in Las Vegas. He was born in Fresno, California, in 1917. Kerkorian is responsible for the development of some of the largest resorts in the gaming industry. His first project was the International, now called the Las Vegas Hilton. Next was the MGM Grand, which is now owned by Bally's. Each was the largest hotel in the world when it opened. In 1993, he opened the new MGM Grand on the Strip. The new Grand is now the largest hotel in the world, with 5,000 rooms. It sits beside a movieland theme park.

Sol Kerzner

The legendary founding force behind Sun International's massive casino empire in southern Africa, Sol Kerzner pioneered the notion of developing a megaresort around gaming when he developed Sun City in 1978. His idea of an entirely self-contained resort complex with a hotel, recreation, and entertainment became the benchmark for U.S. casino developers who followed a decade later.

Don Laughlin

As a child growing up in Owantonne, Minnesota, during the 1940s, Don Laughlin became fascinated with intricate machinery—especially slot machines. He purchased a slot machine through a mail-order catalog and arranged to have it placed in a local VFW Club. He used the profits from the machine to buy another, then another. Soon he was expelled from high school because the principal did not like the fact that Laughlin's illegal gambling earnings exceeded his own salary. Minnesota authorities were very lax about enforcing gaming laws until the federal government passed the Sullivan Act in 1950. A crackdown ensued, and it became impossible to get new slot machines shipped into the state. Laughlin moved to Las Vegas in 1952, and two years later he owned a small bar and casino. For ten years he ground out profits and saved for a bigger investment. That investment turned out to be a run-down motel and casino on the Arizona border at the southernmost point of Nevada, 90 miles south of Las Vegas. Laughlin prospered by catering to drive-in visitors from Arizona and California, especially senior citizens who wintered in the Southwest. With Laughlin's vision, a new gaming town—Laughlin, Nevada—grew. Today, it boasts many large casinos, including a Hilton, a Golden Nugget, and a Circus Circus. Some of these properties have upward of 2,000 hotel rooms.

Frank Modica

On 28 February 1995, Frank Modica retired as the president and chief executive officer of the Showboat Casino in Las Vegas. During a 45-year career in gaming, Modica introduced many innovative ideas for both Las Vegas and Atlantic City casinos, including the utilization of a casino property as a general entertainment center. The Las Vegas Showboat boasts the largest bowling center in the world, and the Atlantic City property has the only movie theater in that city. Modica also guided the Showboat organization into many new ventures in new gaming jurisdictions around the world.

Warren Nelson

Warren Nelson started his 45-year gaming career in his home state of Montana; he had been born in Great Falls in 1913. He quickly moved on from Montana to Reno, Nevada. Nelson came to Reno in 1936 to work at the Palace Club. He is responsible for bringing Keno into the casinos for the first time. During World War II, Nelson served in the Marines, but he returned to Reno afterward. In the early 1960s, he purchased the Cal-Neva Club in Reno; later he bought the Comstock in Reno. Nelson also held interests in Las Vegas casinos. Among gaming pioneers, he was a leader who was able to attract people before the national marketing days of modern corporate Nevada.

Donald (Mike) O'Callaghan

From 1971 to 1979, Mike O'Callaghan served as governor of Nevada. This was a period of incredible casino expansion, as O'Callaghan assumed office just as the state began to allow corporate ownership of casinos. O'Callaghan was born in La Crosse, Wisconsin, in 1929, was a decorated Korean War veteran, and came to Nevada as a schoolteacher. He held many administrative posts that finally led to the governorship of the state. As governor he helped guide such major companies as Hilton and MGM into casino gaming. O'Callaghan established the Gaming Policy Committee and helped the state adjust its policies in the face of new competition from Atlantic City. Following his two terms as governor, he became the managing editor of the *Las Vegas Sun*.

Bill Pennington

Bill Pennington spent many years in the Las Vegas casino industry running slot route operations before teaming up with William Bennett in 1974 when Pennington was 51. The two men pooled $40,000 in savings and purchased the Circus Circus casino on the Las Vegas Strip at a time when the operation was on the verge of bankruptcy. They reorganized operations and focused the property with a family orientation. Their success was phenomenal. They later expanded into Reno and Laughlin as well as developing other new megaresorts in Las Vegas. Pennington suffered major injuries in a boat accident in 1984, and his business involvement with Circus Circus subsided. He retired as chief executive officer in 1988 but remained active on the board of directors into the mid-1990s.

Leonard Prescott

In the space of ten years, Leonard Prescott rose from the position of manual laborer on the Shakopee Mdewakanton Dakota reservation in Minnesota to that of recognized leader of Indian gaming in the United States. In 1987, he became tribal chairman and in 1991 chief executive officer of the tribe's Little Six gaming property. The property developed into the Mystic Lake Casino, one of the premier gambling facilities in the United States. In terms of revenues, Mystic Lake was second only to Foxwood's Casino among all Indian casinos. Prescott was a founding member of the National Indian Gaming Association. Although Prescott's leadership was essential in the development of Indian gambling, he lost his reelection bid for tribal chairman in 1994, and he retired as the primary gambling officer for his tribe.

Si Redd

The "Emperor of Slots" was born in Philadelphia, Mississippi, in 1911. For many years he was a slot machine distributor for Bally's Gaming. In the 1970s, he developed the video gaming machine and independently started his own production with a company that became International Gaming Technologies (IGT). IGT is the leading slot machine company in the world today. Although Redd retired from IGT in the early 1990s, he remained active as a casino entrepreneur, developing gambling properties in Mesquite, Nevada, as well as his native Mississippi.

Michael Rose

Rose was the chairman of the board of Harrah's Entertainment from 1984 through 1996. He joined Holiday Inn Corporation in 1974 and became the president of the corporation in 1976, joining its board of directors in 1978. In 1980, he engineered the purchase of Harrah's Casinos for Holiday Inn. As the chairman of the board of the joint corporation, he then sold Holiday Inns in 1990 and formed the Promus Hotel Corp. Under his leadership Harrah's became the largest gaming company in the United States, with 15 casinos located in all the major gambling locations in the United States.

Jay Sarno

Jay Sarno, who was born in 1921 in St. Joseph, Missouri, attended the University of Missouri before venturing to Nevada after

World War II. Sarno introduced the idea of a theme-based casino resort to the stagnating gambling industry of the 1960s. He built Caesars Palace and operated it from 1966 to 1969. The notion that a casino could be developed around a central idea, such as life in ancient Rome, was novel, and it gave Las Vegas a boost of marketing publicity that was missing at a time when Howard Hughes was accumulating and, in effect, "warehousing" properties. Sarno's vision expanded when he moved north on the Strip and created Circus Circus. Although Sarno did not experience the tremendous profits these properties later realized, his role was essential in the success not only of Caesars and Circus Circus but also of Las Vegas itself during recent years. Sarno died in 1984.

Grant Sawyer

Grant Sawyer graduated from the University of Nevada in 1941. He had been born in Idaho in 1918. After service with the infantry in World War II, Sawyer completed studies at George Washington University Law School. He began practicing law in Elko, Nevada. Sawyer was active in politics and graduated from the position of Elko County district attorney to that of governor in 1958. He served two terms, leaving the office at the end of 1966. During his tenure Sawyer directed the restructuring of casino regulation in the state. Under his leadership, the state maintained its independence in gaming regulation. Attorney General Robert Kennedy attempted to transfer regulatory functions to federal authorities, but Sawyer's negotiating skills prevented this from occurring. In his last year as governor, Sawyer was influential in persuading billionaire Howard Hughes to take over several Las Vegas casinos that had troubled ownerships and were therefore more susceptible to federal investigations. Sawyer later entered law as a successful partner in one of the world's leading gaming law firms: Lionel, Sawyer, and Collins of Las Vegas. Sawyer died in 1996.

Raymond Smith

Raymond "Pappy" Smith was a California carnival game operator before coming to Reno and opening Harold's Club in 1937. Smith popularized casino gaming by offering lower-stakes games (penny roulette), bright signs, and clean facilities. He also made Nevada gaming an item of nationwide discussion by erecting more than 2,000 highway billboards across the country that proclaimed his motto: Harold's Club or Bust.

E. Parry Thomas

Thomas, who was born and educated in Utah, came to Las Vegas in the 1950s. He founded the Bank of Las Vegas (later called the Valley Bank and now part of the Bank of America) and provided loans for casino development in the 1950s and 1960s. This was a time when banks generally refused to advance funds for gaming operations. Thomas has been called "the most powerful prime mover in Las Vegas" by author Mario Puzo.

Donald Trump

Born in Queens, New York, in 1946, Donald Trump graduated from the Wharton School of Finance at the University of Pennsylvania in 1968. After graduation, he worked with his father's construction and apartment management firm. During the 1970s and early 1980s, Trump was instrumental in developing several New York hotels as well as Trump Tower, the tallest and most expensive reinforced concrete structure in New York City. In the mid-1980s, Trump's attention turned to Atlantic City, where he built Trump Plaza, Trump Castle, and the Taj Mahal. At its opening in 1989, the Taj Mahal was the largest and highest-volume casino in the world. In the 1990s, Trump became firmly entrenched as a leading entrepreneurial force in the Atlantic City gaming market.

Claudine Williams

As a teenager growing up in De Soto Parish, Louisiana, Claudine Williams helped out her family by taking a job in a restaurant bar that offered gaming. She was fascinated by the games, and she set out to learn as much as she could. Soon she had saved enough money to go into the business. At the age of 19, she opened the Bonita Club in Galveston, Texas. The operation was successful for several years, as Texas authorities were reluctant to enforce gaming laws. But in the 1960s, the attitudes of Texas officials changed, and Williams moved to Las Vegas with her husband, who was also employed in the industry. Years of hard work and saving resulted in Williams's investment in a new casino, the Riverboat, which opened on the Strip in 1972. The Riverboat flourished and grew. It became the Holiday Casino in 1983 and, with further growth, the largest Holiday Inn in the world. Later Williams sold the property to the Holiday Corporation, which in turn was taken over by Harrah's.

Steve Wynn

A New York native, Steve Wynn was born in 1942. After graduating from the University of Pennsylvania, he took over a family bingo operation in Maryland. He came to Las Vegas in 1966 and got involved in several business ventures. In the early 1970s, he was able to parlay a land purchase from Howard Hughes and its subsequent resale into the capital necessary for a substantial investment in the Golden Nugget. Soon he gained a seat on the Nugget's corporate board, and he used the position to win control of the operation. Under Wynn's leadership, the Golden Nugget become a leading player in the casino industry, acquiring first a New Jersey property and later building the Mirage on the Las Vegas Strip—one of the most profitable and glamorous megaresorts in the world. The Mirage opened in December 1989. It was the first new casino on the Las Vegas Strip since 1973. The facility ushered in a period of revival and boom that continues on the Strip today. Soon other megaresorts followed, including Wynn's own Treasure Island and his Belagio resort, which is scheduled to open in 1998.

Operators and Investors

Don Barden

Don Barden was born in 1944 in Ohio and rose out of poverty to become one of the richest African Americans in the United States (his estimated worth is $2.3 billion). He attended Central State University in Ohio and then began working with George Steinbrenner's American Shipbuilding Company in Lorain, Ohio. He served two terms on the Lorain City council, as he began his own ventures into the entertainment world. At age 23 he started a record store and then a weekly entertainment newspaper. He rose to become the leading entrepreneur behind the creation of the Black Entertainment Network on cable television. He also established *Black Entertainment* magazine. He is now the major partner in a $116 million casino project in Gary, Indiana, and also a leading figure in new casino development for the city of Detroit.

Richard Canfield

Described in *The Encyclopedia of Gambling* as the most success-ful gambler the United States ever produced, Richard Canfield, as with other casino owners, would have denied that he was a gam-bler, knowing that the odds were always in his favor. Born in New Bedford, Massachusetts, in 1855, he began working as a teenager in seaside gaming resorts. By age 18 he had learned enough to take control of operations at a Providence, Rhode Island, poker hall. Then he set about learning the trade by visiting the leading casinos of Europe. With his new knowledge he returned to the United States, established illegal casinos in a series of towns, and later set up shop in New York City. Canfield ran the Big Apple's most exclusive casino during the 1880s and 1890s. In 1902, he opened another exclusive gaming hall in Saratoga, New York. There he ran very high stakes games, especially during the racing season at the local track. When reform politicians won office, Canfield was finally forced to close doors in 1907. He devoted the final years of his life to philanthropy and his art col-lection; he died in 1914.

Morris Bernard (Moe) Dalitz

Moe Dalitz was active in many businesses in Michigan and Ohio in the 1920s and 1930s. He had been born in Detroit in 1908. Dalitz allegedly played a role in Midwest bootlegging operations during Prohibition. He came to Las Vegas in the late 1940s and arranged the financing of the Desert Inn Casino Resort. Dalitz is considered to be the man responsible for developing much of the glamorous image, as well as the growth, of Las Vegas. He brought headliner entertainment to the casinos as well as championship golf. Addi-tionally, Dalitz developed housing projects and a major hospital and shopping center. He died in Las Vegas in 1989.

John Davis

The Encyclopedia of Gambling has described John Davis as "America's first casino operator." In 1827, he opened a casino on Bourbon Street in the French Quarter of New Orleans. His 24-hour establishment offered luxurious appointments to the aristocratic players of the day. Davis served the finest French wines, food, and cigars in a style that today is reserved for the highest-rolling casino players. Competing gambling dens in New Orleans and in other riverside towns were down-market dives in comparison. Davis's establishment operated until reformers succeeded in prohibiting casino gambling in the Crescent City in 1835.

Edward John DeBartolo Jr.

Edward DeBartolo has been a major investor on the gambling scene for several years. He is the leader of a set of family interests that includes horse race tracks, riverboat casinos, and real estate development. He is perhaps best known as the owner of the San Francisco 49ers football team. He was born in Youngstown, Ohio, in 1946 and attended the University of Notre Dame.

Howard Robard Hughes

Howard Hughes was a leading entrepreneur in the United States in the twentieth century. He was born in 1905. In the 1930s and 1940s, he gained fame as an aviator and a movie producer. He was the major owner of Trans World Airlines but was forced to sell his stock in an antitrust action in 1966. He used the proceeds from the sale in an attempt to gain control over casino gaming on the Las Vegas Strip. At one time Hughes owned a third of the Strip's casinos. His investments have been credited with lending an aura of legitimacy to casino gaming. Hughes died in 1976.

J. Terrance Lanni

Terry Lanni presently serves as the president and chairman of the board of MGM Grand, Inc., operators of the largest hotel-casino in the world. He became chairman of the board on 14 July 1995. Before that time he had been with Caesars World, Inc., for 18 years. He was appointed to the National Gambling Study Commission in 1996 to fill a role as spokesperson for the commercial casino industry. Lanni was born in 1943.

John North

A disreputable character who specialized in crooked gambling, John North worked as the boss of gambling dens in Vicksburg, Mississippi, during the 1820s and 1830s. Many people lost fortunes as a result of his dishonest operations. A group of local vigilantes organized against the gamblers. After exposing a plot by North to take control of all criminal activity from Vicksburg to New Orleans in 1835, they burned down Vicksburg's riverfront gambling halls and executed dozens of operators and players. North escaped but was soon captured by the vigilantes and hanged with a roulette wheel tied to his body.

Jim O'Leary

On 8 October 1871, 18-year-old Louis M. Cohn was shooting craps in a barn owned by the O'Learys. His memoirs indicate that his dice-throwing hand accidentally upset a lantern, which ignited some hay; the fire spread and burned the city of Chicago. The O'Learys, seeking an alibi, came up with the story of an unruly cow kicking over the lantern. The O'Learys' son, Jim, spent his formative years training in the gambling tradition and later opened gambling houses in and around Chicago. In 1904, he operated a gambling boat on Lake Michigan. O'Leary specialized in horse race bookmaking in addition to bets on other sporting events and election results. By the time he died in 1926 he was a multimillionaire.

Edward Pendleton

The nation's capital city has a long history of vice and corruption. Edward Pendleton occupies more than a footnote in this history. In 1832, he opened Pendleton's Palace, a gambling hall that catered to the empowered elite of society. Congressmen, cabinet members, and even President James Buchanan sat at Pendleton's tables. Prior to the Civil War, this gambling arena was declared neutral territory between the emerging Blue and Gray factions. As politicians became indebted to Pendleton, he began to wield considerable political influence and was able to assist in the passage of many bills concerned with private interests. Several leading Democrats were pallbearers at his funeral in 1858, and some of the most powerful figures in the country found themselves relieved that Pendleton's IOUs would not be collected.

Stuart and Clifford Perlman

The Perlman brothers set up a small Miami restaurant specializing in hot dogs in 1956. By the late 1960s, their venture had evolved into Lums, Inc., a restaurant chain with 379 outlets. In

1969, the profitable company purchased the Caesars Palace Casino and Hotel in Las Vegas. Under the Perlmans' guidance, Caesars became the premier casino in the world. They expanded this domain into Lake Tahoe and Atlantic City. However, the Perlmans were unable to win a license to operate the casino in New Jersey, and in 1981 they left the corporation.

Michael "Roxy" Roxborough

As president of Las Vegas Sports Consultants, Roxy Roxborough is one of the most important gambling entrepreneurs in the United States. Three-quarters of all Las Vegas casinos rely on Roxborough to "set the line" for all sports events on which wagers are taken. He determines the handicaps for all football and basketball bettors. He sets the "line" for the Super Bowl and all other major contests. He declared that the Green Bay Packers should be a 14-point favorite over the New England Patriots in the 1997 Super Bowl. Roxborough was born in Vancouver in 1952. He attended American University and the University of Nevada–Las Vegas. His gambling career started early. By 1975, he decided to move to Las Vegas and become a full-time gambler. However, he soon realized that he could do much better working for the casinos rather than betting against them. His odds-setting business flourished as sports betting expanded. He now assists gambling houses worldwide with his services.

Philip Glen Satre

Philip Satre serves as the chief executive officer of Harrah's Gaming Group within the Promus Corporation. Satre was born in Palo Alto, California, in 1949. He graduated from Stanford University in 1971 and received a law degree from the University of California at Davis. As an attorney in Reno, Nevada, he represented Harrah's Casinos during its time of transition, first to becoming a publicly traded corporation and then in its merger with Holiday Inns. Satre's leadership as a senior vice-president and then a corporate president helped Harrah's-Promus become the leading casino company in the United States in terms of its overall revenues and the number of venues in which its casinos were located. He developed strategies for marketing casino products to "Middle America," literally and figuratively: to middle-income players and to players in the middle geographic region of the nation. His leadership also was essential in the development of a model of social responsibility followed by Harrah's. The casino group has pioneered programs to help compulsive and problem gamblers.

Benjamin Siegel

Popularly known as the "man who invented Las Vegas" and nicknamed "Bugsy" (but never to his face), Siegel grew up in New York neighborhoods controlled by mobsters. At an early age he became an associate of Meyer Lansky, and the two launched a lifelong partnership in organized crime. Lansky became the financial master behind organized crime ventures across the United States and the Western world. Siegel's life with the mob led to liaisons with leading Hollywood moguls and movie stars. He launched many illegal gaming operations from his Los Angeles base and developed the notion that a desert casino on the outskirts of Las Vegas could attract the movie industry crowd and the globe's most glamorous jet-setters. Siegel shepherded the construction and early operations of the Flamingo, then the world's most luxurious casino, and Lansky organized financing for the venture, which opened during the Christmas holidays of 1946. However, Lansky discovered that Siegel had been siphoning casino investment funds into his private accounts, and in June 1947 Siegel was murdered in the apartment of his actress girlfriend. The murder sensationalized the Las Vegas casino industry and gave the city a reputation as a place of daring adventure. If Siegel didn't invent Las Vegas, his death certainly put it on the map.

Del Webb

Del Webb was a high school dropout who became a professional baseball player in the 1920s. He had been born in Fresno, California, in 1899. After his short athletic career, he started a construction business that grew to become one of the largest in the world. Among other accomplishments, his firm built Sun City in Arizona. Construction profits allowed Webb to reenter the sports world. In 1945, he purchased one-half interest in the New York Yankees. Webb owned the team during its glory days and sold out to CBS in 1965. In 1946, Webb's company built the Flamingo Hotel and Casino for Benjamin Siegel. He also built a number of other Las Vegas casinos, including the Mint and the Sahara, which were constructed for two friends. When Webb's friends could no longer maintain the properties, Webb created a private dummy corporation in 1961 and purchased the two casinos. Webb soon expanded his gambling interests to Reno, Lake Tahoe, and Atlantic City. He was a major industry player until his death in 1974.

Steven Weiss

The founder of Casino Data Systems (CDS) was born in Miami, Florida, in 1962. When he was 12 years old his family moved to Reno, where he became acquainted with the gambling industry. He was a young mathematical genius and was able to graduate from the University of Oregon before he was 20. He soon became a marketing analyst for the Peppermill Casino in Reno, moving next to Bally's slot machine manufacturers. There he analyzed data collection systems utilized by casinos, and as a result he was able to develop an accounting and player tracking system that could process information immediately as it was collected. His invention became known as OASIS—On-Line, Accounting and Slot Information System. OASIS became the central product of Casino Data Systems when he started the company in 1990. Since then the company has developed a wide array of casino products, including a progressive slot machine system called Cool Millions, Caribbean Stud Video Poker, and graphics and sign services. Today, CDS has its products in over 13 states and in 67 casinos.

Famous Players—Inside and Outside the Gambling Halls

Nicholas Andreas Dandolos

The legendary Nicholas Dandolos is known for having won as much as $50 million in a single evening of play. Yet he also experienced losses just as sizable. Dandolos played this rags-to-riches scenario repeatedly during his life and was popularly known as "Nick the Greek." Dandolos was born on the Greek island of Crete in 1893 and emigrated to the United States at age 18. His gambling activity started with horse tracks in Montreal. He soon earned a reputation across the United States and became an essential fixture on the Las Vegas scene as Nevada casinos expanded. His exploits were well publicized by casinos seeking notoriety. The James Bond movie *Goldfinger* incorporated schemes developed by Nick the Greek. Known as a great philanthropist, Dandolos donated millions to charities throughout his gaming years. He died on Christmas Day, 1966.

George Devol

Considered the most talented of the riverboat gamblers, George Devol was born in 1829 and started gambling quite early, as a ten-year-old cabin boy. He developed cheating techniques that won him more than $2 million over a 40-year career on riverboats and in mining camp saloons and casinos. His favorite schemes involved the game of three-card monte. Devol's escapades are recorded in his autobiography, *40 Years a Gambler on the Mississippi*, published in 1892. Devol reformed in his later years, gave speeches that condemned gambling, and lived a quiet life until his death in 1902.

Alice Duffield

Affectionately known as "Poker Alice," Alice Duffield was born in England during the 1850s. She ventured to the United States at the age of 12. Although educated in a fashionable southern school, Duffield lost all her sophistication when she moved west. Following the death of her husband she taught school, but Duffield found her true calling as a poker player in the saloons of Colorado and other western locales. Her rough and rowdy ways featured a cigar profile, foul mouth, and quick action with a gun. Her final gambling post was in Fort Meade, South Dakota, which operated until reform politicians closed it down in 1920. Thereafter, Poker Alice retired to reminisce and smoke cigars until her death in 1930.

Frank Fahrenkopf Jr.

Frank Fahrenkopf Jr. is the president of the American Gaming Association. He is the primary advocate of the casino industry in front of federal government officials. Prior to representing the gaming industry in this role, Fahrenkopf was a Washington, D.C., attorney specializing in international trade matters. Throughout the 1980s, he served as the national chairman of the Republican Party. Fahrenkopf was born in Nevada in 1941 and graduated from the University of Nevada–Reno in 1962. He received a law degree from the University of California–Berkeley in 1965.

John W. Gates

John W. "Bet-a-Million" Gates was known to have gambled thousands of dollars on events such as the direction of the next train on a track, the speed of a raindrop running down a window pane, or the number of flies to land on a piece of bread. The inveterate risk taker was born in 1855. However, prior to making gambling his avocation, he amassed a great fortune as a manufacturer of barbed wire. With his substantial bankroll, Gates wagered continuously, winning big and losing big. Gates earned his nickname when he attempted to place a million-dollar bet on a single horse in a race. The bookies refused to cover his action, as the wager was made prior to the days of pari-mutuel betting. Gates maintained his business career during his gambling years and was one of the early investors in U.S. Steel. He died in 1911.

James Butler Hickok

The legendary "Wild Bill" Hickok was a lawman, gunman, and notoriously poor poker player. He was born in 1837 and learned to survive as a gambler only through intimidation. Often he persuaded winners to leave their money on the table with threats of a gunfight. His prowess with a gun usually was not challenged. However, while playing poker in Saloon Number 10 in Deadwood, South Dakota, on 2 August 1876, he was shot in the back of the head. Hickok was holding a pair of aces and a pair of eights, a combination that came to be known as "The Dead Man's Hand." It is alleged that his murderer, Jack McCall, had been cheated out of a winning hand earlier by the bullying Hickok.

George Rickard

Although he was known as "Tex," Rickard was born in Kansas City, Missouri. By the age of 23 he was a town marshal in Texas, spending all his leisure time in the gambling halls. The lure of the Yukon gold rush beckoned him north to new gambling opportunities. Rickard invested his winnings in a Dawson City saloon called the Monte Carlo but lost the property in a card game. He returned to the States to become a major boxing promoter and staged fights in New York City and Nevada. When he died in 1929, Rickard was lauded for his reputation as an honest player.

Arnold Rothstein

Arnold Rothstein became the most widely known gambler in the country and left several marks on the gaming industry. He was a high-stakes player. Rothstein is also credited with being an initial organizer of Prohibition-era crime. He worked with the young Meyer Lansky and Lucky Luciano during their nascent criminal stages. Rothstein ran several New York gaming establishments through the 1920s. In 1919, he was reportedly involved in a sports betting operation that fixed the World Series. He or his confederates were able to bribe several members of the Chicago White Sox to lose some series games. Supposedly, Rothstein earned $270,000 by betting against the Sox. Rothstein, who had been born in New York in 1882, was murdered in 1928 during a New York City poker game.

John Scarne

John Scarne became fascinated with cards in his preteen years. But his passion was directed somewhat differently than that of other gamblers. Scarne sought to discover how other gamblers made crooked moves and then developed methods to expose these players. Although he was a gambler himself, his career was devoted to ensuring the honesty of gaming contests. Scarne became an adviser to the FBI and other police agencies as well as to casinos. In an effort to help servicemen avoid being cheated, he advised the U.S. Army during World War II. Scarne left his mark on the industry with the publication of several comprehensive books on gambling rules. Scarne was born in 1903 and died in 1985.

Alvin Clarence Thomas

Known as "Titanic Thompson," Alvin Thomas was "the king of the proposition bet." Born in poverty, he entertained himself as a child by inventing competitive games and mastering the skills necessary to win. He would place bets on shooting at targets, throwing rocks, cards, dice, golf, horse races, or anything else available at the moment. Thomas invariably won the game at hand. His nickname came from an exhausted opponent, who exclaimed, "You must be Titanic; you sink everybody." During the Depression, Thompson was recognized along with Nick the Greek as being one of the most cunning gamblers in the United States.

Kenneth S. Uston

The man who popularized the practice of "counting cards" at blackjack games, Ken Uston was trained as a stockbroker and held degrees from both Yale and Harvard. But in the 1960s, he learned of the method by which a player could track the cards already dealt in blackjack and project the remaining odds that future combinations would be dealt. When there was a high probability that a natural blackjack (one ace and one ten or face card) would be dealt, the deck favored the player. This is because the house will pay a player $3 for each $2 ($3 plus the $2) wager when a natural blackjack falls. However, losing means the player only loses $2, regardless of the cards held by the house dealer. Uston perfected counting techniques and wrote more than a dozen books for blackjack players. He also gave classes for would-be players. As a result of his skilled play, Uston won considerable sums of money at blackjack tables. He was subsequently banned from casino play. He resorted to using disguises and also brought legal action against casinos. Uston won court rulings in New Jersey that forced casinos to open their doors to him. However, his court actions in Nevada were not successful. New Jersey casinos adjusted to the fact that they had to let "counters" play by altering their rules and shuffling decks more frequently. Actually, Uston helped the casinos by popularizing the game. He inspired many players with false hopes that they could beat the house. As a result of the card-counting movement, blackjack is now the most popular table game in U.S. casinos. Uston died in Paris while working on a computer investment project.

Rudolph W. Wanderone

Known as "Minnesota Fats," Rudolph W. Wanderone gained fame under the nickname. Born in 1913, he was an expert at pool and billiards by the time he entered grade school and became an expert hustler. With a 51-inch waist, Fats considered himself the "World's Greatest Athlete." His persona was the model for the pool player portrayed by Jackie Gleason in the 1961 classic film, *The Hustler.* Wanderone died in 1996.

Legislation, Statistics, and Points of View

4

The statutes and cases included in this chapter have been selected as representative of major policy developments in the gaming field. Because legalized gambling was not widely prevalent and there were few laws and cases until the latter half of the twentieth century in the United States and Canada, the majority of legislation in this section is from this period.

As the law continues to evolve, new jurisdictions are entering legalization phases, and old questions addressed by judges—such as responsibility for compulsive gambling—are taking on new meaning as gambling is now widespread across the continent. The synopses of laws and cases are not presented as professional legal opinions regarding the law but rather as a starting point for further research.

National statutory laws in the United States and Canada are presented in chronological order. Selected state and provincial legislation and orders are presented in alphabetical order of jurisdictions. Law cases appear in chronological order.

The laws and cases reviewed in this chapter are rich with statements on the nature of the gambling industry and the gambling phenomenon. The "Points of View" section contains specific passages from this body of information as well as passages from other sources. An attempt has been made to present viewpoints both favorable to and critical of the gambling industry.

U.S. Federal Gaming Legislation

The U.S. Congress has enacted many laws pertaining to gambling. Most have dealt with lotteries and interstate commerce; in recent years, however, attention has been given to casino gambling on Indian reservations and on ships at sea as well as to sports gambling.

The National Gambling Impact and Policy Commission Act of 1996 (Public Law 104-169; 110 U.S. Stat. 1482; 23 July 1996)

The act creates a nine-member national commission to study gambling. Three members are appointed by the president, three by the Senate majority leader, and three by the Speaker of the House. The entire membership is supposed to be balanced among persons with "various points of view." The commission's charge is to "conduct a comprehensive legal and factual study of the social and economic impacts of gambling in the United States." All types of gambling are to be studied. The impacts will include crime, pathological gambling, advertising and gambling, taxation, and Internet gambling. The commission will have a full-time executive director and will utilize the National Research Council and the Advisory Commission on Intergovernmental Relations to conduct research projects. The commission will have subpoena powers. The commission will report its findings to Congress no later than two years after beginning its deliberations.

Professional and Amateur Sports Protection Act (Public Law 102-559, 28 October 1992)

This act prohibits betting on sports events throughout the nation, with the exception of wagering in the casinos of Nevada and in the Oregon sports lottery. Limited sports betting was also allowed to continue in Montana and Delaware. New Jersey was given the option of having sports betting in Atlantic City casinos if it authorized the betting before the end of 1993. New Jersey failed to do so.

Flower Garden Banks National Marine Sanctuary
(Public Law 102-251, 9 March 1992)

This act amends the Gambling Devices Act (Johnson Act) by permitting gambling on ships carrying the American flag but only if they do so outside the waters of a state or with the permission of a state. A state may refuse to allow such a ship to dock unless the ship also docks in a foreign port. This act basically reversed an act of 1948 that prohibited gambling on U.S. ships.

Charity Games Advertising Act of 1988
(Public Law 100-625, 7 November 1988)

The provisions of federal law prohibiting the use of the mail for advertising of gambling events and activities do not apply to charitable gaming.

Indian Gaming Regulatory Act of 1988
(Public Law 100-497, 25 October 1988)

This law established a framework for regulating gambling activities on Indian reservations. Gaming was divided into three classes. Class one gaming consisted of traditional Indian games. These were regulated by the tribes without non-Indian oversight. Class two gaming consisted mainly of bingo games. Initially these were to be regulated by a National Indian Gaming Commission also created by the act, but after two years bingo was to be self-regulated by the tribes. Class three gaming included all other games (casino games, racing, and lotteries, for example) and would be regulated in accordance with compacts negotiated between the tribes and state governments. Indians could conduct games only if they were permitted by the state. The three-member National Indian Gaming Commission included two Indians and one non-Indian. In addition to providing general management of Indian gaming, the Commission was designed to outline gaming rules. In 1996, the U.S. Supreme Court ruled that a portion of the act permitting tribes to sue states in federal courts if states refused to negotiate class three agreements was unconstitutional. See *Seminole Tribe of Florida* v. *State of Florida*.

Lottery Advertising Act of 1975
(Public Law 93-583; 88 U.S. Stat. 1916; 2 January 1975)

State government-run lotteries were exempted from the general prohibition on advertising lotteries through broadcasting or through the mails. However, permissible advertisements could be made only in the state of the lottery and adjacent states that also had lotteries. Advertisements were banned in nonlottery states.

The Organized Crime Control Act of 1970
(Public Law 91-452; 84 U.S. Stat. 938; 1970)

Title VIII of the Organized Crime Control Act made it a federal crime to conduct any gambling that was deemed to be illegal under state or local government law anywhere in the United States. Title VIII also created a 15-member Commission on the Review of the National Policy Toward Gambling. The commission issued its final report in 1976.

Federal Reserve System Act, 1967 Amendments
(Public Law 90-203, 15 December 1967, Section 2)

Prohibited banks from dealing in lottery tickets or advertising or announcing any gambling events.

Gambling Devices Act (Johnson Act)
(Public Law 906, 2 January 1951)

Gambling devices may not be transported across state lines, unless the machines are legal in the states involved. Gambling machines must be licensed and records of sales registered.

Federal Communications Act of 1934
(Public Act 416, 19 June 1934)

Advertisements regarding gambling were prohibited on radio or television broadcasts. However, amendments in 1975 (Public Act 94-526, passed 17 October 1976) made certain exceptions for state-sponsored lotteries.

Mail Frauds Act
(17 U.S. Stat. 302, 8 June 1872)

No letter or circular concerning illegal lotteries shall be carried in the mail. The word *illegal* was taken out of the act in 1876 (19 U.S. Stat. 90).

National Canadian Legislation

The Canadian Parliament's national criminal code has undergone tremendous change, moving from almost total prohibition to delegating responsibilities for gaming regulation to the provinces.

Criminal Code of Canada
(Sections 189, 190, 1985)

Parliament placed the control of gambling activities under the jurisdiction of the provincial governments. The federal government yielded its own authority to run a national lottery in exchange for a collective contribution from provincial lottery revenues of $100 million to support the Calgary Winter Olympic Games. The new law continued a ban on nonprovincial machine gaming (gaming with dice) and wagering on single sports events.

Criminal Code of Canada
(Section 190, 1969)

The provincial governments were given the authority to conduct lottery schemes and to authorize charitable organizations to conduct such schemes for fund-raising purposes. Government-run lotteries began, as did many bingo operations. The notion of a scheme soon expanded to casino-type gaming. However, the code prohibited the use of dice in games as well as betting on single sports events. The code also prohibited organizations other than the provincial governments from utilizing machines for gambling.

Criminal Code of Canada
(Section 189, 1892)

The code prohibited the operation of a gambling house, gambling in public places, and the conduct of lotteries. Cheating was also prohibited in any private game.

Selected State and Provincial Legislation

British Columbia Lottery Act of 1974

British Columbia created a Lottery Branch (which was later placed in the attorney general's office) in order to conduct a provincial lottery and also to license charitable gaming events. In 1987, a British Columbia Gaming Commission was created to establish policy for gaming in the province.

Colorado Limited Gaming Act of 1991
(Colorado Rev. Stat. Ann. Sections 12-47.1-101 to 12-47.1-1401)

Subsequent to a vote of the people in November 1990, the Colorado legislature created the Colorado Limited Gaming Commission, comprising five members and authorized to license casinos in the towns of Black Hawk, Central City, and Cripple Creek. Games of blackjack and poker, as well as machines, are permitted, with individual bets limited to $5. Tax rates for gross gaming proceeds are determined by the commission annually but may not exceed 40 percent.

Illinois Riverboat Gambling Act
(1990 Ill. Laws 86-1029; Ill. Ann. Stat. ch. 120, Sections 2401-2423)

The act created the Illinois Gaming Board and authorized granting of licenses for up to ten casino riverboats in navigable waters of the state—excluding Lake Michigan and rivers in Cook County (Chicago). Casino revenues are taxed at a rate of 20 percent, with one-fourth of the amount going to local governments that permit the boats to take on passengers in their communities.

Iowa Riverboat Gaming Legislation
(1989 Iowa Acts 67, 27 April 1989)

The Iowa State Racing and Gaming Commission is empowered to license casino boats to be docked in communities that approve them. Players may wager up to $5 per bet and no more than $200 during an excursion cruise. Gaming revenues are taxed at rates up to 20 percent.

Louisiana Casino Legislation for New Orleans
(La. Rev. Stat. Ann. Sections 4.601 seq., 1992)

The legislature created the Louisiana Economic Development Gaming Corporation to license one land-based casino to be located at the site of the Rivergate Convention Center in downtown New Orleans. The legislation stated that casino operation must lease the facilities from the city and also pay the state an annual tax of $1 million or 18.5 percent of gaming revenues— whichever is greater.

Louisiana Riverboat Casino Legislation
(La. Rev. Stat. Ann. Sections 4.501 seq., 1991)

The Louisiana legislature authorized unlimited casino gambling on certain rivers and waters of the state. The legislation designated the Riverboat Gaming Commission to grant licenses to as many as 15 boats, with casino revenues taxed at a rate of 18.5 percent.

Manitoba Lotteries Foundation Act (1982)

The Province of Manitoba created a gaming agency to centralize lottery operations and regulations of charity gaming. Subsequent regulations (28-84) gave the foundation the authority to conduct bingo and casino gaming on behalf of charities and Manitoba. The foundation became the sole operator of casinos soon afterward.

Michigan Casino Control and Revenue Act of 1996
(Proposal E, passed by the state electorate, 5 November 1996)

The voters of Michigan passed by legislative initiative a law that established a gaming control board to regulate commercial casino gambling in the state. The law authorized the licensing of three commercial casinos within the city limits of Detroit. The control board selects the operators and regulates the gaming activity. Two of three licenses are designated for organizations that sponsored a 1994 advisory election for casinos in Detroit. The law sets the tax rate at 18 percent of the gross gambling win of the casinos. Fifty-five percent of the gambling tax goes to the Detroit city government, and 45 percent goes to the state school aid fund. Although the act mandated licensing within 90 days of the submission of application, the governor indicated that the licensing processes would take a longer time.

Mississippi Casino Gaming Act of 1991
(Miss. Code Ann. Sections 75-76-7)

In 1991, the state of Mississippi created a three-member commission to license casino vessels for operation in certain designated waterways. The act allowed gaming activity to occur while the boats were permanently docked to the shore instead of only when they were taking cruises, as was the case in other riverboat gambling states. The act also permitted unlimited gaming and established a tax rate of up to 8 percent on gross gambling wins of the casinos.

Nevada Gaming Control Act
(Nevada Rev. Stat. Ann. Sections 463.010 seq. 1955 and
subsequent years, notably 1957, 1959, 1969, and 1983)

The Nevada Gaming Control Act was first passed in 1931. As amended, the act currently states that the three-member Gaming Control Board investigates applicants, makes recommendations for licensing, and oversees gaming in state casinos. The five-member Nevada Gaming Commission is responsible for granting licenses and designing regulations for casino operations. Additionally, casinos pay a 6.25 percent tax on their gross gaming wins.

New Jersey Casino Control Act of 1977
(1977 N.J. Laws, 110; N.J. Stat. Ann. Sections 5-12-1 to 5-12-190)

Following a vote of the people in 1976, the New Jersey legislature enacted a law implementing the legalization of casinos for Atlantic City. The act created the Casino Control Commission to license casinos following recommendations from the Gaming Division within the state attorney general's office. The act maintains strict rules for casino operations and financing. Casino gaming revenues are taxed at a rate of 8 percent of gross gaming wins, plus additional fees for economic development projects for Atlantic City.

New York Off-Track Betting Law
(Laws of New York, Chapters 143, 144, 145, enacted 22 April 1970)

New York established off-track pari-mutuel betting on horse races. Provisions allowed off-track parlors. Two government corporations were created to conduct the activity and to take out percentages of the wagers for tax purposes. Local governments throughout New York State were given the option of allowing parlors in their communities.

Ontario Casino Corporation Act of 1993
(Bill 8)

The Ontario government created a crown agency, the Ontario Casino Corporation. The corporation was given oversight responsibilities for all "lottery schemes" in the province. A regulatory commission was set up with registration, enforcement, and audit divisions. The passage of the act opened the door to widespread charitable casinos as well as permanent government-owned casinos in Windsor and Niagara Falls. It also enabled the province to negotiate an agreement for an Indian casino on the Rama reserve near Orilla.

South Dakota Gaming Control Act
(S.D. Cod. Laws Ann. 42-7B-1 seq., 1988)

South Dakota voters authorized casino gaming for the town of Deadwood. The act allowed casinos to be licensed by the South Dakota Gaming Commission and deemed poker, blackjack, and machine gaming as permissible. Bets on single plays originally were limited to $5, but the maximum limits have increased to $25. Attempts to raise the maximum limits to $100 were later defeated by voters. The act also requires casino revenues to be taxed at a rate of 8 percent.

Major Court Cases

Horner v. United States, 147 U.S. 449 (1893)

The Supreme Court upheld federal legislation ruling that the mails could not be used to transport lottery materials. The Court defined the three elements of a lottery as (1) involving money or something of value (called consideration) be (2) offered in a game with a degree of risk, in hope of (3) securing something of greater value (prize).

Federal Communications Commission v. American Broadcasting Association, 347 U.S. 284 (1954)

The Supreme Court upheld the Federal Communications Commission's regulations prohibiting the broadcasting of information concerning lotteries.

Lewis v. United States, 348 U.S. 419 (1955)

The Court ruled that a federal law providing for an occupational tax on wagering does not give parties the right to conduct gambling operations contrary to state and local regulations—including the regulations of the District of Columbia.

State v. Rosenthal, 93 Nev. 36, 559 P.2d. 830 (1977). Dismissed 434 U.S. 803 (1977)

The court found that there are no general constitutional rights to engage in the business of gambling. It is a privileged business subject to state control.

Seminole Indians v. Butterworth, 658 F. 2d 310 (5th Cir. 1981)

A precursor to the Cabazon case. The court concluded that once a form of gambling is legalized in a state, the state loses the power to regulate such gaming on Indian reservation lands.

Uston v. Resorts International, 445 A. 2d 370 (N.J., 1982)

Ken Uston (see Chapter 3 under "Famous Players") was a "card-counter." He memorized cards as they were being played in blackjack games. He then calculated in his mind the odds that certain remaining cards (ones not yet dealt) would favor the players or the dealers and bet accordingly. Good card-counters can actually have odds in their favor. Several New Jersey casinos told Uston to leave their premises. He challenged their authority to exclude him from games. The New Jersey Supreme Court agreed with Uston. They found nothing in the New Jersey gaming law that allowed a policy of exclusion for a player who was simply using a strategy to try to win a game. Clearly Uston was not cheating. The court held that the New Jersey gaming law would have to be changed if casinos were to be able to exclude these strategy players. In Nevada the gaming law does give the casinos the right to exclude such players if they wish to do so.

State of Nevada v. Glusman, 98 Nev. 412, 615 Pac. 2 ed. 639 (1982); an appeal for a new ruling was turned down by the U.S. Supreme Court, 459 U.S. 1192 (1983)

The Nevada Gaming Commission extended its requirement that an individual seek a gaming license to the owner of a retail store on the premises of a casino hotel. The store owner objected, claiming that he had no involvement in any gaming activities. However, the state supreme court said that as a matter of discretion the commission could require licensing, as the store owner would be in close contact with many of the officials of the casino.

Brown v. Hotel and Restaurant Employees Local 54, 468 U.S. 491 (1984)

The U.S. Supreme Court upheld New Jersey's authority to oversee unions whose members were employees of casino hotels. The state's regulation of the unions was a legitimate part of its regulation of gambling, and it did not conflict with federal law providing that union's activity is regulated by the federal agencies, notably the National Labor Relations Board, and the agencies of the Department of Labor.

Posadas de Puerto Rico Associates v. Tourism Company of Puerto Rico, 478 U.S. 328 (1986)

The U.S. Supreme Court upheld the constitutionality of a Puerto Rico statute that prohibited advertising of casino gambling. The Court reasoned that the casino industry was a special industry and that the commonwealth had the power to protect its citizens by limiting their exposure to the industry.

Cabazon v. California, 480 U.S. 202 (1987)

The U.S. Supreme Court upheld the right of Indian tribes to conduct gaming on their reservations as long as the gaming was not in violation of the general policy and criminal law of the state. The gaming was not subject to the civil regulations of the state, as the state had only criminal jurisdiction on reservation lands. The ruling was an important factor in Congress's decision to pass the Indian Gaming Regulatory Act of 1988, which outlined the regulation of gambling activities on Indian reservations.

GNOC Corp. v. Shmuel Aboud, United States District Court, D. New Jersey; 715 Fed. Supp. 644 (1989)

The Golden Nugget Casino of Atlantic City brought an action against Aboud to recover debts he incurred while a player at the casino. Aboud entered a counterclaim asserting that the casino had intentionally served him alcoholic beverages to intoxicate him so that he would engage in reckless gambling activities. The court stated that it was the casino's duty to refrain from accepting bets from intoxicated players and that the casino could be held liable if they did accepts such bets. The court, however, held for the casino due to the fact that the player was unable to prove his claim. This was the first case indicating that a casino may be liable for encouraging intoxicated people to gamble.

Erickson v. *Desert Palace,* U.S. Court of Appeals for the Ninth Circuit, 21 August 1991. Cert. Denied U.S. Supreme Court

On 5 August 1987, Kirk Erickson, a tourist from Arkansas, played a slot machine at Caesars Palace in Las Vegas, Nevada. Erickson inserted three $1 tokens into a slot machine, pulled the handle, and lined up certain winning symbols. According to the casino's display, he had won $1,061,812. However, Caesars Palace refused to pay Erickson, a 19-year-old, because he was underage. (In Nevada a person must be 21 years old to gamble in a casino.) The court held that the plaintiff (Erickson) must seek relief through administrative law processes in the state of Nevada. The Nevada Gaming Control Board denied Erickson's claim because the debt in question was illegal and hence unenforceable through legal action. Consequently, Erickson received no payment from Caesars Palace.

State of Nevada v. *Rosenthal,* 819 Pac. 2d 1296 (30 October 1991)

Frank "Lefty" Rosenthal was one of the main characters portrayed in the movie *Casino.* He had many associations with people of "bad character" while he was a casino executive in Las Vegas. He was denied a license to remain an executive because of the associations and other unsavory activities during the early 1980s. In 1963, he had been convicted of attempting to "fix" a college basketball game, but his civil liberties were restored in later years. The Nevada Gaming Commission placed his name in the Black Book of persons not allowed to enter any casino in the state. Rosenthal claimed that the state did not have the right to do so, as his only conviction of breaking any law had occurred decades before. The state supreme court said that the matter was one of discretion for the commission; that as long as Rosenthal was given a hearing and an opportunity to state his position, the commission could decide the matter; and that his earlier conviction and his unsavory associations were sufficient for the commission to decide that he should be in the book.

United States v. Edge Broadcasting Co., 509 U.S. 418 (1993)

The 1975 Act of Congress permitting some advertising of state lotteries but banning such advertisements if they went into states without lotteries was challenged. Edge Broadcasting Co. was located in Virginia, a lottery state, but the signals of its radio station could be received in nearby North Carolina, a nonlottery state. Edge asked the courts to rule that the restrictions on its advertisements were unconstitutional restrictions on its commercial speech, which Edge claimed were protected by the First Amendment. The U.S. Supreme Court ruled against Edge and upheld the 1975 act with its restrictions. The Court found that Congress had a substantial interest in supporting the nongambling policy of North Carolina and that a reasonable way of supporting the policy was through the advertising ban.

Skipper v. State of Nevada, 879 Pac. 2d 732 (1994)

While Skipper was playing craps at a Nevada casino, he threw the dice in a manner known as "dice sliding." In that way he could control the resulting numbers in the game. A friend of his distracted the dealer as he made his moves. The entire sequence of activities was recorded on security videotapes. Skipper was prosecuted for cheating. The Nevada Supreme Court upheld his conviction, arguing that Skipper's behavior and that of his accomplice provided sufficient evidence of their intent to defraud the casino by cheating and that any reasonable person could reach that conclusion as all the members of a jury did.

Seminole Tribe of Florida v. State of Florida, 517 U.S. (27 March 1996)

The Seminole Tribe of Florida sued the state of Florida in federal courts. The tribe sought a ruling that would force the state to negotiate an agreement with them to permit them to have a casino. Such lawsuits were authorized by the Indian Gaming Regulatory Act (IGRA) of 1988 for circumstances in which the states were not negotiating with the tribes "in good faith."

Florida challenged the right of the tribe to sue the state. The U.S. Supreme Court upheld the state's challenge, ruling that states could not be sued by tribes in federal courts over such matters. The Court held that part of the IGRA was unconstitutional as a violation of the Eleventh Amendment. However, it refused to judge the constitutionality of the entire act, nor to indicate a mechanism of relief for tribes when states refused to negotiate casino agreements.

44 Liquormart, Inc. v. Rhode Island, 134 L.Ed 711, 116 Sct. 1497 (13 May 1996)

Rhode Island had a law prohibiting the advertisement of retail liquor prices. However, the sale of liquor was permitted in licensed locations. The U.S. Supreme Court struck down the state ban as an unreasonable restriction on commercial free speech, because the court felt that the state could show no compelling public interest being served by the ban. The Court suggested that any ban on advertising of legal products could be permitted only if there was a compelling reason for the ban. In the ruling, several justices suggested that the holding in the Posadas case was no longer a proper ruling and that in the future restrictions on advertising legal gambling products might be held to be unconstitutional.

Points of View

To scrimp and save to lay by a few pounds to see these eroded by inflation, wiped out and exposed in their foolish inadequacy in a sudden family emergency or, worst of all, to leave your few accumulated possessions to be fought over when you die—no other single cause, by all accounts, exerts comparable power as a detonator of family unity—is poor sense. To use this money in the hope of a big strike—who knows, you might even win enough to put down a deposit on a house—is surely superior rationality.

Otto Newman. *Gambling: Hazard and Reward.* Atlantic Highlands, NJ: Athlone, 1972, p. 228.

You must realize that a working-class chap is an under-dog and feels like one. He is not satisfied with present conditions, so he often escapes into a world of dreams. This world he finds in religion, socialism, or gambling. Socialism is a dream for himself personally. He can't hope to save enough to get out of his dreary existence. He can't work himself up, that is open only to a few of the best men. The only way out of the mines, or cotton mills, or foundry work or navvy work on the road, is to win in a big way. Only in that way can he gain his real freedom.

Peter Fuller. *The Psychology of Gambling*. New York: HarperCollins, 1974, p. 35.

"Can't you bleeding well listen to what I say? I tell you no number ending in seven ain't won for over fourteen months." "Yes it 'as, then!" "No, it 'as not!" They were talking about the Lottery. The Lottery was the one public event to which the proles paid serious attention. It was probable that there were some millions of proles for whom the Lottery was the principal if not the only reason for remaining alive. It was their delight, their folly, their intellectual stimulant. Even people who could barely read and write seemed capable of intricate calculations and staggering feats of memory. Everyone in the Party was aware that the prizes were largely imaginary. Only small sums were actually paid out, the winners of the big prizes being non-existent persons.

George Orwell. *1984*. New York: Harcourt, Brace, 1949. (New York: New American Library edition, 1981, pp. 72–73.)

"Why do I gamble? Why do I gamble? As a baseball man, I have a hell of a lot of free time. Begin there. Gambling is enjoyment for me. It fills free time. I go to the race track and I sit with the owner of the track. I like that. I like the company of people with money and I'm competitive. I like to win on the ballfield. I like to win my bets. When I win, a lot of the time I give the money to my wife. I get some pleasure setting her loose in a mall. If I lose my bets, hell I lose. You like classic music. Gambling gives me a charge. What is it that they say, different strokes for different folks?"

Pete Rose (former professional baseball player and manager) in Pete Rose and Roger Kahn. *Pete Rose: My Story*. New York: Macmillan, 1989, p. 261.

Legalized casino gambling has been approved by the citizens of New Jersey as a unique tool of urban redevelopment for Atlantic City to attract new investment capital to New Jersey in general and Atlantic City in particular.

New Jersey Casino Control Act, 1977.

It seems to some of us, such a long time ago, that New Jersey undertook to establish this new industry as a "unique tool of urban redevelopment," the success of which is based upon how successfully that industry marketed its only product. That product is not entertainment or recreation or leisure—it's really Adrenalin—a biological substance capable of producing excitement-highs and generated usually by anticipation or expectation of a future event especially when the outcome of that event is in doubt. I think most of us here today who have had the experience with gambling will agree that no form of risk taking or risk acceptance generates the intensity or can produce the amount of Adrenalin in the shortest period of time than a roll of the dice, spin of the wheel or turning of a card.

Thomas R. O'Brien (director, New Jersey Division of Gaming Enforcement). Speech to the 6th National Conference on Gambling and Risk Taking, Atlantic City, 10 December 1984.

Some people say casino gambling is the best way to get new jobs. New industries and casino gambling simply do not go together. In the last few years, we have built up momentum in bringing new jobs to Florida, because we have fine weather, no personal income tax, and stable government. Casinos will severely damage these efforts to bring challenging, high paying jobs to our people throughout Florida. Casinos are a bad risk. Who needs casino gambling? We don't.

Florida governor Reubin Askew, 1978 anticasino commercial.

You're going to find Mormons here who say, "Oh, I just hate gaming." Well, that's silly. You like the roads you drive on? Gaming paid for them. You like the schools your kids go to? Gaming paid for them. You like the parks? Gaming paid for them. Face it: If you live in Nevada, you have to accept gaming. It pays the bills.

The late Joe Burt (a Mormon and general manager of Aladdin Hotel Casino in Las Vegas). *Las Vegas Review Journal,* 13 July 1992, p. 4B.

There's been a transformation in the way the (Mormon) Church views southern Nevada. The reason gaming and the Church have gotten along so well here is we've grown up together. The business of gaming has attained legitimacy. The Mob is gone. We now have major publicly traded corporations in the business. The whole management fiber of gaming has changed.

Richard Bunker (a Mormon and executive director of the Nevada Resorts Association). *Las Vegas Review Journal*, 13 July 1992, p. 4B.

Visitors to the Shrine of the Most Holy Redeemer often ask the priest: "Father, will you pray for me to win?" Millions of people visit Las Vegas every year from parts of the world to test the whims of Lady Luck. In the warmly lit sanctuary of this Roman Catholic Church, where statues of the Nativity, the Last Supper, and the Crucifixion appear along the walls, gambling proceeds are put to use in the pews: Worshippers put casino chips into the collection plate. "Now and then we'll find a $500 chip in one of the plates," Father Leary of the shrine said. A Roman Catholic Church farther up the Las Vegas Strip served the worshippers for decades, but when the world's largest hotel-casinos—the MGM Grand, the Luxor, the Excalibur, and the Tropicana—were built at the south end of the Strip, the new Shrine of the Most Holy Redeemer was built just one block away. When the priest was asked why this was done, he said: "Why not? That's where the people are."

Awake, 22 September 1995, p. 10.

Regulation is important to assure public confidence in the integrity of the games and to increase public acceptance by removing any perception that criminals have ownership interest in the casinos. Governments should also be aware that regulation can inadvertently stifle the growth of an industry. If the goal of a jurisdiction is to use casino gaming to stimulate tourism and raise revenue, the best regulatory system will achieve its regulatory goals at the least cost to the regulated and with the least interference with the operators' business judgment. This is important in a world economy with increased competition.

Casino operators must be responsible in exercising their business judgment. Casino gaming should be a recreational activity primarily for those on a vacation, not something that government needs or wants to encourage as a tenet of daily life for its residents. If casinos, or governments, in their quest to raise gaming revenues seek not the recreational dollar but their own residents' earnings, the public may soon sour on the experiment.

Grant Sawyer (governor of Nevada, 1959–1967). "Foreword." In *International Casino Law*, 2d ed., edited by Anthony N. Cabot, William N. Thompson, and Andrew Tottenham. Reno: Institute for the Study of Gambline, University of Nevada, 1993.

The casinos now allow Native Americans to be involved in large-scale economy and work in a capitalistic area. You have enough dollars to provide more social services to your people. If you are going to work in a capitalist world, then you have to adapt to the policies of the capitalist world. Not all of them, but most of them.

Leonard Prescott (chairman of the board, Mystic Lake and Little Six Casinos, Shakopee-Mdewakanton Sioux Community, Minnesota). *Indian Gaming,* January 1993, p. 11.

Among the pleasures of gambling, certainly the greatest is winning. Anyone who has ever had a two-dollar bet pay off or the contents of the pot shoved his way knows that special exaltation that comes from a combination of pride in skill and joy at the sense of accomplishment. To beat the system with your own system—that is a fulfilling experience. Of course, there is nothing wrong with winning if you don't have a system. Pure luck, when it descends on you of all people, can give you a feeling of gratified self-importance comparable to few other delights.

David Newman, ed. *Esquire's Book of Gambling.* New York: Harper and Row, 1962, p. 13.

Losing well is important if (a) you want to be invited back, or (b) you want to be known as a good loser. However, if you lose well many times over a period of a year, you might consider the possibility that you are not only a good loser but a loser. Your move then is to learn what you're doing wrong, or curse the fates and take up painting. There are, unfortunately, many gamblers who can't quit that easily. For them, the perils are many and the consequences are devastating. In recent years psychologists have attempted to learn the motivations behind the overpowering need to risk everything on a roll of the dice or a spin of the wheel. When gambling assumes its proper place in the spectrum of behavior, it functions as amusement and furnishes a bit of excitement. But for those who are, in the truest sense, addicted, the enticements become daily and deadly necessities. Such is the lot of the compulsive, the habitual gambler.

David Newman, ed. *Esquire's Book of Gambling.* New York: Harper and Row, 1962, p. 27.

Lottery proponents argue many wagered dollars stimulate local economies through expenditures on advertising and retail sales commissions. However, very few people living in the ghettos and barrios own television networks or newspaper chains.

Likewise, a majority of lottery ticket outlets in the country are owned by corporations. Even independently owned outlets are seldom, if ever owned by anyone in the low-income category. Lottery dollars follow a one-way street out of the poorest neighborhoods, and few, if any of these dollars ever find their way back into the areas from whence they came.

Alan Karcher (former New Jersey state senator). *Lotteries.* New Brunswick, NJ: Transaction Publishers, 1989, pp. 96–97.

It is essential to recognize that the lotteries, in the absence of a destructive scandal, are here to stay. It is just as important to acknowledge that lotteries have had some undeniable, though limited, benefits. Lottery revenues have eased some budget pressures, and to a limited degree, allowed for the real expansion of some worthwhile programs. But these benefits have only been realized at a cost—a cost that is becoming increasingly heavier when measured in terms of existing abuses, potential exploitation that must come with a system driven by the imperative for increased revenue, and the risk of budgetary disorder inherent in the advance appropriation of speculative income.

Alan Karcher (former New Jersey state senator). *Lotteries.* New Brunswick, NJ: Transaction Publishers, 1989, p. 113.

It is fundamentally immoral to encourage the belief by the people as a whole in gambling as a source of family income. It would be immoral for government to make available to all of its people a statewide gambling apparatus with the implied assumption that the gains of chance were a fair substitute for or supplement to the honorable business of producing the goods and services by which the people of the nation live. It would be an indecent thing for government to finance itself so largely out of the weaknesses of the people which it had deliberately encouraged that a large share of its revenue would come from gambling. I recognize that the state and some municipalities now receive a comparatively small revenue from pari-mutuel betting at race tracks. I have always had personal doubts about the wisdom or the morality of this system but it is confined to those who are actually able to be present at the track and therefore is not a lure dangled before all people in all walks of life and near every home.

Thomas E. Dewey (former New York governor). Special address to the New York State Legislature, 16 January 1950.

Ultimately, pathological gambling results in crime. Studies uncovered a wide variety of illegal behaviors among the compulsive gamblers interviewed. Compulsive gamblers were involved in check forgery, embezzlement and employee theft, larceny, armed robbery, bookmaking, hustling, running con games, and fencing stolen goods. I also found gamblers engaged in systematic loan fraud, tax evasion, burglary, pimping, prostitution, illicit drug sales, and hustling at pool, golf, bowling, cards, and dice. Compulsive gamblers are engaged in a spiral of options and involvement wherein legal avenues for funding are utilized until they are closed off. As involvement in gambling intensifies, options for legal funding are closed. Depending on personal value systems, legitimate and illegitimate opportunities, perceptions of risk, the existence of threats (for example, by loan sharks), and chance, many compulsive gamblers became involved in more and more serious illegal activity. For some of them, the amount of money runs into millions of dollars.

Henry Lesieur. "Pathological Gambling in Canada." In *Gambling in Canada: Golden Goose or Trojan Horse?* edited by Colin S. Campbell and John Lowman. Burnaby, BC: Simon Fraser University, 1989, p. 230.

Historically gambling has been considered a vice and even in many modern societies where legal gambling exists, it still remains morally tainted. Part of the reason for this censure concerns the risk that gambling necessarily involves. In one sense, gambling is nothing more than risk taking in the hope of realizing some reward. The question is, if gambling is to be considered immoral or unethical because it involves a certain degree of risk, why are other activities involving risk not likewise considered unethical? We are constantly exposed to choices involving different degrees and types of risk. The level of risk which is comfortable for one person may be totally foolhardy by others. Risk merely means that a decision is made to engage in an activity with an uncertain outcome. In the case of gambling the uncertainty relates to the receipt of a monetary reward, and it is this which makes it different from other forms of entertainment.

Charles Singer. "The Ethics of Gambling." In *Gambling in Canada: Golden Goose or Trojan Horse?* edited by Colin S. Campbell and John Lowman. Burnaby, BC: Simon Fraser University, 1989, pp. 277–278.

The most powerful argument put forward by the critics of large-scale gambling—particularly by the political left and welfare groups—is the fear that social and moral structures will be undermined by forms of commercial gambling. Concern was expressed that Canada's traditional emphasis on charity gambling will be brutalized or swallowed up by competitive commercialism. They warn that the generous social programs built up over the years from gambling revenues could be abandoned by future governments as Canadian gambling becomes private and corporate.

Jan McMillen. "The Future." In *Gambling in Canada: Golden Goose or Trojan Horse?* edited by Colin S. Campbell and John Lowman. Burnaby, BC: Simon Fraser University, 1989, p. 397.

Tonya Harding couldn't have invented a better story to help change her image. Now the deposed figure skating champion is a lifesaver. Harding believes God was behind her last-second decision Sunday to stop at a suburban bar in Portland, Ore., for a few minutes to play video poker. Shortly after she arrived, an 81-year-old woman collapsed and stopped breathing. Harding revived her by giving mouth to mouth resuscitation. "It was very very scary," Harding said. "I kept my calm and cool and knew what I was doing. I had to do this. I thank God that I was there. Nobody else in the bar knew what to do."

Las Vegas Review Journal, 29 October 1996, p. 10-A.

Fifty-five million in Florida. Sixty-two million in California. Sixty-nine million in Illinois. And now $115 million in Pennsylvania. Wonderful for the states, and even more wonderful for the few lucky winners, but in the long run these astronomical jackpots may not be good for the lottery industry. For despite widespread public acceptance of lotteries, there are still those who hold the get-rich-quick lure of the lottery is a repudiation of the cherished American work ethic. Those sentiments gain currency whenever lotto jackpots reach stratospheric levels. And they're encouraged by inevitable media accounts of would-be multimillionaires mortgaging their homes to buy tickets. Perhaps the time has come for the lottery industry to reconsider the concept of capping prizes at some reasonable level—say $50 million—before the naysayers begin to make sense.

Paul Dworin (editor). *Gaming and Wagering Business*, 15 May 1989, p. 5.

Casino Niagara took in more than $1 million a day in December. After its Dec 9 [1996] opening, the Falls Avenue gambling hall was visited by 473,200 people who spent $28.7 million. It

averaged 20,600 visitors daily, higher than the 16,000 predicted
for its first year. Had it been open for the full month rather than
just 23 days, it likely would have grossed another $9.6 million.
The gross revenues represent the money left over after winnings
have been paid out. At Casino Niagara, the $28.7 million is
divided into several hands. The provincial government receives a
20% win tax, and a portion of both the gross and net revenues
goes to the Navagante Group, which was hired by the Ontario
Casino Corporation to operate the casino. Also from the gross
revenues, the casino pays its costs for employee salaries, leases,
customer and employee shuffles and police expenses. What's left
over goes to the provincial government.

Niagara Falls (Ontario) *Review*, 11 January 1997, p. 1.

More Americans are playing lotteries than any other form of
gambling, according to [a 1996] gaming survey...[sixty-nine
percent] of U.S. adults played the lottery last year. Lotteries
continue to win the approval of most Americans as 72% of
respondents supported them, while 65% see lotteries as an
acceptable form of entertainment. A majority of respondents
living in non-lottery states (57%) would favor a state lottery in
their state. Interestingly, 64% of respondents indicated that state
lotteries should be privatized.

International Gaming and Wagering Business, October 1996, p. 14.

Overall the Las Vegas hotel industry is the largest and strongest
in the country. The Strip, a three-and-a-half mile stretch of Las
Vegas Boulevard, alone offers more than 66,000 rooms. More
than 10,000 new hotel rooms opened on the Strip [in 1996],
including the 2,035-room New York, New York. The $450-million
project, which includes a re-creation of the New York skyline
with a roller-coaster weaving through Gotham landmarks, was a
joint development of MGM Grand and Primadonna Resorts. In
1998, Mirage Resorts is expected to open the Bellagio, a hotel
with 3,000 rooms and an Italian theme. A few hundred yards to
the north, Bally Entertainment Corporation is building Paris, a
3,000-room casino/resort. Last year two other Strip landmarks,
the Sands and Hacienda, were destroyed to make way for new
resorts. Despite the growth, the annual occupancy rate on the
Strip is still close to 90 percent. Conventions bring in more than
three million visitors a year.

Kevin Brass. "Casino Hotels Grow on Strip's Outskirts." *New York Times*,
2 February 1997, p. Y25.

Economic sovereignty will eventually bring about financial independence for those tribes that are able to game on their reservations. This new self-sufficiency is fostering self-esteem and pride among Native Americans. Gaming revenues are providing for better housing, health, and education. Education is becoming more important, and tribes are realizing that the "New Buffalo," that many term gaming, is really education beyond an eighth grade or a high school diploma. Many dollars are now being used for educational growth. Education will enable the Native American to compete in the larger society; it will also build unity among Indians and non-Indians as well as unity within factionalized tribal communities. The movement to stop Indian gaming continues, but its positive impact on tribes should be reason enough to let it grow.

F. William Johnson. "Legalized Gambling: Economic Sovereignty for Native Americans." *Indian Gaming Magazine*, December 1996, p. 16.

[Mickey] Brown [C.E.O. of Foxwoods Native American Casino—America's number one casino in terms of revenues] says he relishes the differences between working in a casino in the traditional gaming industry and a tribal casino. "In a tribal facility, the concern is for the benefits of the tribe, specifically, to tribal goals and the tribal heritage. Making money is a consideration, but it's not the primary consideration. The primary consideration is the benefit of the tribe long-range. They're concerned about how it will affect the community in which they live, because the casino is on the reservation. Not many shareholders have Treasure Island in their backyard. But this is their neighborhood. They don't want a bunch of neon lights. They want something that blends into the community. They would not want a waterfall or a volcano eruption every 15 minutes. They do like attractiveness, but it has to blend into the community."

Roger Gros. "Forever Foxwoods." *Casino Journal*, August 1996, p. 46.

Indian peoples have known for many years sovereignty is a double-edged sword. On one hand, it gives Native Americans advantages, at least in the world of gaming, that non-Indians don't enjoy. In states where commercial, non-Indian casinos are illegal, Indian tribes often can use sovereignty as a tool to launch their own casinos. And the tax burden for Indian-run casinos is far less than a commercial business would have to bear. That's the positive side of sovereignty. It is the side of the issue that has given reservation economies an enormous boost and allowed

Indian tribes to escape the grinding cycle of poverty and despair. But now millions of dollars are flowing through Indian reservation casinos every day. People who have for years known nothing but deprivation are suddenly having unimaginably huge amounts of money thrown at them, sometimes by unscrupulous individuals. Tribal leaders are being lavished with attentions they're not all used to. Entertaining potential clients and offering them little gifts is certainly within the bounds of standard business practices. But the danger occurs if the tribal leadership becomes too cozy with a management company that doesn't have the tribe's best interest in mind. So tribal members who suspect their elected leadership has been co-opted by a corrupt management company have almost no recourse. State and federal government bodies, when dealing with tribes, are really dealing with tribal councils, whether or not those councils are acting in the best interests of the tribe. That is not to say organized crime infiltration of Indian casinos is commonplace or that every tribal government is corrupt. But, just as with any government official, it does exist.

Matt Connor. *Gaming and Wagering Business,* 15 October–14 November 1993, pp. 1, 55.

That position is strongly disputed by Rick Hill, the newly elected chairman of the National Indian Gaming Association. Referring to a report last year from the Department of Justice that said the "perception in the media and elsewhere that Indian gaming operations are rife with serious criminality does not stand up under close examination," Hill flatly denied charges of organized crime infiltration of reservation casinos. "There is no organized crime, reorganized crime, or disorganized crime on Indian reservations," Hill said. "What critics of Indian gaming are really afraid of is organized Indians."

Matt Connor. *Gaming and Wagering Business,* 15 July–14 August 1993, pp. 44–45.

For what we sincerely believe were the best and most noble reasons—to redress ancient wrongs and to eliminate grinding poverty and abject deprivation on Indian reservations—all branches of the federal government have acted to grant Indians certain rights in the context of gaming, which they would have preferred to avoid. The contention which exists over Indian gaming is so intense that it threatens to inspire a political force strong enough—and perhaps more importantly, angry enough—to threaten not only Indian gaming but all forms of legalized gambling in the nation. [I]f the federal government genuinely and sincerely wishes to improve the lot of America's Indian tribes (and this is perhaps the biggest "if" of all) it would be well-advised, both morally and pragmatically, to do so directly and positively and not in ways which impose burdens upon non-Indians, specifically by forcing state governments to act contrary to the desires and interests of their non-Indian citizens.

J. Mark Reifer. "Indian Gaming: Some Legislative Guidelines." *Casino Journal*, July 1996, p. 8.

Illegal sports betting in the United States is a huge business. Last year alone, bettors wagered billions of dollars with illegal book makers. Every major newspaper prints wagering information. Customers spend millions of dollars on services that claim to have an advantage in picking winners based on the current line. Some even claim that illegal betting is the reason that professional sports have gained the popularity that they enjoy. The problem with keeping sports betting illegal is that the illegality itself does not solve the problem. Persons do not cease to bet on sports simply because it is illegal. This is because in most societies, the enforcement of crimes usually falls into two categories: zero tolerance or decriminalized. The former is reserved for crimes that are strictly and severely punished, with the goal of total eradication. The latter are tolerated crimes that occur almost freely, and aren't severely punished when pursued. Sports wagering is the latter. The problem with decriminalized crimes is that, by definition, criminals run the operation. Money derived from these operations can be funneled into other criminal activities. Police are more likely to accept graft to protect the illegal operators. Regular citizens lose respect for the criminal justice system. And just as important, no regulatory system insures the honesty of the operations. Because of the involvement of the criminal element in the wagering activities, sports are more apt, not less likely, to be tainted with scandal.

Anthony Cabot. *Casino Journal*, December 1993, p. 12.

When you don't have control over your betting habit, it's an illness, like alcoholism or nicotine dependency. The main symptom is likely to be depression. If you bet money that you can't afford to lose, and then you lose, you are going to feel down. How do you come up with the money when you don't have it? Borrow? Hell, just double your previous bet! That way you still end up winning, right? Wrong! You never know how long your bad luck will last. If it lasts too long, and you can't afford to play, you might find yourself in a heap of trouble. It's not something that you ever want to experience.

Vincent Kray (a Toronto gambler). Quoted in *You Bet: Canada's Gaming Report*, February 1994, p. 19.

The Cabazon and Morongo Reservations contain no natural resources which can be exploited. The tribal games at present provide the sole source of revenues for the operation of the tribal governments and the provision of tribal services. They are also the major sources of employment on the reservations. Self-determination and economic development are not within reach if the tribes cannot raise revenues and provide employment for their members.

Justice Byron White. *California* v. *Cabazon*, 480 U.S. 202 (1987).

Sec. 2. The Congress finds that (5) Indians have the exclusive right to regulate gaming activity on Indian lands if the gaming activity is not specifically prohibited by federal law and is conducted within a state which does not, as a matter of criminal law and public policy, prohibit such gaming activity.

    Sec. 3. The purpose of this Act is—(1) to provide a statutory basis for the operation of gaming by Indian tribes as a means of promoting tribal economic development, self-sufficiency, and strong tribal governments; (2) to provide a statutory basis for the regulation of gaming by an Indian tribe adequate to shield it from organized crime and other corrupting influences, to ensure that the Indian tribe is the primary beneficiary of the gaming operation, and to assure that gaming is conducted fairly and honestly by both the operator and players.

Indian Gaming Regulatory Act, Public Law 100-497 (17 October 1988).

Gambling is the only business, legal or illegal, where the product being sold is cash, with no paper record. Organized crime is always attracted to cash businesses, but so is unorganized crime. The high-tech security systems found in every large casino are there to watch for cheating and stealing by employees more than by players. Every government that has legalized gambling has soon realized that it has had to institute tough controls, and most have found that the criminals can be a lot smarter than the regulators.

I. Nelson Rose (professor of law at Whittier College of Law). Quoted in *Indian Gaming and the Law*, edited by William R. Eadington. Reno: Institute for the Study of Gaming, University of Nevada–Reno, 1990, pp. 6–7.

It's no secret that I was opposed to expanding gaming on Indian Lands. I think that it is still a poor tool for economic development in Indian Country and the social ills that it is likely to bring with it may completely overshadow any economic benefits. In Nevada, we understand the social costs associated with large scale commercial gaming, and we've learned over the more than fifty years of its legal existence to deal with it and compensate for it.

U.S. senator Harry Reid (Nevada). Quoted in *Indian Gaming and the Law*, edited by William R. Eadington. Reno: Institute for the Study of Gaming, University of Nevada–Reno, 1990, p. 15.

The gradual decline in police responsibility for gambling enforcement has many roots. The entry of state governments into various forms of gambling certainly was important. So was the federal campaign against large-scale gambling organizations. I would also speculate that increased popular understanding of the inevitable failure of gambling enforcement and a concern that police devote their limited resources to other, more pressing activities may have been the most significant factors. [G]ambling is no longer a major problem for local police. Few resources are devoted to it; except for the occasional large-scale raid, it is given little attention. Narcotics enforcement has apparently taken its place as the responsibility that poses the greatest threat to police autonomy.

Peter Reuter. "Police Regulation of Illegal Gambling." *Annals of the American Academy of Political and Social Sciences*, July 1984, 47.

The prostitute, the pimp, the peddler of dope, the operator of the gambling hall, the vendor of obscene pictures, the bootlegger, the abortionist, all are productive, all produce goods or services which people desire and for which they are willing to pay. It happens that society has put these goods and services under the ban, but people go on producing them and people go on consuming them, and an act of the legislature does not make them any less a part of the economic system.

Edward Hawkins and Willard W. Waller. *Critical Notes on the Cost of Crime*, 1936, pp. 684–685.

The police have concerns about the escalation of gambling activity in this country. There will inevitably be attempts by criminal elements and organized crime to infiltrate, despite the safeguards established by regulatory bodies. Organized crime has historically been involved in gambling, prostitution, and drug trafficking. We would have to be very naive to expect organized crime to relinquish its interest in gambling just because governments legalize the activity. Studies by our neighbors to the south have shown that with the escalation of legalized gambling, we can expect an increase in illegal gambling activity. One former overseer of mob gambling stated, "during my career there has always existed one solid constant—any new form of expansion of legal gambling always increased our client base."

Sgt. Bob McDonald (Royal Canadian Mounted Police). Quoted in Colin Campbell. *Gambling in Canada: The Bottomline.* Burnaby, BC: Simon Fraser University, 1994, p. 186.

Leonard Tose, the former owner of the Philadelphia Eagles National Football League team, admitted on the witness stand in federal court in Camden yesterday that the first time he signed a marker for $30,000 at the Sands Casino in Atlantic City he was too drunk to remember it. Tose, 77, is suing to recover some of the $14 million he admits losing there. Tose claims casino employees encouraged him to drink and then took advantage of him while he was intoxicated. His suit lists 42 dates between 16 June 1981 and 31 December 1982, when he lost $9,740,000 at the Sands, and 30 dates between 10 May 1985 and 2 April 1986 when he lost an additional $4,930,000.

Joseph D. McCaffrey. *The Star Ledger*, 18 February 1993.

Frank Twiggs, a certified compulsive gambling counselor and a member of the Council on Compulsive Gambling in New Jersey, said Monday that statistics indicate underage gambling is a serious problem. In 1991, the casinos reported that nearly 200,000 people under age 21 were turned away at the doors, while 20,000 others were asked to leave the floor, Twiggs said. "Everybody acknowledges that it's a problem," he said. "The numbers of kids who are gambling—any form of gambling—is reaching 100%."

Trudy Walz. *The Record* (North Jersey), 31 August 1993.

In every case of a casino opening near a race track, the track has either closed or is fighting for its life. In every case. There are no exceptions. The action is much faster. At the track, you have to wait 15 minutes to a half hour before the next race. At the casino, events occur all the time. It takes a certain knowledge to wager on horse betting. The bettor can get a little bored wondering where the action is. At a casino, if you lose your last bet, 15 seconds later you have another chance to win.

Barry Meadow. *Casino Executive*. June 1995, p. 38.

A lot of the stigma surrounding the industry has been eliminated. It would not hurt my image, and I could make quite a bit of money in a short period of time.

Don Barden (owner of the Black Entertainment Network, on becoming an owner of a casino). *Casino Executive*, November 1995, p. 54.

Crime is down, employment is up. Business is expanding. Population and housing starts are on the rise. A capital improvement plan is accelerating even as tax rates decline. The city debt is disappearing faster than a runaway river barge. Even since casinos came to Joliet, Illinois, the city's renewal has been unstoppable. In the 1990's explosion of legalized gambling, Joliet seems to have emerged as a model of success—the example that city fathers in other jurisdictions point to as the embodiment of their hopes and dreams of what gaming can bring to their communities.

John Grochowski. *Casino Executive*, June 1966, pp. 42–43.

Big money is trying to sell legislators on casinos as family entertainment, a treacherous trend that cries for regulation. I'm not a prohibitionist. But you don't have to be a puritan to question whether kids should be exposed to gambling as family entertainment. Gambling is an addiction for many, a fantasy for many, it creates no new wealth and yet, for the first time in our economic history, this nonproductive sector is being proposed as an anchor of growth. With anarchy, hunger, racism and joblessness rising all over the globe, what does it say about our character that we devote so much of our high tech potential to inventing better gambling machines? Gambling, not religion, is the opiate of the people, and those sponsoring it are the new Neros. Above all, there is the cancer of political corruption spread by gambling. Even clean, publicly traded gambling corporations can corrupt and dominate the democratic process with their massive lobbying efforts, usually conducted against penniless opposition.

Tom Hayden (California state senator). *Los Angeles Times*, 12 September 1994, p. B-7.

Upping the ante against opponents of casino expansion, gambling industry lobbyists are betting that influential friends in Washington will reverse the industry's run of bad luck in the states...gambling concerns have banded together to establish the American Gaming Association. The head of the year-old lobbying group is Frank J. Fahrenkopf, Jr., a former National Republican Party chairman. Fahrenkopf, a lawyer and political deal-maker, is plugged in both with political leaders in Washington and with gambling's key figures in his native Nevada. From his perch at the head of the AGA, he is expected to cash in his chips with other Washington insiders on behalf of such heavyweight hotel-casino operators as Hilton, ITT, Circus Circus and MGM Grand.

"The gaming industry was one of the few major industries that was not at all represented in Washington," Fahrenkopf said. "Every industry from automobiles to pasta companies is represented with a lobbyist or law office. We're just keeping up with the times and the growth of our industry."

Sam Fulwood III. "Gaming Industry Raises Stakes on Foes." *Los Angeles Times*, 9 July 1996, p. A-5.

Casino gambling is alive and flourishing at Bishop Gorman High School, according to some sources: gambling that even involves some teacher/student connections. One senior boy, who declined to be named, stated, "I'd say that about twenty-five to thirty percent of the guys in the junior and senior class gamble regularly at casinos here in town. They either take the money themselves or give it to a teacher."

The Lance (student paper, Bishop Gorman High School, Las Vegas, Nevada), February 1985.

Growing up in Las Vegas, I have a special appreciation for gambling. The money taxed through gambling paid for my schooling and my lower cost of living as well as giving me a chance to win a $1,000 jackpot from the change after buying a Slurpee. When my friends were hard-up for money, but hungry as lions, any casino would feed us for less than a buck apiece. In addition any education wasn't complete without seeing white lions, a man-made volcano, and King Arthur's castle shooting laser beams into the desert sky. But gambling did have its down-sides. For example, with a town that operates 24 hours a day, there's never any downtime. There was rush hour traffic at three o'clock in the morning, the night sky usually was so bright it looked like an overcast day, and when you asked somebody what they did for a living, they wouldn't say plumber or cook—they said "days," "swing" or "grave." Moreover it put pressure on teenagers that isn't found anywhere else in the country—the temptation to risk hard-earned allowances to win a car or a bucketful of coins. Gambling was looked upon as being a coming of age activity, where those who could handle themselves and act the role of a legal adult were deemed as being more mature than other kids.

Benjamin Raskin. "Gaming Defines State." *The Sagebrush* (University of Nevada–Reno), 1 May 1995.

There are some vices which appear to attract only weak characters, but this is not true of gambling. The strong as well as the weak are attracted to it. It appeals to a certain quality of human nature which is, in itself, highly praiseworthy. The willingness to take risks is a characteristic of all progressive people and is a most valuable characteristic when the risk is one such as is necessarily involved in every great enterprise. Our country has been made by men who dared to risk much in order to attain their ends. Now, the gambling mania is but a perversion of this worthy quality. Men who have the capacity for undertaking difficult enterprises where boldness and daring are required waste their talents in assuming the useless risk of the gambling table. Remove the games and the men will find enjoyment is carrying the risks of legitimate business and in contributing to the progress of the state.

Silas E. Ross. "Prohibit Gambling for the Good of the State." *The Sagebrush* (University of Nevada–Reno), 14 February 1909.

Gambling is the sure way of getting nothing for something.

Wilson Mizner. Quoted in Carl Sifakis. *The Encyclopedia of Gambling.* New York: Facts on File, 1990, p. vii.

As the man was driving to church, he thought to himself, "Wow, life has really turned against me. My wife has left, the mortgage company is about to foreclose on the house, and my business is headed for Chapter Seven bankruptcy." Just then he saw the billboard. It read, "Win the Super Lotto, Turn Your Life Around." He said an "Amen" to that. During the church service the minister asked everyone to be in a moment of personal prayer. God could hear the prayers, "Help the people in Rwanda"; "Look after the children in the hospital"; "Help our missionaries in Central

America." But the man thought as he prayed, "I know others are more deserving, but I have been a good man. I come to church each week. I practice the Golden Rule. Maybe it's O.K. if this time I pray for myself. Dear God, please let me win the Super Lotto." He felt a strange sensation, and then he heard a voice speaking to him. The voice of God replied, "My Son, you have indeed been a good man. It shall be done; you shall win the Super Lotto." But he did not win. His wife called and said she was never coming back, the mortgage company took his house, he also lost his car to the bank, and his business had to close. The next Sunday he walked to church. He was disappointed in God, and at prayer time, he vented his anger. "God, I've been a good man. You promised. But you did not deliver, and now look, my life is ruined." Again he heard the voice of God. "My Son, you have been a good man and indeed I did promise. But my son. You have to meet me half way. You have to buy a ticket."

Old gambling story told in many countries around the world.

Ever since I moved to Las Vegas, my Midwestern friend has been using me as his personal bookie. He is a big fan of college football, and he phones me his bets, and I would go to the casino and place them for him. He used to play football so he knows the intricacies of the game. However, so do the people who set the odds and the "point spreads" in Las Vegas. Late in the Fall after a string of 17 straight losses on Big Ten and NFL games, my friend was desperate. He begged me for information. "Help me. Do you have any information on key injuries? How are the big bettors going on the Bears? What advice can you give me?" I said, "Golly, I really don't have any inside information. The only advice I can give you is maybe you should try hockey." He replied, "Don't be stupid! What do I know about hockey?"

Common experience of people who move to Las Vegas.

I was walking on Fremont Street in downtown Las Vegas. A panhandler came up to me and asked, "Hey Mister, do you have a dollar for a cup of coffee?" In disdain I looked at the poor soul and replied, "Sure! Coffee. Look, I know that as soon as you get the dollar you are heading into the El Cortez Casino and putting it into a slot machine." "No. No. Mister, you have me wrong; I won't gamble the dollar, really." I said, "Yeh, sure! How do I know that." He replied, "See here in my pocket; I got my gambling money already."

Much-repeated nightclub joke in Las Vegas showrooms.

The secret dream of these tenement dwellers had always been to own their own home. My father also dreamed about numbers. He bought numbers books at the newsstands to work out winning combinations. And he still went in everyday with Aunt Beryl. They usually played quarters. Then, one Saturday night, my father dreamed a number, and the next morning the same number appeared on the hymn board [at church]. This, surely, was God taking Luther Powell by the hand and leading him to the Promised Land. Somehow, Pop and Aunt Beryl managed to scrape up $25 to put on the number. And they hit it, straight. I still remember the atmosphere of joy, disbelief, and anxiety when the numbers runner delivered the brown paper bags to our house— $10,000 in tens and twenties, more than three year's pay. And that's how the Powells managed to buy 183-68 Elmira Avenue, in the community of Hollis in the Borough of Queens.

Colin Powell. *An American Journey.* New York: Random House, 1995, pp. 301–303.

In all the states where casinos recently have been established, the rise in employment and the decline in the unemployment rate have been substantially greater than in the same areas before the establishment of casinos. The casino gaming industry employed an estimated 337,000 people in 1995. An additional 328,000 jobs in other industries were generated by the expenditures in casino gaming. Unemployment on Indian reservations has been reduced by as much as 400% since the advent of legalized casino gaming. With the addition of no new casinos over the next decade, direct employment in the casino industry would rise at an average rate of 7.5% per year. Economic activity generated by casino gaming added an estimated $5.9 billion to federal tax receipts in 1995. This figure includes higher personal and corporate income taxes, higher OASHDI taxes and a reduction in unemployment compensation benefits. Total direct tax payments to state and local governments [approximated] $2 billion in 1995.

The Evans Group. *A Study of the Economic Impact of the Gaming Industry through 2005.* Reno, NV: International Gaming Technologies, 1996, pp. 1-1, 1-2.

Figures and Tables

Figure 4.1 is a map portraying casino gaming in the United States. Commercial casino gambling has spread to 11 states, with river-boat casino gambling offered in six states and land-based casinos

Figure 4.1 Casino Gambling in the United States

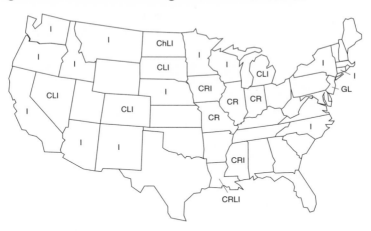

C = Commercial, Ch = Charity—Permanent, G = Government, I = Indian,
L = Land-based, R = Riverboats. There is no legal gambling in Hawaii and only
noncasino charitable gambling in Alaska.

present in six states (Louisiana has authorized both land-based and riverboat casinos). One state offers charity casino games on a daily basis in permanent locations, and Indian reservation casino gaming is now present in 14 states.

Casino gaming has now spread from Quebec westward across the remainder of the Canadian provinces. Although most Canadian gaming is charity based, government-owned casinos have been authorized for Manitoba, Nova Scotia, Ontario, Quebec, and Saskatchewan. Ontario has both riverboat and land-based casinos; all the other casinos are land based. There is also a semipermanent casino in the Yukon Territory. (See Figure 4.2.)

The dates of casino and lottery legalizations demonstrate that policymakers of states and provinces often have a tendency to adopt the same kind of gaming activity that has been legalized in bordering states. Gambling legalization can protect states by offering games that will keep their residents from gambling in other states. However, frequent communication and an increased familiarity with gambling are also factors that lead states to follow policies of nearby states. (See Figures 4.3 and 4.4.)

Thirty-seven states and the District of Columbia have authorized government-run lotteries. In addition, eight of these states plus South Carolina have permitted the placement of video gaming machines in their territories. These machines are typically

Figure 4.2 Casino Gambling in Canada

C = Commercial, Ch = Charity—Permanent, G = Government, I = Indian, L = Land-based, R = Riverboats

Figure 4.3 Dates of Commercial Casino Legalizations

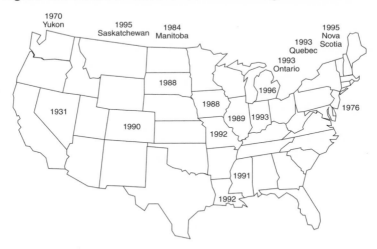

called "video lottery terminals" and are almost identical to video slot machines found in commercial casinos, except that prize money is awarded with tickets rather than with actual coin drops. The gaming machines offer play at simulated games of poker, blackjack, and keno. (See Figure 4.5.)

Figure 4.4 **Dates of Lottery Beginnings**

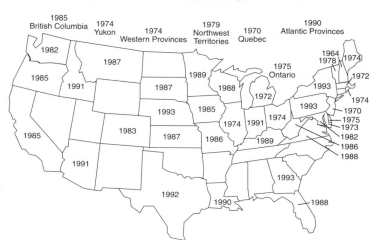

Figure 4.5 **Lotteries in the United States**

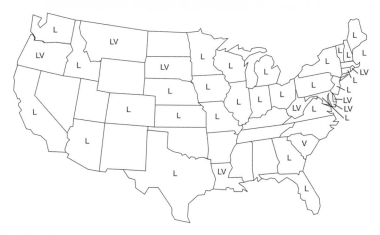

L = Government-Run Lottery, V = Video Lottery Terminals

Every province and each of the territories of Canada has a government-run lottery. Three western provinces—Manitoba, Saskatchewan, and Alberta—and four eastern provinces—New Brunswick, Nova Scotia, Prince Edward Island, and Newfoundland—offer multiprovince lotteries. Individually, these same

Figure 4.6 Lotteries in Canada

L = Government-Run Lottery, V = Video Lottery Terminals

Figure 4.7 Pari-Mutuel Wagering in the United States

D = Dog Racing, H = Horse Racing, I = Intertrack, J = Jai Alai, O = Off-track

seven provinces plus Ontario and Quebec allow video lottery machines similar to those offered in the nine states below the border. (See Figures 4.6 and 4.4.)

Far more than a majority of states offer forms of pari-mutuel betting, a system in which prizes are awarded from a common

Figure 4.8 Pari-Mutuel Wagering in Canada

H = Horse Racing, I = Intertrack, O = Off-track

pool made up of the players' money. Although the betting organization (the track) does not participate in the gambling, it draws a fee from the pool for administering the wagering among the players. The most popular form of pari-mutuel betting is on horse races; the next most popular is on dog races. Four states permit such betting on jai alai matches. Many states have legalized off-track betting and intertrack betting (a player at one track bets on races at other tracks). (See Figure 4.7.)

In Canada, every province and territorial government permits horse race betting. There is no dog race or jai alai betting in Canada. Each government also permits intertrack betting, and all the jurisdictions except Newfoundland and Prince Edward Island have off-track betting. (See Figure 4.8.)

Gross gaming revenues have increased fourfold in the last 15 years. On the one hand, the revenues from both lotteries and casinos have risen dramatically. Also, the entry of Indian gaming in the later 1980s caused a phenomenal rise in gaming revenues. On the other hand, pari-mutuel wagering has remained for the most part static. Only with the advent of off-track and intertrack wagering has this sector managed to grow at all. (See Figure 4.9.)

In 1994, casinos surpassed lotteries as the leading form of gaming in terms of revenues. In future years more dramatic

Figure 4.9 Gross Gaming Wins by Category, 1982–1995

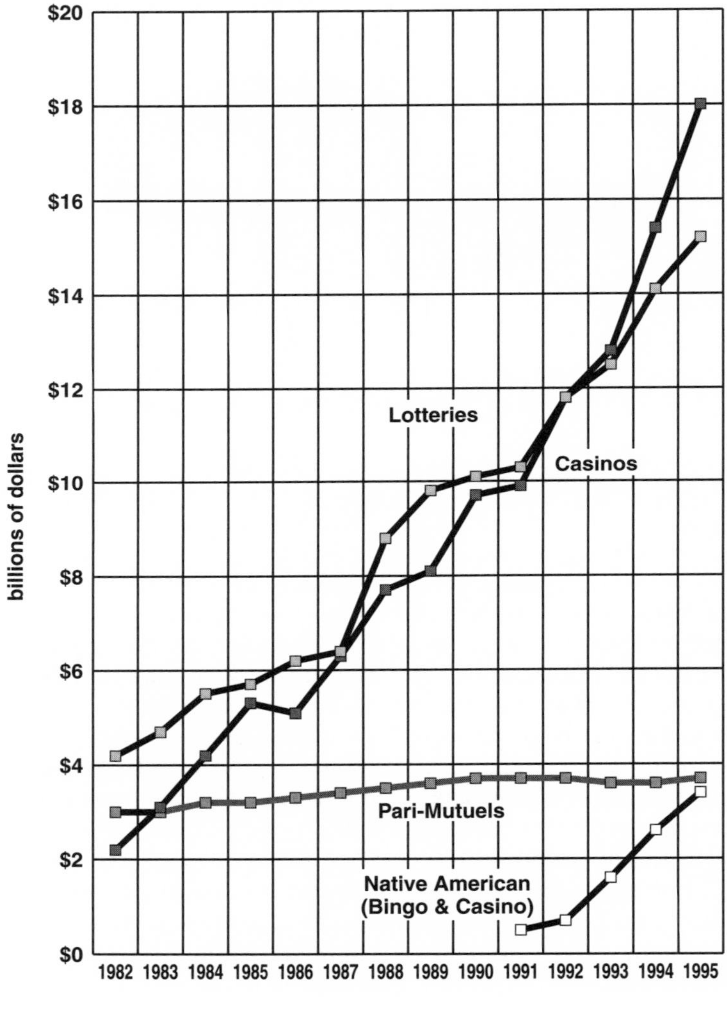

increases in Indian reservation revenues are expected, as many more new casino facilities are being opened by American Indians. (See Figure 4.10.)

The road to a compulsive gambling career, a road of selfish false dreams, is often a very quick journey. In contrast, recovery is a slow path toward reality and concern for others. A leading

Figure 4.10 Gross Revenue from Legal Gambling, 1995

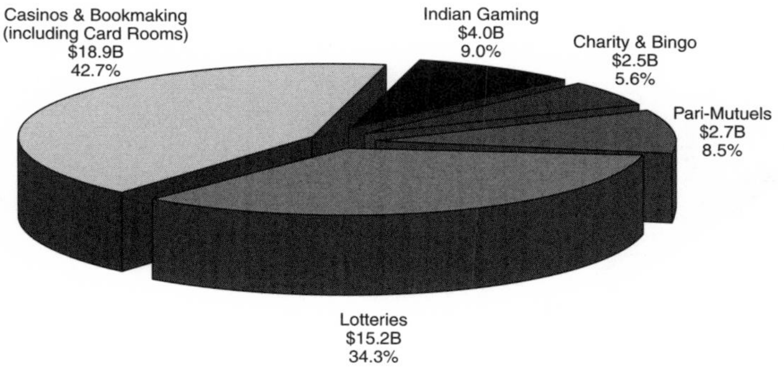

Casinos & Bookmaking
(including Card Rooms)
$18.9B
42.7%

Indian Gaming
$4.0B
9.0%

Charity & Bingo
$2.5B
5.6%

Pari-Mutuels
$2.7B
8.5%

Lotteries
$15.2B
34.3%

Total Revenues $43.3 Billion
Source: *Gaming and Wagering Business* (August–September 1995)

group that supports those in recovery has depicted the many stages on the path toward destruction and the path back to responsibility. (See Figure 4.11.)

Compulsive gambling also has a major impact on family relationships. Figure 4.12 illustrates that the gambler's downward slide into desperation has a parallel effect on the gambler's spouse. The recovery process has mutual benefits as well, as hopelessness is abandoned for a better family life.

Lottery revenues bring billions to state governments. Tables 4.1 and 4.2 show the source of the revenues and their disposition for U.S. and Canadian lotteries. The average per capita ticket sales are just over $100 in the United States (in lottery jurisdictions) and $167 in Canada. Prizes returned to players represent about half of the sales; administrative expenses equaled about 11 percent in the United States and 17 percent in Canada. Governments retain about three-eights of the amounts wagered. (See Tables 4.1 and 4.2.)

Tables 4.3, 4.4, and 4.5 illustrate that voters view various kinds of gambling activity differently. Although there has been a rush toward casino legalizations in recent years, the voters exhibit much more reluctance to legalize casinos than other forms of gambling. Lotteries are quite popular and usually pass with overwhelming votes when placed on the ballot. Election votes on pari-mutuel legalization have mixed results, whereas majorities of the public are most often negative on casino legalization questions. The spread of casino legalization has come, for the most part, from action in state and provincial legislative assemblies.

Figure 4.11 A Chart of Compulsive Gambling and Recovery

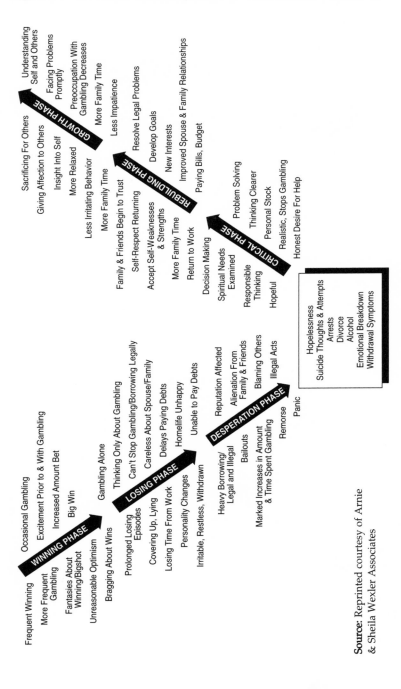

Source: Reprinted courtesy of Arnie & Sheila Wexler Associates

Figure 4.12 A Chart on the Effects of Compulsive Gambling on the Spouse

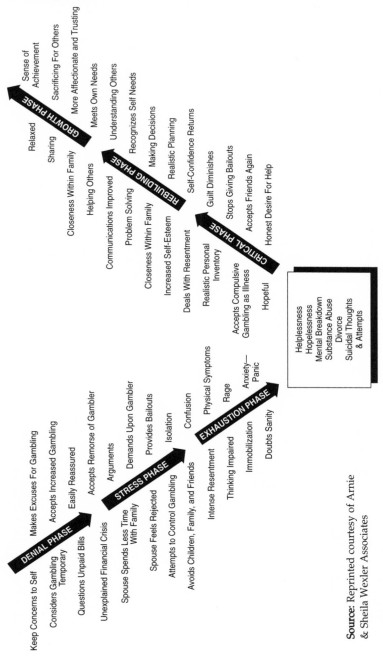

Source: Reprinted courtesy of Arnie & Sheila Wexler Associates

TABLE 4.1
U.S. Lottery Revenues, 1995
(per capita sales in actual dollars; other columns in millions of dollars)

State	Gross Sales	Per Capita Sales	Prizes	Govt. Expenses	Net Revenues
Arizona	286.0	68.10	149.4	44.2	93.2
California	2,166.1	68.55	1,075.2	336.1	754.8
Colorado	351.9	95.11	200.8	50.5	100.6
Connecticut	670.8	203.27	386.3	62.5	222.0
D.C.	230.2	383.67	112.9	29.9	87.4
Delaware	114.1	163.00	56.3	14.5	43.3
Florida	2,303.5	162.22	1,151.7	279.0	872.7
Georgia	1,421.6	197.44	740.3	178.9	502.3
Idaho	88.0	73.33	52.9	16.5	18.6
Illinois	1,629.6	138.10	914.2	129.3	586.2
Indiana	610.7	105.29	349.9	77.6	183.2
Iowa	207.6	74.14	112.6	36.6	58.5
Kansas	177.1	68.12	92.1	27.9	57.1
Kentucky	512.6	131.44	296.3	74.7	141.5
Louisiana	305.3	71.00	152.0	44.1	109.1
Maine	153.2	127.67	88.8	23.2	41.2
Maryland	1,042.0	208.40	545.0	107.8	389.2
Massachusetts	2,793.2	457.90	1,937.6	214.2	641.5
Michigan	1,381.5	145.20	715.4	111.9	554.2
Minnesota	335.9	73.02	196.1	79.9	59.9
Missouri	411.7	77.68	221.8	60.5	129.4
Montana	32.8	36.44	16.2	8.0	8.6
Nebraska	79.0	43.38	39.3	15.4	24.3
New Hampshire	141.0	128.18	80.2	17.2	43.6
New Jersey	1,576.0	199.49	809.5	117.6	648.9
New York	3,028.6	167.33	1,470.6	314.2	1,243.8
Ohio	2,182.3	194.85	1,236.8	234.3	711.2
Oregon*	3,323.0	1,071.93	2,860.3	191.4	271.3
Pennsylvania	1,591.8	131.55	812.7	149.8	629.3
Rhode Island	334.5	334.50	207.4	50.4	76.7
South Dakota*	378.2	540.29	236.8	85.6	55.8
Texas	3,036.5	162.38	1,689.3	333.5	1,013.7
Virginia	902.5	136.74	487.3	103.5	311.6
Vermont	71.7	119.50	42.0	7.5	22.2
Washington	400.9	74.24	207.6	56.6	136.7
Wisconsin	518.9	101.75	298.8	55.8	164.3
West Virginia	481.5	267.50	385.7	40.6	55.3
Total for lottery venues	35,271.8	155.19	20,428.10	3,781.2	11,063.2
	100.0%		57.9%	10.7%	31.4%

*Figures for Oregon and South Dakota include video machines. The figures for other jurisdictions are for "traditional" lottery sales.
Sources: Information is drawn in part from U.S. Census data and from *International Gaming and Wagering Business*, July 1996, pp. S1–S38.

TABLE 4.2a
Canadian Lotteries, 1995
(in millions of Canadian dollars)

Province	Sales	Prizes	Expenses	Net to Province
Alberta	814.8	189.6	120.4	504.8
British Columbia	776.4	403.8	131.8	240.8
Manitoba	304.3	136.9	55.7	111.7
New Brunswick	190.1	89.7	36.5	63.9
Newfoundland	188.7	85.0	34.5	69.2
Nova Scotia	243.1	105.9	43.1	94.1
Ontario	1,942.0	958.0	357.4	626.6
Prince Edward Is.	34.3	15.4	6.2	12.7
Quebec	1,553.8	735.2	319.6	499.0
Saskatchewan	249.3	112.2	45.6	91.5
Total	6,296.8	2,831.7	1,150.8	2,314.3

Source: International Gaming and Wagering Business, July 1996, pp. S32–S38. Where statistics were incomplete, data were interpolated on the basis of general ratios derived from sales ratios to other factors in provinces where information was complete.

TABLE 4.2b
1995 Pari-Mutuel Betting in Canada (On-Track)
(in millions of Canadian dollars)

Province	Amount Wagered	Take-Out Rate (%)	Taxation Rate (%)
Alberta	169.01	8.9	5.0
British Columbia	257.32	1.5	7.0
Manitoba	10.42	4.7	9.5
New Brunswick	4.12	8.7	11.0
Newfoundland	53.52	9.0	11.0
Nova Scotia	10.22	8.8	11.0
Ontario	1,222.03	3.3	7.6
Prince Edward Is.	4.73	0.9	13.6
Quebec	172.42	3.4	7.1
Saskatchewan	7.12	5.5	10.0
Total	1,910.91		

*Note: Amount wagered is amount bet on horses. This amount less the take-out is returned to the winning bettors. The tax rate is applied to the amount wagered, but it is part of the take-out.
Source: International Gaming and Wagering Business, July 1996, pp. S32–S38.

TABLE 4.2c
Gross Gaming Revenues of
Canadian Commercial Casinos, 1994–1997[a]
(in millions of Canadian dollars)

Casino	1994	1995	1996	1997[h]
Halifax	–	–	34.9[c]	36.2
Sydney	–	–	13.3[f]	19.1
Montreal	137.1[b]	347.8	336.7	297.0
Charlevoix	–	15.4[c]	24.5	19.7
Hull	–	–	2.2[g]	110.5
Windsor	–	418.9[d]	526.2	350.1
Northern Belle	–	–	51.1[e]	130.3
Niagara	–	–	–	28.7[i]
Rama	–	–	–	156.0[k]
Crystal	34.4	19.6	17.5	7.5[l]
Club Regent	25.6[c]	36.0	36.8	23.7[l]
McPhillips Street Station	29.1[c]	42.9	46.3	22.6[l]
Regina	–	–	7.0[l]	20.8[b]
Total	226.2	880.6	1,096.5	1,222.2

[a] Fiscal year ended 31 March; [b] 6 months; [c] 10 months; [d] 11 months; [e] 4 months; [f] 8 months; [g] 1 week; [h] 9 months; [i] 3 weeks; [k] 5 months; [l] estimate.
Source: Reports of Provincial Gaming Corporations, reported in Christian Marfels, "The Rapid Growth of Casino Gambling in Canada," paper presented to Tenth International Conference on Gambling and Risk Taking, 1 June 1997.

TABLE 4.2d
Charitable Gaming in Canada, 1995
(in millions of Canadian dollars)

Province	Gross Win	Net to Charity
Alberta	$188.4	$97.3
British Columbia	$220.1	$123.9
Manitoba	$32.7	$17.6
New Brunswick	$23.0	$15.8
Newfoundland	$23.3	$13.4
Nova Scotia	$36.3	$22.5
Ontario	N.A.	
	($2,370.0 wagered)	
Prince Edward Island	$3.5	$1.8
Quebec	$90.4	$60.4
Saskatchewan	N.A.	
	($285.0 wagered)	$49.7

Source: International Gaming and Wagering Business, July 1996, pp. S32–S38.

TABLE 4.3
Selected Popular Referenda Votes (Lotteries)

Year	State	Percentage
1996	Arkansas (Combined with casino)	39 (Defeated)
1994	New Mexico	Passed, but suspended on constitutional grounds
1992	Nebraska	62
	Georgia	52
1991	Texas	65
1990	Louisiana	69
1988	Missouri	58
	Indiana	62
	Minnesota	59
	Kentucky	61
	Idaho	52
1987	Virginia	57
	Wisconsin	65
1986	Florida	64
	Montana	69
	South Dakota	60
	North Dakota	44 (Defeated)
1984	Missouri	68
	California	58
	Oregon	66
	West Virginia	66
1973	Rhode Island	76
	Ohio	64
	Maine	72
1972	Maryland	77
	Michigan	73
	Iowa	67
	Washington	62
1966	New Jersey	81

TABLE 4.4
Selected Popular Referenda Votes (Horse Racing)

Year	State	Percentage
1996	Nebraska (off-track betting)	38 (Defeated)
1988	Tennessee (local)	49 (Defeated)
	Virginia	56
	Nebraska	62
1987	Texas	56
1986	Kansas	58
1984	Missouri	60
1982	Minnesota	58
	Oklahoma	58
1978	Virginia	48 (Defeated)
1974	Oklahoma	46 (Defeated)
1971	Missouri	46 (Defeated)
1968	Indiana	47 (Defeated)
1963	New York (off-track betting)	76
1956	Arkansas	53

TABLE 4.5
Selected Popular Referenda Votes (Casinos)

Year	State	Percentage
1996	Arkansas	39 (Defeated)
	Colorado (for additional towns)	32 (Defeated)
	Michigan (for Detroit)	52
	North Dakota (slot machines in bars)	32 (Defeated)
	Ohio (riverboat casinos)	38 (Defeated)
	Washington (Indian slot machines)	44 (Defeated)
	Arizona (additional Indian casinos)	63
	West Virginia (race track slot machines)	55
1994	Florida	38 (Defeated)
	Missouri	49 (Defeated)
	Missouri (revote)	56
1992	Missouri	58
1990	Colorado	56
	Ohio	42 (Defeated)
	Alaska	40 (Defeated)
	North Dakota	35 (Defeated)
1988	South Dakota	64
1986	Florida	32 (Defeated)
1984	Colorado	33 (Defeated)
	Arkansas	29 (Defeated)
1978	Florida	27 (Defeated)
1976	New Jersey	56
1974	New Jersey	40 (Defeated)
1964	Arkansas	39 (Defeated)

Directory of Organizations

Private Organizations

American Gaming Association
555 13th Street NW
Washington, DC 20004
(202) 637-5676

This organization represents the casino industry in Washington, D.C. It sponsors research on gambling subjects and supports programs to help the industry and individuals deal with problem gambling behaviors.

Publications: The Responsible Gaming Resource Guide.

American Quarter Horse Association
2736 West Tenth
Amarillo, TX 79168
(806) 376-4811

This association maintains the registry for all racing quarter horses and publishes rules for quarter horse racing.

Publications: Rules for quarter horse racing.

Association of Racing Commissioners International, Inc.
Kentucky Horse Park
4067 Iron Works Pike

179

Lexington, KY 40511
(606) 278-5460

An association of government regulatory bodies. Its essential purpose is to exchange regulatory information and guarantee the security of the racing industry.

Publications: A weekly newsletter and annual compilation of statistics on racetrack activity in North America.

Canadian Foundation on Compulsive Gambling
505 Consumers Road, #605
Willowdale, Ontario
Canada M2J 4V8
(416) 499-9800

The foundation supports the study of problem gambling and lobbies governments for funding of treatment programs.

Canadian Trotting Association
2150 Meadowdale Boulevard
Mississauga, Ontario
Canada L5N 6R6
(416) 858-3060

An association founded in 1939 to record and distribute information on harness racing in Canada. Members include track and horse owners, drivers, and trainers.

Publications: The monthly magazine *Trot* and a registry for standardbred horses in Canada.

Gam-Anon International Service Office
P.O. Box 157
Whitestone, NY 11357
(718) 352-1671

Gam-Anon works with members of families affected by pathological gambling. It is a support group that provides understanding about compulsive gambling.

Publications: Gam-a-News, a quarterly newsletter, as well as a variety of pamphlets and information sheets.

Gamblers Anonymous
California Organization
P.O. Box 17173

Los Angeles, CA 90017
(213) 386-8789

Founded in 1957, Gamblers Anonymous has over 900 chapters worldwide. It is a self-help operation for problem gamblers and is patterned after Alcoholics Anonymous. Related chapters serve members of problem gamblers' families.

Publications: An annual directory, a monthly bulletin, and several monographs and pamphlets.

The Gambler's Book Club
630 South 11th Street
Las Vegas, NV 89101
(702) 382-7555

The Gambler's Book Club carries the world's largest supply of gaming books and related materials for sale.

Publications: A newsletter and catalogs listing the club's stock of books.

Harness Tracks of America, Inc.
35 Airport Road
Morristown, NJ 07960
(201) 285-9090

An association of track owners concerned with various aspects of harness racing, including marketing, security, and government relations.

Publications: A weekly newsletter.

The Institute for the Study of Gambling and Commercial Gaming
University of Nevada
Reno, NV 89557
(702) 784-1477

The institute conducts seminars for the gaming industry and sponsors international gaming conferences, which bring together scholars and industry leaders from around the world.

Publications: The proceedings from the conferences and a newsletter. The institute is also copublisher of the *Journal of Gambling Studies.*

International Association of Gaming Attorneys
P.O. Box 7438
Las Vegas, NV 89125
(702) 384-3840

The association conducts seminars and annual conventions for attorneys from around the world.

Publications: Treatises on gaming topics and information related to the current legal status of gaming in all jurisdictions.

International Association of State Lotteries
500 Sherbrooke Street, West, Suite 2000
Montreal, Quebec
Canada H3A 3G6
(514) 282-8000

Founded in 1958, the association fosters the exchange of ideas related to the technical aspects of lottery organization and operation.

Publications: A directory and industry review.

International Gaming Institute (IGI)
University of Nevada–Las Vegas
Las Vegas, NV 89154-6037
(702) 895-3966

The IGI conducts ongoing seminars for members of the gaming industry and for government regulators of gambling from throughout the world. The seminars are coordinated with college degree courses offered at the university.

Publications: Gaming Research and Review Journal and books, including Anthony Cabot's *Casino Gaming: Policy, Economics, and Regulation.*

The Jockey Club
380 Madison Avenue
New York, NY 10017
(212) 599-1919

One of the original organizations created to monitor the integrity of racing in the United States. Founded in 1894, it serves a crucial function of maintaining a registry of thoroughbred race horses. The rules of the Jockey Club are a nationwide model for racing rules. The organization is patterned after the Jockey Club of the United Kingdom.

Publications: Registry of thoroughbred horses.

National Council on Compulsive Gambling
445 West 59th Street, Room 1521
New York, NY 10019
(212) 763-3833

The council encourages public support for treatment programs for problem gamblers and holds regular educational conferences. There are 29 state-affiliated groups.

Publications: Copublishes the leading academic journal on gambling issues, the *Journal of Gambling Studies.*

National Greyhound Association
Box 543
Abilene, KS 67410
(913) 263-4660

The association maintains a registry of racing dogs and promotes the industry by lobbying and sponsoring seminars.

Publications: The monthly *Greyhound Review.*

National Indian Gaming Association
904 Pennsylvania Avenue SE
Washington, DC 20003
(202) 546-7711

An association composed of tribes and associated members engaged in gaming enterprises on reservations. The association promotes integrity in Indian gaming and advocacy issues in tribal sovereignty.

Publications: The monthly *Indian Gaming Magazine* in cooperation with the Public Gaming Research Institute.

Nevada Gaming Attorneys Association
325 South 3rd, Suite 1-310
Las Vegas, NV 89101

An association of attorneys that holds regular seminars covering developments in casino gaming law.

Publications: A newsletter, *Nevada Gaming Counsel.*

Nevada Resorts Association
2300 West Sahara, Suite 440-32
Las Vegas, NV 89102
(702) 362-2472

The Nevada Resorts Association represents the 40 major casinos of southern Nevada in front of various governmental forums, primarily at the state and local level.

North American Association of State and Provincial Lotteries
1726 M Street NW
Washington, DC 20036
(202) 223-4223

An organization of government lottery directors that conducts meetings to exchange information on security, internal controls, and marketing of lottery products. The association also assists new jurisdictions that wish to establish lotteries.

Publications: An annual report and directory.

North American Gaming Regulators Association
P.O. Box 21886
Lincoln, NE 68542
(402) 474-4261

A council of government officials and industry participants that conducts research utilizing existing state or provincial regulatory staffs and holds seminars and general meetings for staff members.

Publications: NAGRA Newsletter (monthly).

Public Gaming Research Institute
4020 Lake Washington Blvd. NE, Suite 100
Kirkland, WA 98033
(425) 803-2900

This institute holds industry seminars and trade shows.

Publications: A series of magazines, including *Casino Gaming*, *Public Gaming*, *Lottery Journal*, and *Indian Gaming Magazine* (with the National Indian Gaming Association).

Race Track Industry Program
College of Agriculture
University of Arizona
Tucson, AZ 85721
(602) 621-4639

This university organization conducts seminars and short courses for the horse and dog racing industries. It also collects and disseminates information to interested parties.

Racetracks of Canada, Inc.
80 Bloor Street, West
Toronto, Ontario
Canada M5S 2V1
(416) 964-7976

An association focusing on information exchange related to the security, marketing, and financial operations of horse tracks.

Publications: A monthly magazine called *Track Talk.*

Special Collections Library (Gaming Resource Center)
University of Nevada–Las Vegas
4505 Maryland Parkway
Las Vegas, NV 89154
(702) 895-3252

This library houses the world's largest publicly accessible collection of gambling books and materials. Materials may be used at the library site only; however, the library responds to telephone inquiries.

Thoroughbred Racing Associations
3000 Marcus Avenue, Suite 2W4
Lake Success, NY 11042
(516) 328-2660

This organization of racing associations advances the cause of racing through governmental relations and dissemination of public information. It adopts a Code of Standards for the industry. A subsidiary organization, the Thoroughbred Racing Protective Bureau, seeks to prevent corruption in the industry through investigations and records of track offenses.

United States Trotting Association
750 Michigan Avenue
Columbus, OH 43215
(614) 224-2291

This organization maintains the registry for all standardbred racing horses.

Publications: The monthly magazine *Hoofbeats* and the registry for standardbred horses.

Government Organizations

Alaska Division of Charitable Gaming
Department of Revenue
P.O. Box 110440
Juneau, AK 99811-0440
(907) 465-2581

Alberta Gaming Commission
Brownlee Bldg., 10365 97th Street
Edmonton, Alberta
Canada T5J 3W7
(403) 427-9796

Alberta Racing Commission
P.O. Box 5684, Station A
Calgary, Alberta
Canada T2H 1Y2
(403) 297-6551

Arizona Department of Racing
15 South 15th, Suite 100
Phoenix, AZ 85007
(602) 542-5151

Arizona Lottery
4740 East University Drive
Phoenix, AZ 85034
(602) 921-4400

Arizona State Gaming Agency
15 South 15th, Suite 100
Phoenix, AZ 85007
(602) 542-5151

Arkansas Racing Commission
P.O. Box 3076
Little Rock, AR 72203
(501) 682-1467

Atlantic Lottery Corporation
770 St. George Boulevard

P.O. Box 5500
Moncton, New Brunswick
Canada E1C 8W6
(506) 853-5800

British Columbia Gaming Commission
848 Courtney Street, 2nd Floor
Victoria, British Columbia
Canada V8V 1X4
(604) 356-2797

British Columbia Lottery Corporation
74 West Seymour Street
Kamloops, British Columbia
Canada V2C 1E2
(604) 828-5500

California Gaming Registration Program
California Department of Justice
P.O. Box 163029
Sacramento, CA 95816
(916) 227-4246

California Horse Racing Board
1010 Hurley Way, Room 190
Sacramento, CA 95825
(916) 263-6000

California State Lottery
600 North Tenth Street
Sacramento, CA 95814
(916) 323-7095

Colorado Limited Gaming Control Commission
Division of Gaming
720 South Colorado Boulevard, Suite 540-S
Denver, CO 80222
(303) 757-7555

Colorado Lottery
201 West 8th Street, Suite 600
Pueblo, CO 81003
(719) 546-2400

Colorado Racing Commission
1560 Broadway, Suite 1540
Denver, CO 80202
(303) 894-2990

Connecticut Charitable Games
85 Alumni Road
Newington, CT 06111
(203) 667-5023

Connecticut Gambling Regulation
P.O. Box 11424
Newington, CT 06111
(203) 566-3949

Connecticut Off Track Betting
P.O. Box 11424
Newington, CT 06111
(203) 566-3949

Connecticut State Lottery
P.O. Box 11424, Russell Road
Newington, CT 06111
(203) 566-2912

DC Lottery & Charitable Games Control Board
2101 M. L. King Jr. SE
Washington, DC 20020
(202) 645-8000/(202) 645-8071

Delaware Gaming Control Commission
P.O. Box 1401
Cannon Bldg., Suite 203
Dover, DE 19903
(302) 739-4522

Delaware Harness Racing Commission
2320 Dupont Highway
Dover, DE 19901-5515
(302) 739-4811

Delaware State Lottery
McKee Business Park, Suite 102
1575 McKee Road

Dover, DE 19901
(302) 739-5291

Delaware Thoroughbred Racing Commission
2320 South Dupont Highway
Dover, DE 19901
(302) 739-4811

Florida Division of Pari-Mutuel Wagering
1940 Monroe, Northwood Court
Tallahassee, FL 32399-1036
(904) 488-9125

Florida Lottery
Capitol Complex
Tallahassee, FL 32399
(904) 487-7725

Georgia Lottery Commission
230 Peachtree Street NW, Suite 250
Atlanta, GA 30303
(405) 577-0600

Greene County Racing Commission
P.O. Box 542
Eutaw, AL 35462
(205) 372-4213

Idaho Lottery
P.O. Box 6537
Boise, ID 83707
(208) 334-2600

Idaho State Horse Racing Commission
P.O. Box 700
Meridan ID 83680-0070
(208) 884-7080

Illinois Gaming Board
P.O. Box 19474
State Office Complex
Springfield, IL 62794-9474
(217) 524-0226

Illinois Office of Bingo and Charitable Games
P.O. Box 19480
Springfield, IL 62794-9840
(217) 524-4164

Illinois Racing Board
100 West Randolph, Suite 11-100
Chicago, IL 60601
(312) 814-2600

Illinois State Lottery
201 East Madison
Springfield, IL 62702
(217) 524-5155

Indiana Horse Racing Commission
Ista Center, Suite 412
150 West Market Street
Indianapolis, IN 46204
(317) 233-3119

Indiana Lottery
201 South Capitol Avenue, Suite 1100
Indianapolis, IN 46225
(317) 264-4800

Iowa Lottery
2015 Grand Avenue
Des Moines, IA 60312
(515) 281-7900

Iowa Racing & Gaming Commission
Lucas State Office Bldg.
Des Moines, IA 50319
(515) 281-7352

Kansas Bingo Enforcement
4 Townsite Plaza, Suite 210
200 Southeast Sixth Street
Topeka, KS 66603-3512
(913) 296-3825

Kansas State Lottery
128 North Kansas Avenue
Topeka, KS 66603
(913) 296-5700

Kentucky Lottery Corporation
6040 Dutchman's Lane, Suite 400
Louisville, KY 40205
(502) 473-2200

Kentucky Racing Commission
4063 Iron Works Pike, Bldg. B
Lexington, KY 40511
(606) 255-2448

Loto—Quebec Societe des loteries et coursed du Quebec
500 Sherbrooke ouest, Bureau 2000
Montreal, Quebec
Canada H3A 3G6
(514) 282-8000

Louisiana Charitable Gaming Division
Office of State Police
P.O. Box 66614
Baton Rouge, LA 70896
(504) 925-1835

Louisiana Economic Development Gaming Corporation
Louisiana Gaming Enforcement Division
Department of Public Safety
265 South Foster
Baton Rouge, LA 70806
(504) 925-4799

Louisiana Lottery Corporation
P.O. Box 90008
Baton Rouge, LA 70879
(504) 297-2000

Louisiana State Racing Commission
320 North Carrollton Avenue, Suite 2-B
New Orleans, LA 70119
(504) 483-4000

Louisiana Video Gaming Division
Office of State Police
P.O. Box 66614
Baton Rouge, LA 70896
(504) 925-1900

Maine State Harness Racing Commission
State House Station #28
Augusta, ME 04333
(207) 289-3221

Maine State Lottery Commission
State House Station #8
Augusta, ME 04333
(207) 624-6700

Manitoba Horse Racing Commission
Box 40, Postal Station A
Winnipeg, Manitoba
Canada R3K 1Z9
(204) 885-7770

Manitoba Lottery Corporation
830 Empress Street
Winnipeg, Manitoba
Canada R3G 3H3
(204) 967-2638

Maryland State Lottery
6776 Reisterstown Road, Suite 204
Baltimore, MD 21215
(410) 764-5700

Maryland State Racing Commission
Stanbalt Bldg., 10th Floor
501 St. Paul Place
Baltimore, MD 21202
(301) 333-6267

Massachusetts State Lottery Commission
60 Columbian Street
Braintree, MA 02184
(617) 849-5555

Massachusetts State Racing Commission
1 Ashburton Place, Room 1313
Boston, MA 02108
(617) 727-2581

Michigan Bureau of State Lottery
101 East Hillsdale
P.O. Box 30023
Lansing, MI 48909
(517) 335-5600

Michigan Charitable Gaming Division
101 East Hillsdale
Lansing, MI 48909
(517) 335-5780

Michigan Office of Racing Commissioner
37650 Professional Center Drive, 105A
Livonia, MI 48154-1100
(313) 462-2400

Minnesota Gaming Control Board
1711 West County Road B, Suite 300 South
Roseville, MN 55113
(612) 639-4000

Minnesota Lottery
2645 Long Lake Road
Roseville, MN 55113
(612) 635-8100

Minnesota Racing Commission
7825 Washington Avenue South, Suite 800
Bloomington, MN 55439
(612) 341-7555

Mississippi Gaming Commission
P.O. Box 23577
Jackson, MS 39225-3577
(601) 961-4400

Missouri Gaming Commission
1616 Industry Drive
Jefferson City, MO 65109
(314) 526-5370 (Bingo Division)
(314) 526-4080 (Riverboat Division)

Missouri State Lottery Commission
1900 Craigshire Road
St. Louis, MO 63146
(314) 579-0900

Montana Board of Horse Racing
P.O. Box 200512
Helena, MT 59620-0512
(406) 444-4287

Montana Gaming Control Division
P.O. Box 201424
Helena, MT 59620-1424
(406) 444-1971

Montana State Lottery
2525 North Montana Avenue
Helena, MT 59601
(406) 444-5825

National Indian Gaming Commission
1850 M Street NW
Washington DC 20036
(202) 632-7003

Nebraska Division of Charitable Gaming
P.O. Box 94818
Lincoln, NE 68509
(402) 471-5937

Nebraska Horse Racing Commission
P.O. Box 95014
Lincoln, NE 68509
(402) 471-4155

Nebraska Lottery
P.O. Box 98901
Lincoln, NE 68509-8901
(402) 471-6102

Nevada Gaming Commission
1150 East Williams
Carson City, NV 89710
(702) 687-6500

(Nevada) State Gaming Control Board
1150 East Williams
Carson City, NV 89710
(702) 687-6500

New Hampshire Bureau of Gaming Enforcement
10 Hazen Drive
Concord, NH 03305
(603) 271-3354

New Hampshire Lottery
Box 1208
Concord, NH 03302
(603) 271-3391

New Hampshire Racing Commission
244 North Main Street
3rd Floor, Carrigan Commons
Concord, NH 03301-5041
(603) 271-2158

New Jersey Casino Control Commission
Tennessee and the Boardwalk
Atlantic City, NJ 08401
(609) 441-3422

New Jersey Division of Gaming Enforcement
140 East Front Street, C.N. 047
Trenton, NJ 08625
(609) 292-9394

New Jersey Legalized Games of Chance Control Commission
P.O. Box 46000
Newark, NJ 07101
(201) 648-2710

New Jersey State Lottery Commission
140 East Front Street, C.N. 041
Trenton, NJ 08625
(609) 599-5800

New Mexico Division of Alcohol and Gaming
P.O. Box 25101
Santa Fe, NM 87504-5101
(505) 827-7066

New Mexico State Racing Commission
P.O. Box 8576 Highland Station
Albuquerque, NM 87198
(505) 841-6400

New York State Lottery
One Broadway Center, Box 7500
Schenectady, NY 12301-7500
(518) 388-3300

New York State Racing & Wagering Board
120 Broadway, 13th Floor
New York, NY 10271
(212) 417-4200

North Dakota Gaming Section
Office of Attorney General
600 East Boulevard
Bismarck, ND 58505-0040
(701) 224-4848

Off-Track Betting—Suffolk Region
Suffolk Regional Off-Track Betting Corporation
5 David's Drive
Hauppauge, NY 11788
(516) 434-4500

Off-Track Betting—Western Region
Western Regional Off-Track Betting Corporation
700 Ellicott Street
Batavia, NY 14020
(716) 343-1423

Ohio Lottery Commission
615 West Superior Avenue
Cleveland, OH 44113
(216) 787-3200

Ohio Racing Commission
77 South High Street, 18th Floor
Columbus, OH 43266-0416
(614) 466-2757

Oklahoma Horse Racing Commission
6501 North Broadway, Suite 100
Oklahoma City, OK 73116
(405) 848-0404

Ontario Lottery Corporation
2 Floor Street, West, Suite 2400
Toronto, Ontario
Canada M4W 38H
(416) 961-6262

Ontario Racing Commission
180 Dundas Street, West, 14th Floor
Toronto, Ontario
Canada M5G 1Z8
(416) 963-0520

Oregon Lottery
2767 22nd Street SE
P.O. Box 12649
Salem, OR 97309
(503) 373-0202

Oregon Racing Commission
800 NE Oregon Street, #11
Portland, OR 97232
(503) 229-5820

Pennsylvania Racing Commission
2301 North Cameron Street, Room 304
Harrisburg, PA 17110
(717) 787-1942

Pennsylvania State Lottery
2850 Turnpike Industrial Drive
Middletown, PA 17057
(717) 986-4052

Rhode Island Division of Games of Chance
311 Danielson Park
North Scituate, RI 02857
(401) 444-1000

Rhode Island Lottery
1425 Pontiac Avenue
Cranston, RI 02920
(401) 463-6500

(South Carolina) Gaming Division
South Carolina Department of Revenue
P.O. Box 125
Columbia, SC 29214
(803) 737-4767

South Dakota Commission on Gaming
118 East Missouri
Pierre, SD 57501
(605) 773-6050

South Dakota Lottery
207 East Capitol, Suite 200
Pierre, SD 57501
(605) 773-5770

South Dakota Racing Commission
118 West Capitol Avenue
Pierre, SD 57501
(605) 773-3179

Texas Lottery Division
P.O. Box 16630
Austin, TX 78761-6630
(512) 323-3700

Texas Racing Commission
9420 Research Echelon 3, Suite 200
Austin, TX 78759
(512) 794-8461

Vermont Lottery Commission
P.O. Box 420
South Barre, VT 05670
(802) 479-5686

Vermont Racing Commission
State Office Building
120 State Street
Rutland, VT 05602
(802) 786-5050

Virginia Racing Commission
P.O. Box 1123
Richmond, VA 23208
(804) 371-7363

Virginia State Lottery
900 East Main Street
Richmond, VA 23219
(804) 692-7000

Washington Horse Racing Commission
7912 Martin Way, Suite D
Olympia, WA 98506
(206) 459-6462

Washington State Gambling Commission
P.O. Box 42400
Olympia, WA 98504-2400
(206) 438-7685

Washington State Lottery
814 Fourth Avenue
Olympia, WA 98506
(206) 753-1412

West Virginia Lottery Commission
P.O. Box 2067
Charleston, WV 25327
(304) 558-0500

West Virginia Racing Commission
P.O. Box 3327
Charleston, WV 25333
(304) 558-2150

Western Canada Lottery Corporation
125 Garry Street
Winnipeg, Manitoba
Canada R3C 4J1
(204) 942-8217

Wisconsin Gaming Commission
1802 West Beltline Highway
P.O. Box 8941
Madison, WI 53708-8941
(608) 266-7777
(608) 261-8800 (Office of Indian Gaming)

Wisconsin Lottery
1802 West Beltline Highway
P.O. Box 8941
Madison, WI 53708-8941
(608) 929-2063

Wisconsin Racing Board
150 East Gilman Street
P.O. Box 7975
Madison, WI 53707
(608) 276-3291

Wyoming Pari-Mutuel Commission
2301 Central Avenue
Barrett Bldg., 3rd Floor
Cheyenne, WY 82002
(307) 777-5887

Selected Print Resources

6

Governments in North America have issued studies and reports on gambling for more than a century and a half. These studies have focused on all aspects of the phenomenon, as discussed in the earlier chapters of this book.

One of the first government reports was presented to the public by the Committee of Twenty Four Citizens of the City of Richmond, Virginia, in 1833. A committee majority felt that the evils of gambling in the fair city could be overcome only with total legal suppression. However, three committee members dissented and issued their own report, which called for deliberate licensing of one or more gambling houses. With limited legalization, the minority's report stated, gambling could be controlled and its evil contained, but total suppression could never be effective.

The debate has continued ever since, and opinions remain divided on how to manage gambling in society. This annotated bibliography begins with a listing of selected government-sponsored studies and other special research reports on this controversial topic. The next section presents an annotated selection of single-volume works devoted to the topic of gambling. The last two sections cover journals concerned with gambling and Web sites devoted to gambling issues.

Research Documents and Government Reports

Abrahamson, Mark, and John Wright. **Gambling in Connecticut: A Research Report.** Storrs: Connecticut State Commission on Special Revenues, 1977.

This study is based upon a survey of Connecticut residents and an examination of gaming literature. The authors conclude that legalized gambling will not lead to massive compulsions but that gambling taxes will be regressive. They see legalization as a deterrent to some illegal activity but not as an ironclad barricade to criminal elements.

Abrams, Robert. **Report of Attorney General Robert Abrams in Opposition to Legalized Casino Gambling in New York State.** Albany: State of New York, 1981.

This report is credited with stopping a casino movement in New York State. Attorney General Abrams makes a scathing attack on the integrity of the Atlantic City casino industry, suggesting that similar problems of organized crime and political corruption would face New York if casinos were legalized.

Anderson, Arthur, LLP. **Economic Impacts of Casino Gaming in the United States.** Prepared for the American Gaming Association, Washington, D.C., 1996. Washington, DC: American Gaming Association, 1996.

The purpose of this report is to demonstrate the many positive contributions of casino gambling for the U.S. economy. Data are presented on the numbers of jobs, amount of wages, and tax revenues produced as well as capital expenditures. Everything is positive: 300,000 direct jobs in the industry plus another 400,000 indirect jobs; $2.9 billion in taxes; jobs that pay well; capital investments of over $4 billion annually. The report thus purports to give political leaders the "true" benefits of this growing industry. Although social costs are not ignored, they are brushed off as matters that cannot be proven or accurately recorded. The author says that "this study makes no attempt to analyze the socioeconomic effects of casino gaming, because such effects are largely based on anecdotal evidence and credible and verifiable data on those effects do not exist. We did not attempt primary research because such effects are particularly difficult to quantify on a macroeconomic basis."

Beare, Margaret, and Howard Hampton. **Legalized Gambling: An Overview.** A Report of the Solicitor General of Canada. Ottawa, Ont.: Ministry Secretariat, 1984. (Report 1983-13).

Beare and Hampton present an in-depth study of casino, lottery, race track, and off-track betting in the Canadian provinces. They also compare their findings with gaming operations in other jurisdictions.

British Columbia Gaming Commission. **The Status of Gaming in British Columbia.** A Report to the Attorney General by the British Columbia Gaming Commission. Victoria, BC: Queen's Printer, 1988.

This is a comprehensive overview of legalized gambling in the province. It examines the history of gambling in British Columbia and the philosophy and social structure of provincial gaming.

City of Detroit, Casino Gaming Study Commission. **Final Report.** Detroit: Casino Gaming Study Commission, 1988.

The Detroit city government has faced monumental fiscal crises for several decades. In the 1970s, casino advocates began suggesting that legalized gambling could cure the budget woes of the city. This study concurs with the pro-casino view that casinos would bring jobs and tax revenues to the city and suggests that casinos have positive social impacts on families because unemployed people have the chance to hold jobs. Shortly after the report was issued, the voters of Detroit said no to casinos in an advisory vote. However, the issue would not go away. In 1994, Detroit voters said yes, and in 1996 the state voters gave the final approval for casinos in Detroit.

Commission on the Review of the National Policy Toward Gambling. **Gambling in America: Final Report.** Washington, DC: Government Printing Office, 1976.

Congress created this commission with the Organized Crime Control Act of 1970. The commission gathered a wide range of information from 1974 through 1976. It concluded that gambling was inevitable and recommended that it be controlled by state and local governments. The commission also suggested that winnings from legal games not be taxed and that casinos be privately owned and located in remote areas away from city populations.

————. **Gambling in America: Final Report, Appendix 1.** Staff and Consultant Papers, Model Statutes, Bibliography, Correspondence. Washington, DC: Government Printing Office, 1976.

This 1,397-page volume offers expert views on all aspects of gambling. Included is an 80-page report on the views of major religious organizations.

————. **Gambling in America: Final Report, Appendix 2.** Survey of American Attitudes and Behavior. Washington, DC: Government Printing Office, 1976.

This volume reports results of the first comprehensive national survey on gambling behavior. The survey was conducted for the commission in 1974.

————. **Gambling in America: Final Report, Appendix 3.** Summaries of Commission Hearings. Washington, DC: Government Printing Office, 1976.

Between 3 April 1974 and 23 September 1976, the commission held 37 days of hearings and received testimonies from over 265 witnesses. This volume summarizes those testimonies.

Council of the City of New York, Committee on Economic Development. **Report Exploring Legalized Casino Gambling and a Local Lottery for New York City.** New York: City of New York, 1990.

This research effort shows that expanded gambling in New York City could create opportunities for economic development. Gambling benefits include new jobs and increased public revenues without having new taxes. Although a majority of the 567 respondents to a questionnaire favored casinos, a substantial minority (40 percent) felt that casino gambling would bring more compulsive gambling, and 35 percent felt that more crime would result.

————. **Marketing Casino Gambling and a Local Lottery.** New York: City of New York, 1991.

The report finds that the economic climate for casinos in New York City is "relatively favorable." A discussion of potential social problems concentrates upon neighborhood dislocations and crime. Problem gambling is overlooked. A casual reference is made to "excessive" gambling, suggesting that "it would be hard to predict" the effects of the problem.

Dombrink, John D., and William. N. Thompson. **The Report of the 1985–86 President's Commission on Organized Crime.** 1986. (A review of the *Report* is in Dombrink and Thompson, "The Report of the Commission on Organized Crime and Its Implications for Commercial Gambling in America," *Nevada Public Affairs Review* 1986, no. 2, pp. 70–75.)

The unpublished *Report* illustrates the manner in which criminal interests, organized and unorganized, infiltrate the environs of gambling operations. It argues that the manner of infiltration is not fully understood and that the precise relationship between gambling and crime is somewhat elusive. This being the case, the nation should slow down its embrace of legalized gambling while detailed studies are made of various aspects of the crime and gambling interface. The authors suggest that a moratorium on new legalization is in order. They also suggest that during a period of a moratorium, standards for the proper regulations of all forms of gambling should be developed and applied nationwide. However, the authors indicate that the enforcement of the standards should be in the hands of the states, and not the federal government, unless the states abdicate responsibilities for keeping the gambling industry clean.

The Evans Group (Dr. Michael Evans, principal). **A Study of the Economic Impact of the Gaming Industry through 2005.** Sponsored by the International Gaming Technologies, Inc. Reno. Reno, NV: International Gaming Technologies, 1996.

The Evans Group's study presents taxation and employment figures in the U.S. casino industry in recent years. The study projects figures for ten years. All economic indicators are positive ones. The study also suggests that crime rates have fallen with the introduction of casinos into local areas. However, in nearly 100 pages of data and textual analysis, the issue of problem gambling receives only casual mention: "Occasional and anecdotal evidence does not prove anything. The fact that some gamblers, from time to time, lose all their money does not imply that the total money has increased with the expansion of the casino gaming industry."

Executive Office of the Governor of Florida. **Casinos in Florida: An Analysis of the Economic and Social Impacts.** Tallahassee: Office of Planning and Budget, State of Florida, 1994.

A comparison is made in this study between the potential benefits of casinos in terms of jobs and tax revenues and costs such as crime, compulsive gambling, and business losses. The study finds that the costs exceed the benefits. The costs of crime and compulsive gambling are projected to be $2.16 billion, whereas tax revenues receive a "high range" estimate of $276 million.

Hospitality Advisors (Marquette Partners, Minneapolis). **The Impact of Indian Gaming in Minnesota.** Sponsored by Sodak Gaming Suppliers, Inc., 1991. Minneapolis: Marquette Partners, 1991.

Indian casinos, according to this report, are providing jobs and payroll and employee taxes as well as purchasing power in local Minnesota communities. The report also discusses how tribes are using casino revenues. Information was gathered from direct interviews with the operators of the gaming facilities and state agencies. There is no mention of problem gambling.

KPMG-Peat Marwick. **Economic Benefits of Tribal Gaming in Minnesota.** Minneapolis: KPMG-Peat Marwick, 1992.

This report looks at revenues generated by the Indian casinos of Minnesota and how tribes are disposing of the funds. The report indicates that welfare rolls have fallen in the rural counties with casinos.

Mangalmurti, Sandeep, and Robert Allan Cooke. **State Lotteries: Seducing the Less Fortunate?** Chicago: The Heartland Institute, 1991. (Policy Study 35).

The researchers offer a very well documented report on how government lotteries market their products to poor people, the young, and people who are susceptible to problem gambling. The report is very critical of this kind of gambling.

Murray, James M. **The Economic Benefits of American Indian Gaming Facilities in Wisconsin.** Madison: Wisconsin Cooperative Extension Service, University of Wisconsin, and Wisconsin Indian Gaming Association, 1993.

The author, of the University of Wisconsin–Green Bay, makes an input-output economic analysis of casino gambling operations conducted by 11 tribes in Wisconsin. Information is taken exclusively from the tribes. The analysis looks at employment, taxation, and purchasing. By applying economic multipliers, he concludes that the casinos are producing major positive benefits. Reduced unemployment and construction funding are among the collateral benefits. Problem gambling is not examined.

New York State Task Force on Casino Gambling. **Report to the Governor.** Albany: State of New York, 1996.

Governor Pataki commissioned a study of casino gambling in recognition of the need for information for pending policy debates. The New York legislature has approved one constitutional proposal for casinos, and in 1997 they will be asked to approve a second proposal. If they do so, the state's voters will then decide whether or not the state will have casinos. Over 300 pages of text are supplemented with another 100 pages of charts. The study committee held four hearings in New York City, Buffalo, and Albany, and they also collected testimony from scores of individuals. Although economic factors dominate the report, the researchers give considerable attention to the issues of pathological and problem gambling. They include reviews of many studies of prevalence rates and costs. The issue of relationships between crime and casinos is also well covered, along with specific attention to crime and compulsive gambling. The report recommends increased funding for education and awareness programs, for treatment, and for continued research in the area of compulsive gambling. It also recommended that the state adopt a policy of permitting persons to exclude themselves from casino facilities.

Ryan, Timothy P., Patricia J. Connor, and Janet F. Speyrer. **The Impact of Casino Gambling in New Orleans.** New Orleans: Bureau of Business and Economic Research, University of New Orleans, 1990.

The researchers utilized crime statistics from 80 different cities as they measured impacts of casino gambling. They applied a sophisticated data analysis and concluded that the presence of casino gambling in a city "leads to an increase of 132.8 crimes per 1,000 residents." The type of crime most affected by gambling is larceny and theft.

Societe d'exploitation des lotteries et courses du Quebec (Loto Quebec). **Casinos. Summary of the Final Report.** Montreal: Loto Quebec, 1978.

Quebec has been considering the legalization of casinos since New Jersey voters approved gambling in 1976. This initial provincial study recommended serious consideration of a European-style casino with restricted membership (or entrance requirements), dress codes, and limited hours of operation.

State of Nevada, Legislative Commission, Subcommittee to Study Gambling. **Study of Gambling: Final Report.** Carson City: Nevada Legislative Counsel Bureau, 1992.

The legislature of Nevada became concerned about how the spread of gambling throughout North America would impact its own casino industry. After studying the issue, they issued this report that outlined efforts to attract more foreign gamblers to Nevada, recommended curbs on Indian gambling—giving states more power to control the gaming, and recommended a continued ban on lotteries within Nevada. Needless to say, the impact of the report was felt almost entirely within the state of Nevada.

State of New York, Casino Gambling Study Panel. **Final Report, August 1979.** Albany: State of New York, 1979.

A panel of experts was appointed by Governor Hugh Carey in February 1979. The panel held public hearings, interviewed experts, and traveled to several communities with casinos. They concluded that casino gaming could bring economic benefits to New York State and recommended that certain communities be allowed to have casinos if approved in local referendum elections.

Thompson, William N., Ricardo Gazel, and Dan Rickman. **The Economic Impact of Native American Gaming in Wisconsin.** Milwaukee: Wisconsin Policy Research Institute, 1995.

This report offers an economic impact analysis of 17 Indian casinos in Wisconsin. The analysis utilizes an input-output economic model. Data were gathered from many independent sources. Nearly 700 players were interviewed regarding their behavior. They were asked how they would spend funds if they were not gambling. One-fourth indicated household goods; 10 percent said food. Casino revenues were projected from comparable data (based upon square footage and number of gambling positions), as were expenditures. Data from the Wisconsin Cooperative Extension report were also utilized. Automobile license tags were used with interviews to assess the geographical source of spending at the casinos.

Although the study did not focus upon problem gambling costs, these were estimated and used as a supplement to suggest that the positive economic impacts found in the input-output model were incomplete and were certainly more positive than they would be if social costs were considered.

Two subsequent reports by Thompson, Gazel, and Rickman were published in 1996 by the Wisconsin Policy Research Institute (now located in Thiensville, Wisconsin): *The Social Costs of Gambling in Wisconsin* and *Casinos and Crime in Wisconsin*. These two reports focused specifically on social costs, analyzing a prevalence survey and a survey of members of Gamblers Anonymous groups as well as statistical data on crime in all Wisconsin counties from 1981 to 1995.

Touche-Ross, Inc. **Casino Industry's Economic Impact on New Jersey.** New York: Touche-Ross, 1987.

This is an economic impact study performed under the sponsorship of the Atlantic City Casino Association. The report indicates that economic impact results have "far exceeded expectations." Public revenues for senior citizens and the disabled are cited as areas where outputs were greater than anticipated. Property values went up at a higher rate than predicted, and the number of visitors was much greater. No mention is made of compulsive gambling or any other social costs that might have accompanied the introduction of casino gambling into New Jersey.

University Associates. **Economic Impact of Michigan Indian Gaming Enterprises.** Lansing, MI: University Associates, 1992.

This report was written to support the legal position of tribes engaged in litigation against the state of Michigan over the establishment of casino gaming in the state under provisions of the Indian Gaming Regulatory Act of 1988. Seven Michigan tribes had already begun limited casino operations that in 1992 were in a state of "legal limbo." The report looked at employment and payroll and other employee taxes. It concluded that the casinos had a very positive impact upon the economically depressed areas of northern Michigan where most were located.

U.S. Congress, Senate, Committee on Government Operations. **Report: Gambling and Organized Crime, March 28, 1962.** Washington, DC: Government Printing Office, 1962.

This Senate committee, chaired by Senator John McClellan, investigated organized crime connections to gambling at the request of

Attorney General Robert F. Kennedy. The committee focused largely on the use of interstate telephone lines to assist illegal gamblers. The report recommended that wiretap evidence be used in the fight against illegal gambling.

Books on Gambling

Abt, Vicki, James Smith, and Eugene Christiansen. **The Business of Risk: Commercial Gambling in Mainstreet America.** Lawrence: University Press of Kansas, 1985. 286p.

The authors closely examine the structure of casinos, lotteries, and pari-mutuels. The book describes the range of gambling behaviors, including recreational and occasional gamblers, obsessive-compulsive gamblers, and professional gamblers. It pleads with politicians to examine the general public interest as they consider legalization questions. Attention to factual data is rigorous, as is the level of analysis. This is one of the most important academic treatments of the gambling industry and is valuable to scholars, politicians, and those interested in gambling as a public policy issue.

Allen, David D. **The Nature of Gambling.** New York: Coward-McCann, 1952. 249p.

This is a dated survey of gambling, beginning with an anthropological and psychological consideration of the subject. The book examines the nature of gambling in the United States and foreign countries at the turn of the century. It is valuable for those interested in historical developments.

American Gaming Association [AGA]. **Responsible Gaming Resource Guide.** Washington, DC: AGA, 1996. 111p.

In recognition of a growing awareness that the casino industry must deal with the issue of problem gambling, the AGA has prepared this volume of materials for the industry. The book defines the issues of problem gambling, strategies for dealing with the problem inside and outside of casinos, strategies to prevent teenage gambling, and cooperative strategies to utilize with government agencies. An appendix provides materials actually used by several gaming companies to address the issues at their facilities and in their communities.

Asbury, Herbert. **Sucker's Progress.** New York: Dodd, Mead, 1938. 493p.

This is a very complete survey of all forms of gambling in the United States, from colonial days to the end of the nineteenth century. Although jammed with information on games and personalities, the work lacks a focused point of view.

Barnhart, Russell. **Gamblers of Yesteryear.** Las Vegas, NV: Gamblers Book Club Press, 1983. 239p.

Gaming historian Barnhart presents eighteenth- and nineteenth-century accounts of gaming enterprises at Bath, England; Spa, Belgium; Baden-Baden and Bad Homburg, Germany; and Monte Carlo, Monaco. The emphasis is on major personalities of the early casino era, including Beau Nash, Peter the Great, and Fyodor Dostoyevsky.

Berger, A. J., and Nancy Bruning. **Lady Luck's Companion: How to Play, How to Enjoy, How to Bet, How to Win.** New York: Harper and Row, 1979. 280p.

An introduction to the full spectrum of gambling, intended for the player, the spectator, and the interested citizen. Written in layperson's terminology, it offers detailed and interesting facts about history, personalities, and gaming rules.

Bergler, Edmund. **The Psychology of Gambling.** New York: International Universities Press, 1958. 244p.

This landmark volume portrays the problem gambler as a neurotic individual with an unconscious wish to lose. According to this work, the gambler habitually takes chances, allows games to preclude all other activity, brims with optimism, never stops while ahead, experiences a great deal of pleasure and pain while playing, and achieves his or her victories in masochistic forms.

Berman, Susan. **Easy Street: The True Story of a Mob Family.** New York: Dial Press, 1981. 214p.

The daughter of one of the early "mob" figures in Las Vegas casino gambling writes about the atmosphere surrounding her family. David Berman was the individual selected to operate the Flamingo upon the death of "Bugsy" Siegel. The book provides an interesting discussion of the forces that guided a small western town toward becoming a world tourist mecca.

Braidwaite, Larry. **Gambling: A Deadly Game.** Nashville, TN: Broadman Press, 1985. 220p.

This church-sponsored publication seeks to build a case against the spread of legalized gambling. The author examines forces behind the expansion, focusing on the Reagan administration's shift of fiscal burdens from the federal to state governments and the emergence of a corporate presence in the gaming industry. Braidwaite believes that the legalization of gambling stimulates illegal gambling. The book examines lotteries, pari-mutuel wagering, casinos, sports betting, compulsive gambling, and moral questions concerning personal gambling behaviors.

Brailey, F. W. L. **Gambling in Canada.** Toronto: United Church of Canada, 1958. 31p.

This religious tract argues against gambling. It contains references to Canadian law and church edicts.

Brenner, Reuven, with Gabrielle Brenner. **Gambling and Speculation: A Theory, a History, and a Future of Some Human Decisions.** New York: Cambridge University Press, 1990. 286p.

The Brenners place gambling activities into the realm of all human decision making. They view commercial gambling as they view any other commercial activity: an exchange of goods and services from those with supplies to those with demands. They categorically reject notions that gambling is a sin—an activity that must be prohibited. Indeed, they state that society is best served with legalization, as gambling products meet consumer demands and serve human needs. They utilize much historical evidence as they build a strong justification for governmental lotteries. The book represents one of the strongest defenses of lotteries that can be found.

Cabot, Anthony N. **Casino Gaming: Policy, Economics, and Regulation.** Las Vegas: University of Nevada–Las Vegas International Gaming Institute, 1996. 527p.

Anthony Cabot is one of the leading gambling attorneys in the United States. In this volume he has drawn together a wealth of knowledge on many facets of the casino gaming industry. The book has a decidedly social-science perspective, with chapters focusing on the history of gaming, religion and gambling, the economics of gambling, ownership patterns, and policy models for gaming law and for regulatory systems. However, the last half of the book does provide a detailed overview of the specific regulatory processes in North American and other jurisdictions. Chapters are devoted to the licensing process, investigations, regulation of gaming devices, casino accounting and record keeping, taxation, and casino crimes. This is clearly the best single-volume textbook treatment of casino gambling and its regulation.

Cabot, Anthony, William Thompson, and Andrew Tottenham, eds. **International Casino Law.** 2d ed. Reno: Institute for the Study of Gaming, University of Nevada–Reno, 1993. 565p.

This is a collection of essays by various authors. Each examines the casino law of a particular country or political subunit of a country. Essays present historical information on the development of casinos, laws, and government enforcement agencies. The book offers a comprehensive body of information regarding licensing rules, taxation, and game regulations.

Campbell, Colin, ed. **Gambling in Canada: The Bottomline.** Burnaby, BC: Simon Fraser University, 1994. 198p.

Campbell's volume offers an edited collection of 19 papers that were presented to the Second National Symposium on Gambling in Canada, held in Vancouver in 1993. The articles are written by academicians, gambling operators, and government regulators. William Eadington and Garry Smith lead with overviews of policy in the gaming industry; then I, Diana Dever, and Rick Ponting offer discussions of Indian gambling. Henry Lesieur, Elizabeth George, Rachel Volberg, and Sue Fisher discuss compulsive gambling. Regulators discuss projects in British Columbia, Saskatchewan, Ontario, and New Brunswick. The interesting collection offers readers a rare opportunity to gain overall perspectives on the Canadian gambling scene.

Campbell, Colin S., and John Lowman. **Gambling in Canada: Golden Goose or Trojan Horse?** Burnaby, BC: Simon Fraser University, 1989. 417p.

This book is a collection of presentations made to the First Canadian National Symposium on Lotteries and Gambling, held in 1988. Like the United States, Canada has witnessed an explosion of growth in gaming. The essays consider the development of Canadian gaming law, lottery operations, horse racing, and charity gaming in various provinces and on Indian reserves.

Carroll, David. *Playboy's* **Illustrated Treasury of Gambling.** New York: Crown, 1977. 255p.

This survey of gambling suggests that the activity is an appropriate recreational pursuit. Games are illustrated, and advice is provided on how to play them.

Chafetz, Henry. **Play the Devil: A History of Gambling in the United States from 1492 to 1955.** New York: Potter Publishers, 1960. 475p.

From land, gold, and silver rushes to lotteries for the Selective Service draft, the United States has always been a nation of gamblers. This very readable book examines many aspects of our gambling history. Chapters look at colonial lotteries, riverboat gamblers, mining town casinos, and developments in horse racing. The book is packed with information but lacks footnotes. A strong bibliography does make up somewhat for this deficiency.

Clotfelter, Charles T., and Philip J. Cook. **Selling Hope: State Lotteries in America.** Cambridge, MA: Harvard University Press, 1989. 323p.

Clotfelter and Cook's comprehensive study reviews the history of lottery gambling and many of the public policy questions surrounding lotteries. Americans' overwhelming acceptance of lotteries is conditioned by powerful lobbies, which include suppliers and beneficiaries of earmarked funds from the activity. The authors see lotteries as methods for regressive taxation and an acceptable means of raising money. They suggest that other forms of taxation should be considered as alternatives to the further growth of lotteries.

Coggins, Ross, ed. **The Gambling Menace.** Nashville, TN: Broadman Press, 1966. 128p.

This collection of essays presents historical, social, economic, and psychological aspects of gambling with a religious slant. The well-written and well-documented articles are unsupportive of gambling. The editor accurately foresees a national drive for legalization. Evidently his plan to stop gambling expansion fell short of his goal.

Custer, Robert L., and Harry Milt. **When Luck Runs Out.** New York: Facts on File, 1985. 239p.

The late Robert Custer is considered a pioneer in the development of treatment programs for compulsive gamblers. In this book he and Harry Milt present a comprehensive statement built around the medical notion that compulsive gambling is a disease. The authors examine the roots of problem gambling, phases of the gambler's career, impacts of gambling behavior on families, and treatment programs available for problem gamblers. The final chapter is devoted to the female compulsive gambler.

David, Florence Nightingale. **Games, Gods, and Gambling: The Origins and History of Probability and Statistical Ideas from the Earliest Times to the Newtonian Era.** New York: Haefner Publishing, 1962. 275p.

The author ties the history of gambling to notions of mathematics and probability. The book discusses Galileo's experiments with dice, Pascal's use of roulette wheels, and Cardano's attention to games in a manner designed to make mathematics fun for the layperson. Nonetheless, this is a serious research work.

Davis, Bertha. **Gambling in America: A Growth Industry.** New York: Franklin Watts, 1992. 112p.

This volume was published for young adult audiences. It provides a comprehensive survey of gambling enterprises throughout the United States. Specific attention is given to the pros and cons of legalized gambling, including issues such as taxation and compulsive gambling.

Demaris, Ovid. **The Boardwalk Jungle.** New York: Bantam Books, 1986. 436p.

The coauthor of *The Greenfelt Jungle* strikes again with an exposé of organized crime in Atlantic City. More fun reading, but again the story is one sided and very selective. It does provide a good overview of the seamy side of Atlantic City's casino origins.

Demaris, Ovid, and Ed Reid. **The Green Felt Jungle.** New York: Pocket Books, 1964. 244p.

According to this account, the purpose of Las Vegas is to fleece money out of a gullible public. Reid and Demaris provide a one-sided view, suggesting that Las Vegas is controlled by organized crime families and politicians who do their bidding. It makes for fun reading, as long as the reader keeps in mind that the story is slanted and that it was put together more than three decades ago.

Dombrink, John Dennis. **Outlaw Businessmen: Organized Crime and the Legalization of Casino Gambling.** Ph.D. dissertation, University of California–Berkeley, 1981. 362p.

This study examines twentieth-century developments in the casino industry. Dombrink devotes close attention to political support for casino legalization in Florida and New Jersey, emphasizing the central campaign issues of crime.

Dombrink, John, and William N. Thompson. **The Last Resort: Success and Failure in Campaigns for Casinos.** Reno: University of Nevada Press, 1990. 220p.

This book analyzes campaigns to legalize casino gambling in 20 states from the 1960s through the 1980s. The authors theorize why of these the 1976 New Jersey effort was the only successful campaign. Failure to legalize high-stakes casino gambling occurred in states where government-run lotteries were being established simultaneously. The authors suggest that casino legalization efforts were subjected to a veto model—if one factor in a list of critical factors was negative, the campaign would fail. However, with lottery legalization issues, politicians and voters merely weighed the evidence. Using a "gravity model," they supported legalization if more facts favored gambling than opposed gambling. The series of factors included support from political and business elites, reputation of sponsors of legalization efforts, campaign financing, and dominance of economics as the key campaign issue. As the book went to press, Iowa and South Dakota authorized limited-stakes ($5) betting on casino games. The authors suggest that in the future voters may regard limited forms of casino gaming as favorably as they did lotteries in the past.

Dostoyevsky, Fyodor. **The Gambler.** Original publication date: 1866. Translated by Victor Terras. Chicago: University of Chicago Press, 1972. 164p.

This is a novel, close to being autobiographical, about a compulsive gambler. Dostoyevsky often wrote to finance his self-destructive habits. His novel offers readers a very personal understanding of pathological gambling. Psychological motivations for gaming—including need for stimulation, feelings of social inferiority, and low self-esteem—are revealed, as are the physiological effects of the habit (trembling, sweating, imagined temperature changes). Scholars from Freud to contemporary sociologists have used the book as a benchmark for their studies of compulsive behaviors.

Eadington, William R. **Gambling and Society: Interdisciplinary Studies on the Subject of Gambling.** Papers from the First Annual Conference on Gambling, Las Vegas, June 1974. Springfield, IL: Charles Thomas, 1976. 466p.

Proceedings and papers from the Second Annual Conference on Gambling, Lake Tahoe, June 1975; the Third Annual Conference on Gambling, Las Vegas, December 1976; and the Fourth National Conference on Gambling, Reno, December 1978 were not published in single collections. Individual papers are available through Special Collections Libraries of the University of Nevada at Reno and Las Vegas.

————, ed. **The Gambling Papers.** Proceedings of the Fifth National Conference on Gambling and Risk Taking, Lake Tahoe, October 1981. Reno: Department of Economics, University of Nevada, 1982.

Thirteen volumes include papers on pathological gambling, the business of gambling, gambling legislation and regulations, and analysis of playing strategies, gaming stocks, and industry trends.

————, ed. **The Gambling Studies.** Proceedings of the Sixth National Conference on Gambling and Risk Taking, Atlantic City, December 1984. Reno: Bureau of Business and Economic Research, University of Nevada, 1985.

These five volumes cover gambling and public policy, economic issues, and pathological gambling.

————, ed. **Gambling Research.** Proceedings of the Seventh International Conference on Gambling and Risk Taking, Reno, August 1987. Reno: Bureau of Business and Economic Research, University of Nevada, 1988.

Five volumes on business activity, government policy, and playing behavior in the gaming industry.

————, ed. **Indian Gaming and the Law.** Reno: Institute for the Study of Gaming, University of Nevada–Reno, 1990. 298p.

Reservation gambling increased rapidly after Florida Seminoles initiated high-stakes bingo games in the late 1970s. In 1987, the

U.S. Supreme Court ruled that states could not regulate gambling on Indian reservations unless the games were illegal under state criminal law. The ruling prompted Congress to pass the Indian Gaming Regulatory Act of 1988, which paved the way for some measure of regulation over reservation gambling. In 1989, the University of Nevada sponsored a symposium on the new law. This book includes the papers presented there.

Eadington, William R., and Judy A. Cornelius, eds. **Gambling and Public Policy: International Perspectives.** Reno: Institute for the Study of Gambling and Commercial Gaming, University of Nevada, 1991. 688p.

———. **Gambling and Commercial Gaming: Essays in Business, Economics, Philosophy, and Science.** Reno: Institute for the Study of Gambling and Commercial Gaming, University of Nevada, 1992. 656p.

This and the previous volume contain papers delivered to the Eighth International Conference on Gambling and Risk Taking, held in London in August 1990.

Eadington, William R., and John Rosecrance, eds. **Betting on the Future: Gambling in Nevada and Elsewhere.** *Nevada Public Affairs Review*, vol. 2 (special issue), 1986.

This is a collection of essays on the gaming industry from a mid-1980s point of view. Two of the articles consider obsessive-compulsive gambling in Nevada; others deal with constitutional questions surrounding casino regulation, the competition of the California lottery with Nevada casinos, casino activity in Europe, and the gambling report of the President's Commission on Organized Crime.

Ezell, John S. **Fortune's Merry Wheel.** Cambridge, MA: Harvard University Press, 1960. 331p.

This is a comprehensive academic history of lotteries in the United States from the early days of Jamestown Colony until the end of the nineteenth century. The author closely examines causes for the establishment of lotteries in many settings as well as the decline of the infamous Louisiana Lottery. The book presents a mass of well-documented material and is a valuable reference work. Its lack of a basic theme, however, detracts from its merit.

Farrell, Ronald A., and Carole Case. **The Black Book and the Mob: The Untold Story of the Control of Nevada's Casinos.** Madison: University of Wisconsin Press, 1995. 286p.

In the late 1950s, the state of Nevada greatly strengthened its controls over the casino industry. The state had come under detailed scrutiny from federal investigators for allowing "Mob" (organized crime) involvement in its casinos. State leaders felt they had to free the state from this Mob image if they were to avoid wholesale federal regulation of its casinos—or worse, perhaps even a national prohibition on casino gambling. After creating a new Gaming Control Board and the Nevada Gaming Commission, the state legislature started the Black Book. Officially designated the List of Excluded Persons, the Black Book named individuals who were considered so notorious that they had to be banned from entering any Nevada gaming hall. Farrell and Case provide an excellent historical account of how the Black Book was created and how each name came to be entered into the book. They suggest that the intention of the Black Book was more cosmetic than it was to actually control bad things in casinos. They suggest that the state purposefully selected "mobsters" with Italian names for inclusion and left other mobsters out. By doing so the state acquiesced to false stereotypes of the state held by national officials.

Findlay, John M. **People of Chance.** New York: Oxford University Press, 1986. 272p.

The United States was colonized by European adventurers, risk takers, and opportunists. Such people moved westward from the seventeenth to the twentieth centuries. Findlay explores the development of gambling against this frontier backdrop. The book concludes with three chapters devoted almost entirely to events in Las Vegas after the 1931 legalization of casinos. Findlay shows how the events reflect the broader culture of Americans as a "people of chance."

Fowler, Floyd J., Thomas Mangione, and Frederick Pratter. **Gambling Law Enforcement in Major American Cities.** Washington, DC: National Institute of Law Enforcement and Criminal Justice, 1978. 357p.

This work reports on an intensive study of how police and prosecutors approach the topic of illegal gambling. The authors conclude that legalization is an ineffective remedy for the problem and concede that current enforcement efforts need careful review.

Frey, James H., and William R. Eadington, eds. **Gambling: Views from the Social Sciences.** *Annals of the American Academy of Political and Social Science* 474 (July 1984). 233p.

This is a valuable collection of research studies. Of particular importance is editor James Frey's sociological review of gambling and James Smith and Vicki Abt's examination of gambling as play. Also of note is Roy Kaplan's study of the social and economic impacts of lotteries. Other articles examine police enforcement of antigambling statutes, urban development and Atlantic City casinos, and the psychology of gambling.

Galliher, John, and John Cross. **Morals Legislation without Morality: The Case of Nevada.** New Brunswick, NJ: Rutgers University Press, 1983. 163p.

The authors explore a paradox. Nevada has had very strict laws on drug usage, a constitutional prohibition on lotteries, and strict laws on prostitution in Las Vegas and Reno. At the same time, the state supports itself with casino gambling revenues, permits legal brothels in rural areas, and permits the public sale of alcoholic beverages 24 hours a day, every day. After a thorough analysis of many policy issues concerned with "morality," the authors conclude that the state is not concerned with political theory or philosophy. Instead, the state has one central goal: protect the gambling industry with policies consistent with that protection.

Geis, Gilbert. **Not the Law's Business.** New York: Schocken, 1979. 262p.

A comprehensive analysis of "victimless" crimes in the United States. Gambling is presented in context of other such crimes, such as those related to alcohol and drug use, homosexuality, and illegal abortion.

Goodman, Robert. **The Luck Business: The Devastating Consequences of Broken Promises of America's Gambling Explosion.** New York: The Free Press (Martin Kessler Books), 1995. 273p.

A journalist (formerly with the *Boston Globe*) turned academician attacks the growing gambling industry in America. Although the pages of Robert Goodman's book seem to push every known argument against gambling ever made, they do contain a collection of valuable information. The arguments, even when not decisive, are backed by solid information gathered from the existing body of research on gambling today. Goodman considers the economic impacts of gambling by examining who does the gambling and who wins the games. He looks closely at interrelationships between politicians and the gambling industry. On one level, politicians seek to find new tax revenues; on another level, they have their hands out for campaign contributions or in some cases something worse (bribes). Goodman presents data on the many social costs of gambling for communities: compulsive gambling, a lessening of the work ethic, crime, and infrastructure costs. Even though the book is one sided, it offers the reader a very good collection of information on the issues of gambling.

Halliday, Jon, and Peter Fuller, eds. **The Psychology of Gambling.** London: Allen Lane, 1974. 310p.

A collection of writings on compulsive gambling. Sigmund Freud's major study of Dostoyevsky is included. The book also offers a comprehensive bibliography.

Hashimoto, Kathryn, Sheryl Fried Kline, and George Fenich, eds. **Casino Management for the '90s.** Dubuque, IA: Kendall-Hunt, 1996. 514p.

This text presents a well-edited and blended volume of more than 70 old and new essays on the practical aspects of casino gambling management. The three coeditors are also coauthors, as they write effective introductions for each section of the book. The book is arranged to be used in the college classroom. The book is supplemented with a collection of case studies and exercises on a computer disk. The package also includes transparencies and lists of examination questions. The book is divided into six sections: the casino industry, games, casino organizational structure, marketing, the future, and nongaming operations.

Haskins, Jim. **Gambling, Who Really Wins?** New York: Franklin Watts, 1979. 64p.

An easy-to-read description of the gambling enterprise. The book concludes with a chapter about compulsive gambling, its treatment, and a warning to gamble safely and in moderation. However, the book deals only in generalities and lacks a plan of action for those desiring to recover from gambling problems.

Haubrich-Casperson, Jane, with Doug Van Nispen. **Coping with Teen Gambling.** New York: Rosen Publishing Group, 1993. 147p.

The authors call compulsive gambling the "hidden disease" of the United States. They see the sickness attacking the nation's youth. In an initial chapter, cowriter Van Nispen documents his experiences as a young pathological gambler. Other chapters discuss the spread of gambling, the kinds of personalities drawn to gambling and prone to become problem gamblers, the stages of the gambling "disease," and programs for making society aware of problem gambling and also for treating the "disease."

Heineman, Mary. **Losing Your Shirt: Recovery for Compulsive Gamblers and Their Families.** Minneapolis: Compcare Publishers, 1992. 191p.

This is a very readable handbook for people trying to cope with gambling pathologies. The book presents many vignettes and case studies suggesting the value of 12-step recovery programs such as those offered by Gamblers Anonymous.

Herman, Robert D. **Gamblers and Gambling: Motives, Institutions, and Controls.** Lexington, MA: D. C. Heath, 1976. 142p.

This book synthesizes the views of many academic scholars on the subject of compulsive gambling. The author also looks at horse racing and other gambling operations.

———, ed. **Gambling.** New York: Harper and Row, 1967. 264p.

Although this collection was put together 30 years ago, the essays still hold value for today's students of gambling. Many of the articles emphasize social science approaches. Authors include Thorstein Veblen, William F. Whyte, and Edmund Bergler. Other articles on public policy include one by the late Robert F. Kennedy.

Hotaling, Edward. **They're Off! Horse Racing at Saratoga.** Syracuse, NY: Syracuse University Press, 1995. 368p.

Edward Hotaling presents a well-written and thoroughly documented history of one of the most important gambling institutions in the history of the United States, the racing track at Saratoga, New York. Races began in earnest at Saratoga in the early 1900s. For nearly a century Saratoga was the destination of choice for gamblers from New York City. Track betting stimulated the creation of a large illegal casino that became a model for later casino development. The book offers clues as to why the casino institution has experienced its greatest growth on the North American continent.

Hulse, James W. **Forty Years in the Wilderness.** Reno: University of Nevada Press, 1986. 141p.

Hulse says that Nevada is and always has been the only state with the true character of a "company town." Nevada was once controlled by mining companies, but today it is the gambling corporations that maintain significant influence in the state. Hulse says that regulation of the industry by the government is weak at best. He traces industry development from the "Mob" days, through the Howard Hughes period, to the advent of large corporations. Hulse perceives a need for radical change, which includes federal gambling regulation.

The International Casino Guide. 3d ed. Port Washington, NY: BDIT, 1992. 349p.

Where are the casinos, what are their games, and how many tables and slot machines do they offer players? This reference book lists virtually every casino property in the world, along with information regarding currency controls, regulatory agencies, transportation, hotel, and restaurant facilities.

Johnston, David. **Temples of Chance: How America Inc. Bought Out Murder Inc. to Win Control of the Casino Business.** New York: Doubleday, 1992. 312p.

For many years the author has been the gambling reporter for the *Philadelphia Inquirer*. As such he has reported on the manner in which corporations came to dominate political leaders in Atlantic City. The stories he relates here are as fascinating as those in Demaris's and Reid's books, and they are presented in a thoroughly researched manner. This book raises questions about how politicians can be compromised by greed, as they are by members of crime organizations.

Jones, J. Philip. **Gambling: Yesterday and Today, A Complete History.** Devon, UK: David and Charles, 1973. 192p.

Because this overview of gambling was written almost 25 years ago, much of its material is dated. However, several chapters devoted to historical surveys remain valuable. These include histories of playing cards and animal and bird sports—subjects usually not covered well in other gambling surveys. A basic theme in the book is the notion that the gambling phenomenon has links with the early development of human beings. The early members of the human species had to risk safety and comfort every day in order to secure food and the other necessities of life. The author states that a risk-taking genetic structure—inherited from our Adam and Eve—draws us toward gambling today.

Kaplan, H. Roy. **Lottery Winners.** New York: Harper and Row, 1978. 173p.

Kaplan tracked down and interviewed winners of $1 million or more. In this fascinating analysis he reveals that nearly three-fourths of the big winners quit their jobs. He views lotteries as governmental devices that aim to divert people from the banalities of their daily lives by allowing them to "dream the impossible dream."

Karcher, Alan. **Lotteries.** New Brunswick, NJ: Transaction Publishers, 1989. 116p.

Karcher, a former New Jersey state senator, approaches the subject of lotteries from the perspective of a government official. He assesses the economic value of lotteries as public revenue sources as well as the dangers present in the marketing of lottery products. His final chapter suggests changes in lottery operation, which include increased payouts, restricted sales to minors and intoxicated ticket buyers, and bans on sales of gambling products over the telephone. Karcher also urges restrictions on lottery advertising.

Kefauver, Estes. **Crime in America.** Garden City, NY: Doubleday, 1951. 333p.

U.S. Senator Estes Kefauver of Tennessee conducted extensive and well-publicized hearings on the role of organized crime in U.S. society and concluded that illegal gambling was the major activity of the national criminal network. The book relates his impressions of the hearings in a sobering fashion and is designed to stimulate public outrage and indignation.

Kelly, Joseph, ed. **New York School Journal of International and Comparative Law: Special Issue on Gambling.** Vol. 8, No. 1, Winter 1986. 192p.

Five essays detail the passage and implementation of casino law in Great Britain, British methods of gaming debt collection, gambling on the high seas, the evolution of gambling in Australia, and the impact of U.S. law on casino development in other jurisdictions. The articles are thoroughly documented, and each is a useful resource for those desiring to pursue these topics more intensively.

King, R. T., ed. **Playing the Cards That Are Dealt: Mead Dixon, the Law, and Casino Gambling.** Reno: University of Nevada Oral History Program, 1992. 276p.

This is a biography based on 32 hours of interviews with Mead Dixon, who was the chief legal counsel for Bill Harrah. Dixon took the individually owned casino company public after the death of Harrah. He then engineered the merger of Harrah's with Holiday Inn Corporation. The resulting company (Promus, Inc.) became the largest casino-oriented business in the United States, with gambling operations in all of the major casino markets. Dixon provides insights into the different thought processes of individual gambling entrepreneurs on the one hand and corporate entities on the other.

————. **Hang Tough! Grant Sawyer: An Activist in the Governor's Mansion.** Reno: University of Nevada Oral History Program, 1993. 256p.

This book is based on over 30 hours of interviews with Grant Sawyer as he reminisced about his years as governor of Nevada from 1959 through the end of 1966. The years were critical for the development of the casino gambling industry, as Sawyer had to maneuver the state into a posture of strict regulation of casinos and away from a laissez-faire attitude that had existed since 1931. The book examines how Sawyer saved the industry from federal attacks by taking steps to assure the U.S. public that casinos could be run in an honest manner.

————. **Always Bet on the Butcher: Warren Nelson and Casino Gambling, 1930s–1980s.** Reno: University of Nevada Oral History Program, 1994. 242p.

This biography examines a major industry actor in the gaming industry from his days as a dealer in illegal "joints" in Montana and California to his time as a corporate leader in northern Nevada casinos. The account of Nelson's life takes the reader through the days when it was quite acceptable for casinos to cheat players to a time when the casinos sought to give good customer service—and honest games—to the players. Nelson learned early the truth that occasionally a lamb may get the best of those in the slaughterhouse, but if you are a bettor, "always bet on the butcher." He helped develop the philosophy that has popularized gambling and keeps players coming back: You can only skin a lamb once, but with care and concern you can shear wool from a lamb forever.

King, Rufus. **Gambling and Organized Crime.** Washington, DC: Public Affairs Press, 1969. 239p.

Attorney Rufus King prepared an extensive report on gambling and organized crime for President Lyndon Johnson's Crime Commission. Here he expands on the report by examining all aspects of crime and gambling. King looks at operators, the gambling utilized by crime networks, and the relationships between legal and illegal gambling and suggests that these problems cannot be solved solely by local government. He also rejects the notion that legalization is a solution, pointing to the criminal involvement in legal casinos, and calls for the creation of a new federal agency with extensive authority to conduct wiretaps of crime organizations.

Kusyszyn, Igor, ed. **Studies in the Psychology of Gambling.** New York: Simon and Schuster, 1972. 172p.

Kusyszyn offers a set of academic writings that were originally published in the late 1960s. Especially valuable are articles that survey various psychological findings on the subject of compulsive gambling and its treatment.

Lehne, Richard. **Casino Policy.** New Brunswick, NJ: Rutgers University Press, 1986. 268p.

Lehne examines the processes by which New Jersey engineered regulatory structures and rules for casino gaming after the state approved casinos in Atlantic City. Thirty elements in the Casino Control Act of 1977 are closely examined. The author assesses whether each was implemented according to the legislature's intentions. The analysis provides insight into the failure of Atlantic City to achieve the dream of urban revitalization.

Lesieur, Henry R. **The Chase: Career of the Compulsive Gambler.** Cambridge, MA: Schenkman, 1984. 323p.

Henry Lesieur is the editor of the *Journal of Gambling Studies* (formerly the *Journal of Gambling Behavior*). In this book, he describes the development stages in compulsive gambling behavior. The problem gambler plays games early in his lifetime and experiences early big wins—wins accompanied by psychological highs. In subsequent career stages, the gambler is perpetually chasing bad bets with more bets of higher amounts. He is in a feverish quest to retrieve a new psychological high equal to that experienced as a younger person. This is the chase.

Lester, David, ed. **Gambling Today.** Springfield, IL: C. C. Thomas, 1979. 149p.

Lester has coordinated the writing of nine separate essays into a comprehensive look at the impacts of casino gambling on society. The essays treat economic impacts of Atlantic City casinos, crime and gambling, and the social impacts of compulsive gambling as well as the motivations for gambling.

Lionel Sawyer and Collins [law firm]. **Nevada Gaming Law.** 2d ed. Las Vegas, NV: Lionel Sawyer and Collins, 1995. 442p.

Members of the world's largest gaming law firm present an in-depth analysis of all aspects of the legal requirements for the gaming industry in Nevada. This expanded edition of a book first published in 1990 (Jerome Vallen, ed.) provides a wealth of insights and understandings about the application of gaming law in the one state where gaming is the dominant industry.

Long, Patrick, Jo Clark, and Derick Liston. **Win, Lose, or Draw? Gambling with America's Small Towns.** Washington, DC: Aspen Institute, 1994. 97p.

Three authors from the University of Colorado explore the impacts of a new casino industry upon three mountain towns in their state: Blackhawk, Central City, and Cripple Creek. They also look at Deadwood, South Dakota. They find that obvious economic benefits have been at least partially offset by social dislocations and changes that are not all beneficial.

Longstreet, Stephen. **Win or Lose: A Social History of Gambling.** Indianapolis, IN: Bobbs-Merrill, 1977. 268p.

Win or Lose offers an extensive body of information about games and gambling in the United States. Although comprehensive in scope, the book lacks documentation, which limits its value as a research tool. Nevertheless, for the general reader it merits attention.

Maheu, Robert, and Richard Hack. **Next to Hughes: Behind the Power and Tragic Downfall of Howard Hughes by His Closest Advisor.** New York: HarperCollins, 1992. 289p.

This book is essentially an autobiography of Robert Maheu, the key confidant of Howard Hughes during the billionaire's Las Vegas era. Maheu orchestrated Hughes's casino-purchasing activities from 1966 through 1970. Here he provides insights into why Hughes came to Las Vegas and why he wanted to buy casinos. By doing so, Hughes helped Las Vegas rid itself of a Mob-run image and set the stage for major corporations such as Hilton to come into the gambling town.

Mahon, Gigi. **The Company That Bought the Boardwalk.** New York: Random House, 1980. 262p.

Mahon's Atlantic City is the story of how one company, Resorts International, decided to enter the casino gaming business and how it manipulated political leaders in both the Bahamas and New Jersey to gain windfall profits. The book is an exposé. It is well written and documented by the author, who is on the staff of *Barron's Magazine.*

Martinez, Tomas M. **The Gambling Scene: Why People Gamble.** Springfield, IL: C. C. Thomas, 1983. 231p.

The author uses in-depth interviews as well as participant observations as he formulates a sociological definition of compulsive gambling. He looks at the progressive steps of the disease as well as treatment programs. He also explores the many social costs attending government promotion of gambling activities.

Mirkovich, Thomas R., and Allison A. Cowgill. **Casino Gambling in the United States.** Lanham, MD: Scarecrow Press, 1996. 432p.

This very useful resource guide presents the reader with a vast amount of information on casinos in the United States and Canada. The central chapters offer a complete annotated bibliography of 900 sources printed between 1985 and 1994. The sources examine all facets of the gambling industry. Other chapters list both governmental and private gambling organizations.

Moody, Gordon. **Quit Compulsive Gambling: The Action Plan for Gamblers and Their Families.** Wellingborough, UK: Thorsons, 1990. 144p.

According to the author, excessive gamblers are vulnerable people. They are impatient, have active dreamworld imaginations, and are taken over by the action of play. Gordon Moody has worked for decades as a Gamblers Anonymous counselor. Moody employs his personal experience in his discussion of excessive gambling. He explains the recovery path outlined by the Gamblers Anonymous program, specifically the 12-step method adapted from Alcoholics Anonymous.

Morrison, Robert S. **High Stakes to High Risk: The Strange Story of Resorts International and the Taj Mahal.** Ashtabula, OH: Lake Erie Press, 1995. 378p.

The author has a vested interest in telling the seamy side of Donald Trump's gambling operations. Morrison perceived himself as having been "stiffed" by "the Donald." Morrison's company helped construct Atlantic City's largest and most glamorous casino for "the Donald," but Trump didn't pay all the bills. Using the Taj Mahal as his vehicle, Morrison takes the reader through the history of Atlantic City gambling. The first half of the book focuses upon James Crosby, the founder of Resorts International and the person who began the Taj Mahal project. Crosby died in 1986, and his interest in the casino was taken over by Donald Trump. The remainder of the book examines Trump's casino kingdom. To be sure, the author is very critical of Trump.

Newman, David, ed. *Esquire*'s **Book of Gambling.** New York: Harper and Row, 1962. 333p.

This series of articles from *Esquire* magazine covers many aspects of gaming—psychology, rules, and operations.

O'Donnell, John R. **Trumped: The Inside Story of the Real Donald Trump, His Cunning Rise and Spectacular Fall.** New York: Simon and Schuster, 1991. 348p.

The casino industry has always been dominated by individuals. Once Mob leaders dominated the scene, then Howard Hughes. Even after corporations took over, the role of the individual remained important. In the 1980s, three personalities controlled the Atlantic City casino industry—Steve Wynn, Merv Griffin, and

Donald Trump. This book examines Donald Trump as a casino entrepreneur. It is laden with many anecdotes that challenge the image of Trump as a master of good deals. The book reveals many interesting sides of the business practices in the casino industry.

Parmer, Charles B. **For Gold and Glory.** New York: Carrick and Evans, 1939. 352p.

This is the story of horse racing in the United States, from its colonial beginnings in Virginia to the Triple Crown races of the twentieth century. The author provides much incidental information on jockeys, trainers, racing officials, owners, and bettors. A collection of action photographs adds to this enjoyable reading venture.

Peterson, Virgil. **Gambling: Should It Be Legalized?** Springfield, IL: Charles C. Thomas, 1951. 158p.

Virgil Peterson served for many years as the director of the Chicago Crime Commission. As the city's chief watchdog over crime, he observed much illegal gambling. In response to many who advocated legalization as a means to cope with the illegal activity, he argues that legalization exacerbates problems of crime in the community. He finds that all gambling is parasitic, nonproductive activity—whether legal or illegal. This 1951 book is especially valuable as a historical document that reflects the predominant perspective on gambling in the middle of the twentieth century.

Ploscowe, Morris, and Edwin J. Lukas, eds. **Gambling.** *Annals of the American Academy of Political and Social Science.* Special Issue, Vol. 269, May 1950. 209p.

This symposium represents the first serious attempt to collect studies that provide an overall analysis of the gambling problems in society. Articles consider the legal status of gambling, the forms of games offered, the psychology of gambling, and gambling in foreign countries.

Pollock, Michael. **Hostage to Fortune: Atlantic City and Casino Gambling.** Princeton, NJ: Center for the Analysis of Public Issues, 1987. 204p.

Pollock, a newspaper reporter, presents another chronicle of the Atlantic City story. This is a balanced account of the positive results of casino gaming and the failures of this experiment in urban redevelopment. The referenda campaigns of 1974 and 1976 are reviewed along with the steps taken to establish the first casinos. Attention is given to the early work of the Casino Control Commission, the role of organized crime in Atlantic City, and the effects of casino development on local housing and land values.

Robertson, William H.P. **A History of Thoroughbred Racing in America.** Englewood Cliffs, NJ: Prentice-Hall, 1964. 621p.

Robertson has written a detailed history of 300 years of horse racing in the United States. The book is an authoritative document that is both readable and a valuable reference tool.

Romero, John. **Casino Marketing.** New York: International Gaming and Wagering Business, 1994. 268p.

A longtime gambling industry consultant has brought together a series of essays and columns he has written on casino marketing. He offers witticisms and wisdom on a topic of great interest to the gambling industry and to the public interested in the industry.

Rose, I. Nelson. **Gambling and the Law.** Hollywood, CA: Gambling Times Press, 1986. 304p.

This law book for the layperson contains a series of essays by Professor Rose of the Whittier College of Law. The chapters cover a wide variety of subjects, including the organization of gambling regulatory bodies, the law of gambling debts, constitutional questions regarding prohibitions of advertising on gambling, IRS cash transaction reporting requirements, and definitions of gambling. Although the book is not a tight-knit legal treatise, it contains many interpretations that merit the attention of those interested in studying gambling.

Rosecrance, John. **The Degenerates of Lake Tahoe.** New York: Peter Lang, 1985. 169p.

John Rosecrance has been a participant observer of regular horse racing bettors in the racebooks of Lake Tahoe, Nevada, casinos. In his book, he closely examines strategies for selecting horses for bets, for making the actual bets, and for analyzing the results of the races afterward. He finds that most gamblers are acting on a rational decision-making model as they wager—at least in their own minds. They deny that their behavior is compulsive or that they are out of control, even when their losses are excessive. The social structure of the gamblers' environment is offered as an alternative to that in normal society, yet in itself it is also seen as normal.

———. **Gambling without Guilt: The Legitimation of an American Pastime.** Pacific Grove, CA: Brooks/Cole, 1988. 174p.

Rosecrance feels that the gamblers should not experience guilt for gambling, which is quite normal behavior. In this book Rosecrance offers a critique of the medical model of obsessive gambling. He rejects the notion that excessive or problem gambling is a disease with only one remedy—abstinence. This valuable book presents a quick social and historical survey of the entire issue of legalized gambling.

Rosen, Charles. **Scandals of '51: How Gamblers Almost Killed College Basketball.** New York: Henry Holt, 1978. 262p.

The author was formerly a college basketball player in New York City. His love of the game shows as he takes the reader through the first half century of the game and to an era when the greatest teams, many based in New York City, fell apart amid a gambling scandal. Rosen explores the details of the betting scandal that revolved around players "shaving points" so that they would win by close scores and not "cover the spread." The spread is the handicap—a number of points given by a bettor to the underdog team. Rosen paints a picture of greed and power and illustrates the vulnerability of players and games in an atmosphere of widespread gambling activity.

Ross, Gary. **Stung: The Incredible Obsession of Brian Moloney.** Toronto: Stoddart Publishers. (Published in the United States as *No Limit: The Incredible Obsession of Brian Moloney.* New York: Morrow, 1989. 301p.)

Gary Ross provides the most insightful description of a compulsive gambler since Dostoyevsky's *The Gambler* was penned in 1866. *Stung* is the story of Brian Moloney, who as a child went to the race track near his Ontario home. As a college student he served as a bookie for his fellow students. Soon after graduation he was working as a loan officer in a prominent bank. By this time he was "hooked" with the gambling disease. He had gone through the cycles of an early big win, chased by more and more gaming and more and more losses. His work gave him opportunities for embezzlement. But instead of paying off gambling debts and quitting, Moloney just kept gambling. He discovered that casinos offered faster action. Casinos catered to his needs and pleasures with no thought about the source of his money. By the time he was caught, he had lost over $10 million.

Sasuly, Richard. **Bookies and Bettors: Two Hundred Years of Gambling.** New York: Henry Holt, 1982. 266p.

This social history of gambling links today's U.S. gaming enterprise to British establishments from the eighteenth and nineteenth centuries. The emphasis is on horse race betting and Mafia influence among bookies.

Scarne, John. **Scarne's Guide to Casino Gambling.** New York: Simon and Schuster, 1978. 352p.

This is one of several guides to gambling written by a leading authority in the field. The chapters cover history, game descriptions, and observations on the operations of casinos. The author advises players on systems, including card-counting methods for blackjack games.

Scott, Marvin B. **The Racing Game.** Chicago: Aldine, 1968. 186p.

This volume treats horse racing as a social organization tied together by information systems. This academic book will be enjoyed by the serious student of gaming and the "sport of kings." Extensive references to other works on horse racing are provided.

Shaffer, Howard J., Sharon A. Stein, Blase Gambino, and Thomas N. Cummings, eds. **Compulsive Gambling: Theory, Research, and Practice.** Lexington, MA: Lexington Books, 1989. 350p.

This book presents a collection of essays on the status of research knowledge about the problem of compulsive gambling. Special consideration is given to models of treatment. The notion that treatment demands abstinence is contrasted with behavior modification approaches. Actual treatment programs are discussed. The effect of compulsive gambling on family life is explored, as are public policy options for dealing with the pathological behaviors.

Sifakis, Carl. **The Encyclopedia of Gambling.** New York: Facts on File, 1990. 340p.

The author presents descriptions of nearly a thousand items from every kind of game played, the leading personalities in the history of gambling, and specific casinos and casino jurisdictions, to gambling techniques. The very concise and readable entries are supplemented by a glossary of terms and an annotated bibliography.

Skolnick, Jerome. **House of Cards: Legalization and Control of Casino Gambling.** Boston: Little, Brown, 1978. 382p.

This is a sociological analysis of casino gaming operations in Las Vegas. The author looks at the history of Nevada gaming, the operators (individual and corporate), the sources of financing, and the general public attitude toward such an industry. Especially valuable are chapters contributed by John Dombrink on gaming regulation and how criminal elements have compromised gaming.

Smith, John L. **Running Scared: The Life and Treacherous Times of Steven Wynn.** New York: Barricade Books, 1995. 352p.

Newspaper reporter John Smith is a native of Las Vegas. He has grown up in the midst of the gambling industry, rubbed shoulders with its key characters, and observed the growth of the casino industry from its illegitimate roots to the corporate-based legitimacy that it enjoys today. Yet Smith remains concerned that the shady past of Las Vegas may have a hold on its present as well. He attempts to link the two Las Vegas communities in this biographical account of the leading entrepreneur of Las Vegas today, Steven Alan Wynn. The book is written in the tradition of other investigative reporters who gave us *The Green Felt Jungle*, *The Boardwalk Jungle*, and *Temples of Chance*. The book presents many disturbing stories in a very interesting manner. Precise factual support for many rumors is often lacking, as is a conclusion about what a community should do even if a case could be proven that its leading businessman has had past dealings with bad people. There are no suggestions that any corruption has been involved in the gambling operations at Wynn's casinos (where he is CEO)—the Mirage, Treasure Island, or the Golden Nugget properties.

Spanier, David. **Inside the Gambler's Mind.** Reno: University of Nevada Press, 1994. 240p.

A connoisseur of the gambling scene, David Spanier presents a very readable and enjoyable discussion of winners and losers he has met during his frequent visits to the casinos of Europe and the United States. His vignettes include portraits of Edward Thorpe, the math professor who popularized the technique of card-counting for blackjack players; Gordon Moody, the minister who pioneered gambling treatment programs for compulsives in England; and Marie Blanc, the grand lady of gambling at Monte

Carlo in the nineteenth century. Spanier is positive about gambling, and readers will find his stories entertaining. This work was originally published in London in 1987 as *Easy Money: Inside the Gambler's Mind*.

————. **Welcome to the Pleasuredome: Inside Las Vegas.** Reno: University of Nevada Press, 1992, 275p.

In this volume Spanier focuses upon life in Las Vegas as it developed from an outpost community to the center of casino gambling for an entire world. He tells stories of the glamour and glitz but also of the ordinary lives that collectively make Las Vegas the "Pleasuredome."

Sternlieb, George, and James W. Hughes. **The Atlantic City Gamble.** Cambridge, MA: Harvard University Press, 1983. 215p.

A thorough account of the events leading up to the legalization of casinos for Atlantic City and the initial operation of the city's casinos from 1978 to 1983. The authors illustrate the successes and failures of legalization and conclude with a series of recommendations for other jurisdictions.

Teski, Marea, Robert Helsabeck, Franklin Smith, and Charles Yeager. **A City Revitalized: The Elderly Lose at Monopoly.** Lanham, MD: University Press of America, 1983. 191p.

This study examines the way in which Atlantic City casinos changed the urban ecology for elderly residents in neighborhoods near the Boardwalk. The elderly had settled in Atlantic City because the decaying city offered inexpensive lifestyles. However, with the advent of casinos, land values skyrocketed and investors began to crowd out the stores and shops that serviced the senior citizens. The authors suggest that jurisdictions considering legalization of casinos study Atlantic City closely.

Thompson, William, and Michele Comeau. **Casino Customer Service = The WIN WIN Game.** New York: Gaming and Wagering Business, 1997. 332p.

The dilemma faced by gambling establishments is a big one: How do you take money away from people and send them away not only happy but also wanting to return? The answer is to give them entertainment value and to make them feel good. The author and his colleague focus on developing good customer service as a means of giving entertainment value. They discuss mission statements, hiring the right kind of employee, training, motivation, and dealing with complaints. An annotated bibliography reviews the literature of customer service.

Thorpe, Edward O. **Beat the Dealer.** New York: Random House, 1962. 236p.

This is a classic account of how players can actually gain the edge on the casino by keeping track of cards as they are played in blackjack. The book resulted in a craze that has made blackjack the most popular table game in casinos today. It also led to casinos altering their rules to minimize card counting.

Turner, Wallace. **Gambler's Money.** Boston: Houghton-Mifflin, 1965. 306p.

Pulitzer Prize–winning journalist Wallace Turner turns his investigative skills on the legal casino industry of Las Vegas in this exposé. He examines the development of casinos capitalized with Mob and Teamster Union moneys and follows the flow of gaming profits from the hands of players into the hands of gangsters who engage in antisocial activities outside of Nevada. Turner writes that gambling is an immoral business given a "base of legality" in Nevada, and from this foothold gamblers have branched out to change patterns in U.S. life. Turner's judgment that "gambling must be contained" is as relevant now as it was then, and he makes a case for federal regulation of gambling.

Vogel, Harold L. **Entertainment Industry Economics: A Guide for Financial Analysis.** New York: Press Syndicate of the University of Cambridge, 1994. 446p.

This comprehensive volume covers all aspects of the entertainment industry: movies, home videos, television, sports, music, and gambling. Vogel provides the reader with a broad range of statistical data by which the importance of the emerging gambling industry can be judged. The book is especially useful in offering precise definitions of terminology that is treated loosely elsewhere: for example, *drop, win, hold, edge, odds.* The book is also helpful for persons wishing to understand the structure of businesses in the gaming industry. Although the book is written for those with a specific interest in finance, it is beneficial for general audiences as well.

Walker, Michael. **The Psychology of Gambling.** Oxford: Pergamon Press, 1992. 262p.

Michael Walker presents a collection of research studies that support the "cognitive" perspective on gambling behavior. This perspective treats the gambler as a thoughtful person who seeks to behave rationally. Unfortunately, the gambler may also be acting irrationally, as he or she may be acting on the basis of false information, for instance, a false notion of game odds or a false sense of control over game outcomes. The book begins with a discussion of the skills necessary to play several games—horse race betting, bridge, poker, and blackjack. Pure (or nearly pure) chance games are then explored with a focus upon why people play the games. Many explanations for gambling behavior are reviewed, from psychoanalytical theories to conditional learning theories to cultural explanations. Walker gives strong support for his belief that heavy gamblers are drawn into action believing that they can control game outcomes. The last chapters discuss problem gambling and treatment strategies for problem gamblers. Given that problems arise because people believe they are using strategic thinking, treatments must also be based upon thoughtful steps to recovery. This is an excellent one-volume overview of problem gambling.

Watson, Tom. **Don't Bet on It.** Ventura, CA: Regal Books, 1987. 249p.

This is a religiously based book that presents the many negative aspects of gambling from a very biased viewpoint. Nonetheless, the arguments are presented in an organized manner and are supported by factual information. It is well referenced and, as such, should be considered a good resource.

Weinstein, David, and Lillian Deitch. **The Impact of Legalized Gambling: The Socioeconomic Consequences of Lotteries and Off-Track Betting.** New York: Praeger, 1974. 208p.

The authors have conducted the first serious socioeconomic study of two major forms of gambling. They draw conclusions that others are slowly beginning to realize: Lotteries cannot solve the long-run fiscal problems of government, earmarked programs do not really gain from lottery funds, lottery funds are not stable government revenues, and government promotion of gambling can have negative social consequences. The authors outline a list of questions that should be researched by policymakers prior to legalizing more gambling.

Weiss, Ann E. **Lotteries: Who Wins, Who Loses?** Hillside, NJ: Enslow. 1991. 112p.

This young-adult book presents a comprehensive review of the development of lotteries, their advantages and disadvantages, and governmental use of lottery funds. It is a balanced commentary that focuses upon the economic dimensions of lottery enterprises.

Periodicals

Casino Executive. Published by William J. Dorn, 15 South Fifth Street, Suite 900, Minneapolis, MN 55402.

This monthly magazine began publication in 1995 and in a short time has become one of the leading trade publications of the casino industry. Its columns feature analyses of the political and economic atmosphere of gambling from elections to gambling stocks and bonds as well as all other major aspects of casino operations.

Casino Journal. Companion trade publication with *Casino Journal of New Jersey*. Editorial offices: 3100 West Sahara, Suite 209, Las Vegas, NV 89102; Bayport One, Suite 470, West Atlantic City, NJ 08232.

Regular features of this monthly industry publication include articles on gaming law, personalities of the casino industry, casino promotions, and government policies in gaming. The journal is now in its sixth year of publication.

Casino Magazine. Published by William J. Dorn, 15 South Fifth Street, Suite 900, Minneapolis, MN 55402.

A predecessor and now companion publication of *Casino Executive*, this monthly magazine focuses upon the games played at the casino tables and on other aspects of gaming of interest to players as well as to casino operators.

Gaming Research and Review Journal. Published by the University of Nevada–Las Vegas [UNLV] International Gaming Institute, The William F. Harrah College of Hotel Administration, UNLV, Las Vegas, 89154-6037.

A semiannual academic publication, this journal features scholarly articles on all aspects of the gambling industry. Emphasis is on commentary on the business aspects of casino operations.

Gaming Technologies (formerly *Casino Gaming International*). Published by the Public Gaming Research Institute, 15825 Shady Grove Road, Rockville, MD 20850.

A monthly publication devoted to news and features about the commercial casino gaming industry.

The Grogan Casino Report (formerly *The Grogan Report*). Published by Stephen Grogan, 30746 Bryant Drive (P.O.Box 249), Evergreen, CO 80439.

This monthly publication focuses upon business and management aspects of casino operations throughout North America.

Indian Gaming Magazine. Published by the Public Gaming Research Institute for the National Indian Gaming Association, 4020 Lake Washington Blvd. NE, Suite 100, Kirkland, WA 98033.

This monthly publication began in 1991. It focuses upon gambling developments on Indian reservations. In addition to features, it includes regular articles on the law of gaming, marketing, industry news, and profiles of leading industry figures.

International Gaming and Wagering Business. Published by BMT Publications, 7 Penn Plaza, New York, NY 10001-3900.

Started in 1978 as *Gaming Business Magazine*, this monthly publication is recognized as the definitive trade publication for the gaming industry. Its regular features include articles on lotteries, riverboat and Indian casinos, and marketing and customer service in the gaming industry. It also publishes the latest statistical information on all facets of the gaming industry worldwide and directories of gaming establishments and gaming industry suppliers. The periodical reports on new legal developments in this fast-growing industry.

Journal of Gambling Studies. Cosponsored by the National Council on Problem Gambling, 445 West 59th Street, New York, NY 10019, and the Institute for the Study of Gambling and Commercial Gaming, University of Nevada, Reno, NV 89557.

The first U.S. academic journal devoted solely to the gambling phenomenon, this journal (originally called the *Journal of Gambling Behavior*) initially focused on problem gambling and studies of treatment methods. In the later 1980s, the editors sought out more general studies of public policy and gambling and changed the title. The quarterly journal provides not only the latest research studies into gambling but also regular reviews of gambling books.

Passenger Vessel News. Published by Pearson Publication Company, P.O.Box 8662, Metairie, LA 70011.

Passenger Vessel News has been a bimonthly publication since the advent of riverboat gambling in 1989. The magazine features operational aspects of casinos on riverboats, including games management, financial concerns, and marketing. Pearson also publishes *Riverboat Gaming Report*, which offers periodical statistics on gaming results for the boat operations.

Public Gaming International. Published by the Public Gaming Research Institute for the National Indian Gaming Association, 4020 Lake Washington Blvd. NE, Suite 100, Kirkland, WA 98033.

A monthly featuring news reports and stories about lotteries. Formerly called *Public Gaming*, the magazine began in 1973.

Turf and Sports Digest. Published by Turf and Sports International, 118 West Pennsylvania Avenue, Towson, MD 21204.

Published since 1924, this bimonthly magazine contains stories about race track events and personalities. It features statistical records of leading horses.

Web Sites for Examining Gambling Issues

Those interested in gambling issues can find much useful information on Internet Web sites. Many of the sites are commercial enterprises and charge fees for their use. Others are free at the time of this writing (1997), and several of these are listed below. The first three sites provide information on legislation, court cases, and administrative rulings. The next group consists of sites that provide specific information on gambling. Sites that provide information exclusively for players of games are excluded. The third group of three listings directs the Internet "surfer" to newspapers in Canada and the United States.

I offer my appreciation to the source for this information to Joe Richardson of Great Gamble, Inc., Fargo, North Dakota (joe-fargo@aol.com).

Legal Documents

The Canada Pages
(http://www.citenet.net/users/g.vanert/ canada.html)

This site leads to a broad range of government agencies on the federal and provincial levels as well as to some of the best political sites in Canada.

Legal Information Institute, Cornell Law School
(http://www. law.cornell.edu/statutes.html)

This site has strong links to state constitutions, statutes, and codes for those states that provide them without service costs.

Thomas
(http://thomas.loc.gov)

This is a U.S. government supersite. All federal online public information is available within a couple of links from this site.

Gambling-Specific Sites

Gambler's Book Club
(http://www.gamblersbook.com/)

This site gives a more complete listing of books than the preceding site but without descriptions.

Gambler's Bookstore of America
(http://www.gamblersbook.com/gambler/)

This site provides a wide selection of books and videos on a broad range of gambling topics. It includes annotated descriptions of each book along with images of book covers.

Institute for the Study of Gambling and Commercial Gaming, University of Nevada–Reno
(http://www.unr.edu/gaming/index.html)

The site provides much information on the extensive training programs offered by the institute as well as a listing of their many publications.

Winner's Publishing
(http://www.winner.com/index.html)

This is a source that is most useful for linking the "surfer" to many other gaming-related sites.

Online Newspapers

Canoe
(http://www.canoe.ca)

Through this site the network surfer can utilize keywords to find articles on gambling issues in many Canadian newspapers.

Globe Net, The *Globe and Mail*, Toronto
(http://www.globeandmail.ca/)

The *Globe and Mail* is considered to be Canada's "national newspaper" for many. This site gives the browser the capacity to search for articles in the *Globe*.

New Century Network
(http://www.newcentury.net/)

The site provides an alphabetical listing of newspapers in the United States with links to each.

Selected Nonprint Resources

7

Feature Films with Gambling Themes

Hollywood has always represented one of the greatest gambles of life in the United States. Whether the player is a budding starlet from the Midwest, a playwright from the South, or a director looking for a box-office kill, the movie industry holds the same allure as a lottery ticket, a long shot at the racecourse, or the spinning dice in a floating craps game. The glitzy town personifies a thousand parables of fame and another thousand hard-luck tales. Hollywood has always been the story of good luck and bad luck, of winners and losers. It is no wonder, then, that producers have sought out scripts that feature gambling themes or gambling settings. Below are listed films that reveal Hollywood's view of the gambling phenomenon. Descriptions are based on my own viewing, film reviews in popular media, Leonard Maltin's *Movie and Video Guide 1993* and *1995* (New York: Penguin Books, 1992 and 1994), and Video Hound's *Golden Movie Retriever 1996* (Detroit: Visible Ink, 1996). Each film is available on videocassette (VHS format), and many are also available on laser

Price listings are from the Wherehouse, Inc., film catalog or from the price listed by the distributor indicated (whichever was lower). Addresses of the distributors cited are located at the end of the chapter.

Aces and Eights
Type: VHS
Length: 58 minutes
Date: 1936
Cost: $14.95
Source: World Education 2000

A western adventure film that focuses on cheating in a card game. Wild Bill Hickok was holding aces and eights during a poker game when he was shot in the back in a Deadwood, South Dakota, tavern. The film starts with a scene of Hickok discussing cards and fate.

Any Number Can Play
Type: VHS
Length: 102 minutes
Date: 1949
Cost: $19.98
Source: MGM

Clark Gable stars as an elderly dice-rolling gambler facing the crisis of impending death.

The Apple Dumpling Gang
Type: VHS/LD
Length: 100 minutes
Date: 1975
Cost: $19.99
Source: Wherehouse Entertainment, Inc.

A Walt Disney–produced farce that focuses upon the life of a Wild West cardsharp who becomes the guardian for three orphaned children. The gambler takes the children into his world of deception and trickery but then finds himself changing his ways as he accepts the obligations of parenthood.

Atlantic City
Type: VHS/LD
Length: 104 minutes
Date: 1980
Cost: $14.95
Source: Paramount Home Video

Burt Lancaster stars in this dramatic story about changing lives. It is set in Atlantic City in its early days of transition from a decaying resort town to a casino destination. The film portrays the town's traditional ambience as a haven for racketeers and gangsters unaltered by the onslaught of new legal gambling houses. Scenes include profiles of casino employees and their ambitions.

A Big Hand for the Little Lady
Type: VHS/LD
Length: 95 minutes
Date: 1966
Cost: $19.98
Source: Facets Video

This mixture of comedy and tragedy is built around one poker game in the back room of an old western saloon. A single hand of the game consumes an hour of the film. Different types of gamblers and their relationships are explored: the slick professional gambler, the con artist, the playful amateur, and the compulsive gambler.

The Big Town
Type: VHS/LD
Length: 109 minutes
Date: 1987
Cost: $89.98
Source: Vestron Video, Inc.

A story centered on a young, small-town gambler who comes to Chicago in 1957 and continues his "hot streak." With his new bankroll he finds himself attracted to two women. He must choose between a wholesome, unmarried mother and a wild, married striptease dancer. Much of the scenery and plot are designed to make the film a 1950s nostalgia piece.

Billy Bathgate
Type: VHS/LD
Length: 106 minutes
Date: 1991
Cost: $19.99
Source: Touchstone Home Video

This very lucky man was the companion of Dutch Schultz in his many criminal operations, which included gambling ventures. Billy is just a young hanger-on who is drawn into a faction of the Mob just as the faction is on its ascendancy. The scenes reveal the interconnections between gambling activity and other organized crime ventures. A later falling-out with his Mob benefactors leaves Billy Bathgate excluded from the meeting that results in the murder of his former associates by a rival gang.

Bob Le Flambeur (French)

Type: VHS/LD
Length: 102 minutes
Date: 1955
Cost: $39.95
Source: RCA/Columbia Pictures Home Video

This losing gambler gathers his friends together in a plan to rob the Deauville casino in France. The scenery displays the contrasting style of a typical European gaming house and the U.S. casinos of Las Vegas and Atlantic City.

Bugsy

Type: VHS/LD
Length: 135 minutes
Date: 1991
Cost: $14.95
Source: Wherehouse Entertainment, Inc.

A fairly accurate account of how mobster Benjamin Siegel helped develop the famous Las Vegas Strip. This film offers glimpses of Siegel during his rise to gangland success, his interactions with a Lansky-like character during the establishment of the Flamingo, and his fatal attraction to Hollywood starlet Virginia Hill.

Casino

Type: VHS
Length: 179 minutes
Date: 1995
Cost: $14.98
Source: Universal Home Video

This film presents the image of the Mob trying to hold onto a piece of Las Vegas casino action in the 1980s. It is basically a true account of the battles between two "connected" individuals who were childhood friends. One is Frank Rosenthal, a casino manager; the other is Tony Spilatro, a racketeer who seeks to steal from the casinos. Rosenthal is denied his gaming license by the Nevada gaming regulators and leaves town after there is an attempt on his life. Spilatro is not so lucky. He and his brother are assassinated outside of Chicago in 1986. The film glamorizes the "power" of these two men who actually were only minor embarrassments for an industry that had been taken over by corporations by the time they had arrived on the scene.

Casino Royale (British)
Type: VHS/LD
Length: 130 minutes
Date: 1967
Cost: $19.95
Source: RCA/Columbia Pictures Home Video

This is a James Bond spoof, with its many antics leading to the tables of the French Casino Royale. There Bond, an English gaming sharp, confronts a key executive of the spy organization, SMERSH, in a card game. The executive is a cheat, but he finds his match in his baccarat game with Bond.

The Cincinnati Kid
Type: VHS/LD
Length: 113 minutes
Date: 1965
Cost: $19.98
Source: MGM/UA Home Video

This film features the game of stud poker, providing an excellent portrayal of the illicit professional gaming society in New Orleans—complete with the staging of a cockfight. The Cincinnati Kid, played by Steve McQueen, is a young derelict cardsharp who challenges Edward G. Robinson, playing the king of New Orleans gaming, to a marathon duel on the tables. The activity develops slowly and methodically, giving the audience a feel for the emotion of the gaming.

The Color of Money
Type: VHS/LD
Length: 119 minutes
Date: 1986
Cost: $19.95
Source: Touchstone Home Video

A good portrayal of pool-hall hustling, an unorganized but popular form of gambling activity. The film is a 25-year-later sequel to the movie *The Hustler*. It juxtaposes the differing lifestyles between two generations. However, both generations are unified through their occupational lifestyle—pool-hall hustling.

Dead Lucky
Type: VHS
Length: 91 minutes
Date: 1960
Cost: $19.98
Source: Prime

A new gambler experiences "winner's luck" and picks up an easy fortune. Then the difficulties begin, as the film takes us through sequences including murders, scams, and mysterious women.

Deadly Impact (Italian)
Type: VHS/LD
Length: 91 minutes
Date: 1985
Cost: $29.98
Source: Vestron Video, Inc.

In this farce, set in Las Vegas and Phoenix, a young computer whiz develops a system to break casinos' central computer coding. He manipulates the messages on the computer chips, thereby controlling when the slot machines will have winning plays. After winning a large sum of money, he is hunted down by local thugs, and the film degenerates into a cat-and-mouse game.

Diamonds Are Forever
Type: VHS
Length: 120 minutes
Date: 1971
Cost: $19.95
Source: MGM

This 007 James Bond adventure features many Las Vegas gambling scenes, including a wild car chase through the Fremont Street casino area.

Eight Men Out
Type: VHS/LD
Length: 119 minutes
Date: 1988
Cost: $9.98
Source: Orion Home Video

A careful study of the 1919 Black Sox scandal, which involved a gambler's bribing baseball players in the World Series. The film records the social structure of sports betting and how players—

both guilty and innocent—can be compromised if vigilant controls are not in place.

The Electric Horseman
Type: VHS/LD
Length: 120 minutes
Date: 1979
Cost: $14.98
Source: MCA Home Video

Las Vegas becomes the setting for this metaphor of exploitation and innocence. The values of gaming lifestyles and humanity are contrasted as Jane Fonda and Robert Redford team up to steal a horse from a Las Vegas show and head for open grazing land. The film offers excellent footage of Caesars Palace and the Las Vegas Strip, circa 1970s.

Family Players
Type: VHS
Length: 109 minutes
Date: 1991
Cost: $89.95
Source: Columbia Tristar

A family is being torn apart because of the father's uncontrollable gambling problems. The destructive pressures of compulsive gambling are felt by his children and wife.

Fools Rush In
Date: To be released late 1997

Life and love in Las Vegas can be more of a gamble than any bets at a blackjack table. *Fools Rush In* is a romantic comedy that uses the full Las Vegas scene as a backdrop for the plot. Most of the joke routines revolve around the outdoor Las Vegas temperature and the indoor casino floor action.

The Fox and His Friend
Type: VHS/LD
Length: 123 minutes
Date: 1975
Cost: $79.95
Source: Wherehouse Entertainment, Inc.

A carnival performer wins a lottery, but he discovers that his win has become a vehicle for his lover to exploit him. The film focuses on the issues of wealth and poverty and examines how the characters' mindsets are altered by changing circumstance.

The Gambler
Type: VHS/LD
Length: 111 minutes
Date: 1974
Cost: $14.95
Source: Paramount Home Video

This is not the Dostoyevsky story, but it *is* a story about a compulsive gambler. The central character is a college professor with an uncontrollable passion for gambling who will bet on anything simply for the excitement and uncertainty. The portrayal provides a valid case study of the problem gambler.

The Gambler Returns: The Luck of the Draw
Type: VHS
Length: 180 minutes
Date: 1993
Cost: $89.95
Source: Cabin Fever Entertainment

It is Kenny Rogers time again. Here the songster gambler travels across the country in order to participate in another poker game.

Gilda
Type: VHS/LD
Length: 110 minutes
Date: 1946
Cost: $19.95
Source: RCA/Columbia Pictures Home Video

The proprietor of a Buenos Aires casino becomes involved in a Nazi cartel. This intrigue serves as the backdrop for another story that occurs within the gaming hall. The proprietor's wife, played by Rita Hayworth, is also involved with a young gambler employed by her husband. Yet the plot strays off and is difficult to follow.

The Godfather, Part II
Type: VHS/LD
Length: 200 minutes
Date: 1974
Cost: $29.95
Source: Paramount Home Video

As the second part of the *Godfather* trilogy, this film features the Las Vegas connection to Mob families. The production won an Oscar as the best film of the year. Here the sons of the old-time

Mob try to go legitimate by attempting to take over Las Vegas Strip casinos and manipulating Nevada politicians.

The Grasshopper

Type:	VHS/LD
Length:	95 minutes
Date:	1970
Cost:	$19.98
Source:	Powersports/American Video

A Canadian girl comes to Las Vegas with a dream but ends up as a wasted call girl. The film's value is in its portrayal of a side of Las Vegas society not outwardly observable in the gaming halls. Las Vegas shows illustrate the glitter that makes the Strip famous.

The Grifters

Type:	VHS/LD
Length:	114 minutes
Date:	1990
Cost:	$19.95
Source:	HBO Video, Inc.

Scam artists work their trade until it destroys them. Many of their antics revolve around gambling operations, including the sleight-of-hand artist's scheme to win at the racetracks.

Guys and Dolls

Type:	VHS/LD
Length:	150 minutes
Date:	1955
Cost:	$19.98
Source:	CBS/Fox Video

The widely acclaimed Broadway musical about street lives and gambling in New York is brought to the screen. Frank Sinatra portrays Nathan Detroit—a small-time street player caught up in craps games and playing the ponies. Marlon Brando portrays the kingpin of the local gaming rackets.

Harlem Nights

Type:	VHS/LD
Length:	115 minutes
Date:	1989
Cost:	$149.95
Source:	Paramount Home Video

The film, set in New York in the 1930s, presents the efforts of an underground gambling club's owners to stand up to the Mob. Eddie Murphy wrote and directed this sometimes good, sometimes bad effort at comedy. The cast of comedy hall-of-famers includes Redd Foxx, who plays a dealer with poor eyesight, and Richard Pryor, who plays Sugar Ray, one of the casino owners.

Havana

Type:	VHS/LD
Length:	140 minutes
Date:	1990
Cost:	$19.95
Source:	MCA Home Video

Castro is about to take over, but a gambler decides to remain at the casino in order to make his last big win. As the game continues, stories of approaching troops fill the halls. Inevitably, the gambler gets involved in the political intrigue of the moment. The characters foresee the expansion (transfer) of gambling activities to other locales, including London, the Bahamas, and Las Vegas.

Honeymoon in Vegas

Type:	VHS
Length:	95 minutes
Date:	1992
Cost:	$19.95
Source:	RCA/Columbia Pictures Home Video

Nicholas Cage loses his prospective wife in a rigged card game. That is, he loses a lot of money, and the winner agrees that he will settle the debt if he can spend an evening with the future wife. The movie involves the hero's efforts to win back his fiancée. It features many Las Vegas gaming scenes and local personalities, including a troupe of skydiving Elvis impersonators.

The Hustler

Type:	VHS/LD
Length:	135 minutes
Date:	1961
Cost:	$19.98
Source:	CBS/Fox Video

This is the quintessential film about poolroom hustling. Jackie Gleason portrays the legendary Minnesota Fats (see the biography of Rudolph W. Wanderone under "Famous Players" in Chapter 3). Paul Newman is the young pool hustler seeking his fame through his big-time matchup with Fats. The action is gripping between the play on the table and the betting behind the players.

Indecent Proposal
Type: VHS
Length: 119 minutes
Date: 1993
Cost: $19.95
Source: Paramount Home Video

This plot is almost identical to that of *Honeymoon in Vegas*. Woody Harrelson loses a card game to a crooked gambler, Robert Redford. To settle his debts, Harrelson offers his wife, played by Demi Moore, to Redford for an evening. The film is set in Las Vegas.

Jinxed!
Type: VHS/LD
Length: 103 minutes
Date: 1982
Cost: $14.95
Source: MGM/UA Home Video

Bette Midler stars as a Las Vegas singer who becomes involved in an adventure with a man who manages to jinx a blackjack dealer. Set in the casinos of northern Nevada, the film portrays the superstitions that control the lifestyles of many in the gaming industry.

Kenny Rogers as The Gambler
Type: VHS/LD
Length: 94 minutes
Date: 1980
Cost: $14.95
Source: Wood Knapp Video

Rogers acts out the narrative of his famous song. The lines in the song give the basic lesson for the poker-playing gambler. "Every hand's a winner, every hand's a loser." It all depends on how the hands are played. A winner's "gotta know when to hold 'em" and "know when to fold 'em."

Kenny Rogers as The Gambler, Part II
Type: VHS/LD
Length: 200 minutes
Date: 1983
Cost: $14.95
Source: Wood Knapp Video

More adventures with a deck of cards.

Kenny Rogers as The Gambler—The Legend Continues
Type: VHS/LD
Length: 200 minutes
Date: 1987
Cost: $14.95
Source: Wood Knapp Video

Rogers finally decides to "fold 'em," and the trilogy is completed.

Lady from Louisiana
Type: VHS/LD
Length: 82 minutes
Date: 1941
Cost: $14.98
Source: Republic Pictures Home Video

The crooked operations of politicians and grafters in the famous nineteenth-century Louisiana Lottery are captured on film. The hero, played by John Wayne, is sent in to clean up the mess. The plot thickens as he is compromised by a romance with the chief culprit's daughter.

Le Million (French)
Type: VHS/LD
Length: 85 minutes
Date: 1931
Cost: $24.95
Source: Wherehouse Entertainment, Inc.

This adventure revolves around the quest to find a lost lottery ticket.

Let It Ride
Type: VHS/LD
Length: 86 minutes
Date: 1989
Cost: $14.95
Source: Paramount Home Video

This very humorous film looks at the world of horse racing and the gambling addicts that it attracts. Richard Dreyfus, like so many other pathological players, wants just that "one big day at the track." The film is shot at Florida's Hialeah Racetrack. The movie becomes a fantasy when Dreyfus gets his "big day" and somehow avoids gambling all the money back.

Little Miss Marker
Type: VHS

Length: 88 minutes
Date: 1934
Cost: $49.99
Source: MCA Home Video

Little Miss Marker is Shirley Temple. She is used by her guardians as an IOU to guarantee the payment of a gambling debt.

Little Vegas
Type: VHS/LD
Length: 91 minutes
Date: 1990
Cost: $89.95
Source: RCA/Columbia Pictures Home Video

A comedy about the Mob's efforts to invade the area around a trailer park and turn it into an illegal gambling retreat. The movie plays more like a poor television sitcom than a feature with the continuity of a real story line.

Looking to Get Out
Type: VHS
Length: 70 minutes
Date: 1982
Cost: $59.95
Source: Fox Home Entertainment

This is a comedy starring Ann-Margaret and Jon Voight as two gamblers trying to keep ahead of some loan sharks who mean them harm. Much of the action takes place in the Las Vegas MGM casino (now Bally's) on the Strip.

Lost in America
Type: VHS/LD
Length: 91 minutes
Date: 1985
Cost: $19.98
Source: Warner Home Video, Inc.

A married couple drops out of the "rat race" and leaves suburbia to find "America" in their Winnebago. Their first stop is the Desert Inn Casino on the Las Vegas Strip. The couple's "yuppie" dream life quickly comes apart as the wife gambles their entire savings away on a single stint at the tables. The film illustrates how quickly an innocent person can be drawn into pathological playing behavior. The film unflatteringly portrays casino personnel as allowing a compulsion to destroy people.

Lucky Luciano (Italian-French-American)
Type: VHS/LD
Length: 110 minutes
Date: 1974
Cost: $9.95
Source: Nelson Entertainment, Inc.

A screenplay about one of the leading mobsters who ran illegal gaming and other racket ventures.

The Marrying Man
Type: VHS/LD
Length: 118 minutes
Date: 1991
Cost: $19.95
Source: Wherehouse Entertainment, Inc.

Crazy things can happen in Las Vegas. A carefree bachelor goes to Las Vegas with his buddies for one last fling. He ends up falling in love with a lounge singer who just happens to be a casino mobster's girlfriend. They get married, then divorced, then remarried in a senseless plot with a lot of Las Vegas scenery attached.

Mississippi
Type: VHS
Length: 73 minutes
Date: 1935
Cost: $9.95
Source: Wherehouse Entertainment, Inc.

The silver screen takes the audience back a century to a time when the Mississippi River was lined with paddle-wheel boats seeking to lure gamblers aboard. This musical comedy revolves around a riverboat captain and his poker playing. The ambience of riverboat gambling portrayed is in considerable contrast to the slot machines and polished felt tables of Mississippi riverboats today.

Monte Carlo
Type: VHS/LD
Length: 200 minutes
Date: 1986
Cost: $29.95
Source: New World Video

A spy story set around the classic casino. The film offers visuals of the Palace, which once stood above all others as the casino gambling capital of the world.

My Little Chickadee
Type: VHS
Length: 91 minutes
Date: 1940
Cost: $14.98
Source: MCA Home Video

This is a W. C. Fields classic comedy favorite. It is about a professional gambler and a lady of questionable reputation—Mae West. They get married in order to have a front from behind which they attempt to bilk the residents of small-town U.S.A.

The Naughty Nineties
Type: VHS/LD
Length: 76 minutes
Date: 1945
Cost: $14.95
Source: MCA Home Video

Bud Abbott and Lou Costello get into their comic routine antics on a Mississippi riverboat in the 1890s. The plotless script finds the comic duo operating with scheming businessmen and gamblers.

Ocean's Eleven
Type: VHS/LD
Length: 127 minutes
Date: 1960
Cost: $19.98
Source: Warner Home Video, Inc.

This film offers a flashy look at Las Vegas, the tables, the slot machines, and, of course, the show girls. This comedy is about an 11-man team that robs five Las Vegas casinos on New Year's Eve. The film stars Frank Sinatra and his Rat Pack: Dean Martin, Joey Bishop, Peter Lawford, and Sammy Davis Jr.

Pocketful of Miracles
Type: VHS/LD
Length: 136 minutes
Date: 1961
Cost: $14.98
Source: MGM/UA Home Video

Frank Capra remakes his 1933 film *A Lady for a Day*. The king of New York gamblers, Dave the Dude, always buys an apple from Apple Annie just for luck. When he learns that Annie's long-lost daughter is returning home, he decides to help Annie. The daughter does not know that Annie has fallen on bad times, so Dave organizes all his friends in a masquerade designed to convince the daughter that Annie is a society matron.

Queen of Spades (Russian)

Type:	VHS/LD
Length:	100 minutes
Date:	1960
Cost:	$39.95
Source:	Kultur Video

This is a tragedy about pathological gambling. The film is set off by classical music scores by Tchaikovsky, which are performed by the Bolshoi Orchestra. A Russian army officer is torn between his love for an aristocratic lady and his passion to gamble. The plot focuses on his attempts to find out her grandmother's secrets for winning card games.

Rain Man

Type:	VHS/LD
Length:	140 minutes
Date:	1988
Cost:	$19.98
Source:	MGM/UA Home Video

This film depicts Dustin Hoffman as an idiot-savant whose mathematical skill helps his brother (Tom Cruise) beat Caesars Palace. Hoffman's mind is a computer machine that enables him to act as the ultimate card-counter at blackjack games. After achieving large wins, the pair is asked to leave the casino. There are some very good shots of Caesars, its gaming areas, and its other luxurious facilities. However, the Las Vegas setting is only a small part of the film.

The Rocking Horse Winner

Type:	VHS
Length:	91 minutes
Date:	1949
Cost:	$39.95
Source:	Fest

A young boy is able to predict the winners of horse races by riding his rocking horse. His mother gets caught up in the fantasy. However, as she discovers his secret powers she succumbs to greed, and tragedy ensues as she loses control over her gambling on races.

Rover Dangerfield

Type: VHS/LD
Length: 74 minutes
Date: 1991
Cost: $19.98
Source: Warner Home Video, Inc.

As a wisecracking dog cartoon character, Rodney Dangerfield enjoys his life hanging around the casinos in Las Vegas. Unfortunately, he is "dognapped" and taken to a farm in the country. There he must learn to get along with new friends. However, he plots his return to the Las Vegas Strip and his old dog friends.

Run

Type: VHS/LD
Length: 91 minutes
Date: 1990
Cost: $19.99
Source: Wherehouse Entertainment, Inc.

A law student seeks out an illegal casino. While at the casino he becomes embroiled in an argument with the son of a mobster. In the course of a fight the mobster's son falls, accidentally hitting his head, and dies. The gambling scene ends, and the chase scenes begin.

Shadow of the Thin Man

Type: VHS/LD
Length: 97 minutes
Date: 1941
Cost: $19.98
Source: MGM/UA Home Video

The first scene is a racetrack. The betting action surrounds a mysterious murder, and the plot thickens.

Stacy's Knights

Type: VHS/LD
Length: 95 minutes
Date: 1983
Cost: $29.98
Source: Vestron Video, Inc.

A young girl goes to Reno to try her luck at blackjack. She learns card-counting skills, and along with her boyfriend, she wins a large sum from the casinos. The casino retaliates by putting a crooked dealer into the game. The ensuing cat-and-mouse episodes result in her boyfriend's death. She then organizes her own gang of cheats and ultimately beats the casino. The card-playing scenes are mechanical, and the overall flow of action is rather slow.

Strike It Rich (British)

Type: VHS/LD
Length: 87 minutes
Date: 1990
Cost: $89.99
Source: HBO Video, Inc.

An accountant gets caught up in gambling fever when he takes his honeymoon in Monte Carlo. The film offers another graphic study of compulsive gambling behaviors.

Things Change

Type: VHS
Length: 114 minutes
Date: 1988
Cost: $14.95
Source: Columbia Tristar

Don Ameche stars in a film about an old man who agrees to take a "fall" for a mobster by confessing to a crime the mobster committed and by accepting a jail sentence. As part of his payment for this "good deed," the old man is given a special weekend in Las Vegas. That's where the real fun starts.

Thursday's Game

Type: VHS/LD
Length: 100 minutes
Date: 1974
Cost: $69.95
Source: Vidmark Entertainment

Poker-playing buddies commiserate about their business and marital problems.

29th Street

Type: VHS/LD
Length: 101 minutes
Date: 1991
Cost: $19.98
Source: Wherehouse Entertainment, Inc.

An adventure about loan sharks and the winner of the New York State lottery. The film makes a good effort to illustrate how a lottery can cause many people to get caught up in a gambling frenzy. This is a very good action film with an interesting plot and a surprise ending.

The Underneath

Type:	VHS
Length:	99 minutes
Date:	1995
Cost:	$19.90
Source:	Universal Home Video

This story is about a recovering compulsive gambler and his homecoming after treatment. His reunion with his family is emotionally distressing, and he is drawn away once again to a quest for one more "big win."

Vegas Strip Wars

Type:	VHS
Length:	100 minutes
Date:	1984
Cost:	$69.95
Source:	LIV

Rock Hudson stars in his last television movie. He plays a casino owner caught up in a competitive struggle against other owners on the Strip. The film also stars James Earl Jones.

Vegas Vacation

Date:	To be released July 1997

Here come the Griswolds again. This is the third Chevy Chase traveling-with-the-family film. The film is heavy on the sights in Las Vegas and environs. Showroom acts feature Zeigfried and Roy and, of course, Wayne Newton. There is also casino action, a showgirls bar scene, and many outdoor vistas. The plot is simple, and the message is comedy.

Viva Las Vegas

Type:	VHS/LD
Length:	86 minutes
Date:	1964
Cost:	$14.98
Source:	MGM/UA Home Video

Elvis comes to Las Vegas as a race car driver. He then gets into the musical business, using Las Vegas as a set for his songs, and his romance with Ann-Margaret. Scenes include the neon, the tables and machines, and the Hoover Dam. It is not a bad 1960s Las Vegas travelogue. The plot offers Elvis and his music, nothing more.

Wanda Nevada
Type: VHS
Length: 105 minutes
Date: 1979

Peter Fonda plays a gambler who wins Brooke Shields in a poker game. The film features Henry Fonda in the only role he ever played opposite his son.

Videocassette Documentaries on Gambling

The issue of gambling has been the theme of several documentary programs aired by public and commercial television organizations. The following list of such programs and other videotapes on gambling is taken from the Special Collections Department of the James Dickinson Library at the University of Nevada–Las Vegas. Because these videos are not always available for sale to the general public, price information has not been included. The distributors' addresses are listed at the end of this chapter. Inquiries may also be made to local libraries, as the tapes may be available through interlibrary-loan systems.

Accent Las Vegas: The City of Destiny
Type: VHS
Length: 40 minutes
Date: 1985
Source: William Mors Productions

What is Las Vegas really like? This video looks at the history, educational system, housing, and law enforcement as well as the entertainment facilities and casinos of Las Vegas.

American Dreaming: Atlantic City's Casino Gamble
Type: VHS
Length: 52 minutes
Date: 1989
Source: After Image Media Productions

This video discusses the attempt in the late 1980s to revitalize Atlantic City and examines the policy questions surrounding the use of casino gambling as a tool to solve deep-seated urban problems.

Atlantic City: The Queen Takes a Chance
Type: VHS
Length: 60 minutes
Date: 1978
Source: New Jersey Public Television

This video discusses the attempted rebirth of Atlantic City after the legalization of gambling and features interviews with residents and city officials.

Atlantic City: The Ten-Year Gamble
Type: VHS
Length: 58 minutes
Date: 12 February 1988
Source: New Jersey Public Television

This program examines casino gambling in Atlantic City from its inception through its first ten years of operation.

Benny Binion Remembered
Type: VHS
Length: 45 minutes
Date: 10 January 1990
Source: KVBC-TV

A documentary on the life of Benny Binion, casino entrepreneur, developer of the Horseshoe Casino of Las Vegas, and founder of the World Series of Poker. (See Binion's biography under "Gambling Hall of Fame" in Chapter 3.)

Betting on the Lottery
Type: VHS
Length: 58 minutes
Date: 1990
Source: PBS Video

Discusses why people play lotteries and to what extent government treasuries benefit from lotteries.

Big Gamble in Atlantic City
Type: VHS
Length: 50 minutes
Date: 1986
Source: CBS Television News

Bill Moyers conducts conversations with major gaming industry players as well as citizens of Atlantic City in order to assess the accomplishments of legalized gambling in the community.

Compulsive Gambling: Against All Odds
Type: VHS
Length: 27 minutes
Date: 1983
Source: ABC Television

Discusses what a compulsive gambler is and what help is available.

Compulsive Gambling: Betting Their Lives
Type: VHS
Length: 30 minutes
Date: 1983
Source: ABC Television

Focuses upon Gamblers Anonymous, GamAnon, and the treatment programs available at the Johns Hopkins Center for Pathological Gambling.

Deal Me Out
Type: VHS
Length: 28 minutes
Date: 1989
Source: St. Vincent's Medical Center

A docudrama about a compulsive gambler and his struggles and treatment.

Emerald River Resort: Paradise Found
Type: VHS
Length: 53 minutes
Date: 1990
Source: ABC Television

The growth and development of Laughlin, Nevada, and the efforts to build the Emerald River destination resort.

48 Hours in Las Vegas
Type: VHS
Length: 52 minutes
Date: 26 January 1988
Source: CBS Television News

Hosted by Dan Rather, the show discusses gambling on sports and at casino games. Looks at life of teenagers in Las Vegas, growing up in Las Vegas, and weddings in wedding chapels. Includes interviews with entertainers.

Frontline/The Political Power of Gambling
Type: VHS
Length: 60 minutes
Date: 1997
Source: PBS Video

This special on how gambling establishments have entered the political arena and are using big money to influence regulation of their businesses was first aired on PBS *Frontline*, 10 June 1997. The special devotes much attention to the unregulated gambling cardrooms of California.

Future Vision Presents Poker Town
Type: VHS
Length: 25 minutes
Date: 1984
Source: Wombat Film & Video

A documentary on the World Series of Poker held annually at Binion's Horseshoe Casino in Las Vegas.

Going Places—Las Vegas
Type: VHS
Length: 60 minutes
Date: 1997
Source: PBS Video

Al Roker narrates a series of PBS specials on tourist locations around the world. This episode appeared in January 1997. It features the many attractions of Las Vegas, tourist-resort casinos, and locals-oriented casinos as well as showrooms, wedding chapels, and the surrounding scenery—Lake Mead and Red Rocks Canyon.

Horse Race Handicapping
Type: VHS
Length: 111 minutes
Date: 1984
Source: Jacada Publications

A college course on the business of pari-mutuel wagering and handicapping principles.

I Can't Believe I Won the Lottery
Type: VHS
Length: 60 minutes
Date: 1989
Source: Fox Broadcasting Television Stations, Inc.

Explores what happens to the people who win big state lottery prizes.

Las Vegas
Type: VHS
Length: 240 minutes
Date: 1997
Source: Arts and Entertainment Network

This is a special of the Arts and Entertainment network first shown in summer 1996. The program makes an intense analysis of life in the gambling capital of the world, focusing on gaming but also looking at lifestyles, education, recreation, and culture outside the casinos. The special provides a substantial assessment of the impact of casino gambling on a community.

Las Vegas: Only in America
Type: VHS
Length: 52 minutes
Date: 1990
Source: International Video Network

This video discusses gambling and entertainment in Las Vegas as well as the cultural diversity and history of the city.

Laughlin 1988
Type: VHS
Length: 53 minutes
Date: 1988
Source: KLVX-TV

The development of a casino resort community is the focus of this video.

Lucky Number
Type: VHS
Length: 57 minutes
Date: 1990
Source: Maryland Public Television

Explores compulsive gambling and treatment programs.

The Mob on the Run
Type: VHS
Length: 120 minutes
Date: 1987
Source: KLAS-TV

An investigative reporter's history of the involvement of the Mob in gambling in Las Vegas, originally broadcast as segments of KLAS-TV *Eyewitness News*. Includes segments on Moe Dalitz, Allan Dorfman, the Teamsters Union, and members of the Atlantic City and Chicago Mobs.

North American Conference on the Status of Indian Gaming
Type: VHS
Length: 800 minutes
Date: 1989
Source: Institute for the Study of Gambling and Commercial Gaming.

Nine 90-minute tapes of conference speakers, including members of Congress, Indian leaders, former Secretary of the Interior Stewart Udall, and other authorities on gaming. Speeches focus on the Indian Gaming Regulatory Act of 1988.

Statewide Conference on Compulsive Gambling
Type: VHS
Length: 300 minutes
Date: 1985
Source: Council on Compulsive Gambling of New Jersey

A series of tapes of presentations on topics such as crime and compulsive gambling, treatment programs, gambling and sports, and public policy and compulsive gambling.

Steve Forte's Gambling Production Series
Type: VHS
Length: 210 minutes
Date: 1984
Source: BTA Joint Ventures

Four videos expose various methods of cheating at casino card and dice games.

An Unauthorized History of the NFL
Type: VHS
Length: 60 minutes
Date: 1983
Source: WGBH Educational Foundation

Jessica Savitch discusses illegal betting, the role of the Mob in football betting, and connections between owners, coaches, players, and organized crime. Originally shown on *Frontline* on PBS.

Distributors

ABC Television
77 West 66th Street
New York, NY 10023
(212) 456-7777

ABC Wide World of Learning
1330 Avenue of the Americas
New York, NY 10019
(212) 887-1735

After Image Media Productions
(no current location)

BTA Joint Ventures
P.O. Box 80876
Las Vegas, NV 89180

Cabin Fever Entertainment
100 West Putnam Avenue
Greenwich, CT 06830
(203) 863-5200

CBS/Fox Video
P.O. Box 900
Beverly Hills, CA 90213
(562) 373-4800

CBS Television News
51 West 52nd Street
New York, NY 10019
(212) 975-4321

Columbia Tristar
10202 West Washington
Culver City, CA 90232
(310) 280-8000

Council on Compulsive Gambling of New Jersey
1315 West State Street
Trenton, NJ 08618
(609) 599-3299

Facets Video
1517 West Fullerton Avenue
Chicago, IL 60614
(312) 281-9075
(800) 331-6197
FAX (312) 929-5437

Filmmakers Library, Inc.
124 East 40th Street, Suite 901
New York, NY 10016
(212) 808-4880

Fox Broadcasting Television Stations, Inc.
1020 West Pico Boulevard
Los Angeles, CA 90035
(310) 277-2211

Fox Home Entertainment
P.O. Box 900
Beverly Hills, CA 90213
(310) 369-3900

HBO Video, Inc.
1100 Avenue of the Americas
New York, NY 10036
(212) 512-7447
(800) 648-7650
FAX (212) 512-7458

Institute for the Study of Gambling and Commercial Gaming
University of Nevada–Reno
Reno, NV 89557
(702) 782-1477

International Video Network
2242 Camino Ramon
San Ramon, CA 94583
(510) 866-1121

Jacada Publications
P.O. Box 1418
Louisville, KY 40201

KLAS-TV
3228 Channel 8 Drive
Las Vegas, NV 89109
(702) 792-8888

KLVX-TV
4210 Channel 10 Drive
Las Vegas, NV 89119
(702) 737-1010

Kultur Video
Video Division(s): White Star
121 Highway 36
West Long Branch, NJ 07764
(908) 229-2343
(800) 458-5887
FAX (201) 229-0066

KVBC-TV
1500 Foremaster Lane
Las Vegas, NV 89101
(702) 642-3333

Maryland Public Television
11767 Bonita Avenue
Owings Mills, MD 21117
(301) 356-5600

MCA Home Video, Division of MCA, Inc.
11312 Penrose Street
Sun Valley, CA 91352
(818) 768-3520

MGM
2500 Broadway
Santa Monica, CA 90404
(310) 449-3000

MGM/UA Home Video
10000 Washington Boulevard
Culver City, CA 90232-2728
(213) 280-6000
(800) 433-5500, Ext. 792
FAX (213) 836-9627

Nelson Entertainment, Inc.
Video Division: Charter Entertainment
Embassy Home Entertainment
335 North Maple Drive, Suite 350
Beverly Hills, CA 90219-3899
(213) 285-6000

New Jersey Public Television
1573 Parkside Avenue
Trenton, NJ 08638
(609) 882-5252

New World Video
1440 South Sepulveda Boulevard
Los Angeles, CA 90025
(213) 444-8100

Orion Home Video, Division of Orion Pictures Corp.
9 West 57th Street
New York, NY 10019
(212) 980-1117
FAX (212) 688-8197

Paramount Home Video, Division of Paramount Pictures Corp.
5555 Melrose Avenue
Hollywood, CA 90038
(213) 956-5000

PBS Video
1320 Braddock
Alexandria, VA 22314-1698
(703) 739-5380

Powersports/American Video
15700 Dickens Street
Encino, CA 91436
(800) 553-2030; (800) 338-2040 (in California)
FAX (818) 907-0598

RCA/Columbia Pictures Home Video
Subsidiary of Columbia Pictures Industries, Inc.
3500 West Olive Avenue
Burbank, CA 91505
(818) 953-7900
(800) 722-2748
FAX (818) 953-7864

Republic Pictures Home Video, Division of Republic Pictures Corp.
12636 Beatrice Street
Los Angeles, CA 90066-0930
(213) 302-1656
(899) 826-2295 (orders)
FAX (213) 306-8865

St. Vincent's Medical Center
355 Bard Avenue
Richmond, NY 10310-1699
(718) 878-1234

Touchstone Home Video
500 South Buena Vista Street
Burbank, CA 91521
(818) 840-1875

Universal Home Video
70 Universal City Plaza
Los Angeles, CA 91608
(818) 777-6419

Vestron Video, Inc.
Video Division: Lightning Video
1010 Washington Boulevard
Stamford, CT 06901
(203) 978-5400

Vidmark Entertainment
2901 Ocean Park Boulevard, Suite 123
Santa Monica, CA 90405-2906
(213) 399-8877
(800) 424-7070
FAX (213) 399-8877

Warner Home Video, Inc.
Subsidiary of Warner Brothers, Inc.
4000 Warner Boulevard, No. 19
Burbank, CA 91522
(818) 954-6266
(899) 626-9000 (orders)
FAX (818) 954-6540

WGBH Educational Foundation
125 Western Avenue
Boston, MA 02134
(617) 492-2777

Wherehouse Entertainment, Inc.
P.O. Box 2831
Torrance, CA 90509-2831
(310) 538-2314

William Mors Productions
407 Park East Way
Las Vegas, NV 89106
(702) 383-3041

Wombat Film & Video, Division of Cortech Communications, Inc.
250 West 57th Street, Suite 2421
New York, NY 10019
(212) 315-2502
(800) 542-5554
FAX (212) 582-0585

Wood Knapp Video, Division of Wood Knapp & Co.
140 East 45th Street
New York, NY 10017
(212) 983-8192

World Education 2000
P.O. Box 11118
Fort Lauderdale, FL 33339
(305) 565-8888

Glossary

baccarat One of a series of games (baccara, chemin de fer, punto banco) in which the winning hand of cards totals nine or a number closest to nine (tens and face cards count as zero). Two hands are dealt: One is called "the bank hand," the other "the player hand." Players may bet on either hand. In baccarat and punto banco all bets are against the house; in the other forms of the game the players may bet against each other.

bail-out Loaning money to a compulsive gambler in order to help the gambler meet his or her financial obligations. Usually the bail-out is done with a promise that the person will stop gambling. This is a phase of the cycle of pathological gambling.

bank *See* casino.

banking games, nonbanking games A banking game (or a house bank game) is a casino game in which the bettor plays against the casino. These games include blackjack, roulette, craps, baccarat, and machine games. In contrast, in nonbanking games players compete with each other. The casino is not a player in the game, although the house may charge a fee for conducting the game. The most popular nonbanking game is poker. Pari-mutuel games are also nonbanking games.

big wheel (also called big six or wheel of fortune)   This is a game played with a vertical spinning wheel. In Nevada the big wheel has 54 positions, each showing either the face of a paper currency or a joker. The faces include $1, $2, $5, $10, and $20. The bettor wagers that one of the six configurations will end up on the winning place. The payoff odds are very much against the player, and the game is therefore considered a "sucker bet."

bingo   This very popular charity game is usually played with cards containing 24 numbers (from 1 to 75) placed in five columns and five rows. The player purchases the cards before the game begins. A dealer then draws numbers one at a time randomly from a pool of 75 numbers, until one player covers a designated portion of the card with winning numbers—either a row, a column, or a predetermined winning configuration. That winner receives a prize. Bingo is generally conducted as a non-banking game.

blackjack (also called twenty-one)   A card game in which players seek to have a hand with cards totaling 21 or a number close to, but not over, 21. Players wager that their hand will be better than the house or dealer hand. The dealer gives each player two cards. The dealer also displays a single card. The players then may ask for additional cards in hopes of getting a 21 count. Aces may count as either 1 or 11, face cards 10, and other cards their normal values. The term *blackjack* refers specifically to a hand with an ace and a single card with a value of 10.

book, make book, bookie   *Book* is a term that refers to taking bets on races, on sports events, or on numbers. A person who makes book, or takes the bets, is referred to as a bookie, although this term is usually reserved for persons taking bets where gambling is illegal.

California aces   A game developed for use in California Indian casinos. Even though it is similar to blackjack, it is not a banking game. The players compete against one another for the best hand, although the casino assesses a charge against each player for participating. The best hand is a 22 (two aces), and no player can bust. The winning player has the hand closest to 22, with a hand under 22 (for example, 20) being rated better than a hand the same distance over 22 (for example, 24). On ties the "pot" is split among the players with the best hands.

card-counter   A blackjack player who keeps track of all the cards that have been dealt. By doing so, he or she is able to calculate the odds of specific cards being dealt on subsequent plays. Expert counters can actually gain an advantage over the house. Certain casinos refuse to allow players to engage in counting techniques and ask them to leave if they are discovered.

Caribbean stud poker   A banking game variation of stud poker in which each player competes one on one with the house dealer for the best poker hand. Only five cards are dealt to each player and the dealer. Also, players are permitted to make side bets on the value of their hands. Good hands—for example, straight, flush, four of a kind, royal flush—are given prizes that are multiples of the side bet (for example, 50-to-1, 100-to-1). Super prizes are also available as several tables pool side bets, and the first person to have a royal flush wins the super jackpot.

casino (also called house or bank)   A casino is a location—a building or a large room—where games of chance are played with some regularity. Today's casinos feature a variety of card games, dice games, roulette and wheels of fortune, and various slot machines and gambling video games.

chance   An outcome that is determined by a randomly occurring risk that can be calculated. The odds—the probabilities—of a game of chance are known, and a person makes wagers with the knowledge that a random event will determine the outcome. In pure chance games the player cannot affect the outcome with the use of any skill he or she may possess. Similar to the concept of risk.

chase   A losing gambler's practice of betting larger and larger sums of money in hopes of winning back past losses. This reckless kind of play is typical among compulsive or pathological gamblers.

chips   Tokens for gambling used by casinos to represent money.

chuck-a-luck   A game played with three dice. Players bet on whether certain combinations will appear after the dice are rolled. Variations of the game are called "sic bo" and "cussec."

compulsive gambler (used interchangeably with the term *pathological gambler***)**   A gambler who has succumbed to a psychiatric impulse disorder. The disorder is evidenced by a progression of gambling activity that cannot be controlled by the gambler. The gambler becomes intolerant of losing and must keep betting to satisfy his or her inner drives. The gambling preoccupies the gambler's thinking to the point where the consequences of the gambling activity are completely disregarded. The compulsive gambler will have a high score on the South Oaks Gambling Screen.

craps   A very popular casino game in the United States in which players bet on combinations determined by the rolling of two dice. The specific term *craps* refers to a losing combination of numbers 2 (called "snake eyes"), 3, and 12 on the first roll of the dice.

exotic bets   These are combination bets at horse tracks and dog tracks. They include the daily double, exacta, trifecta, and quinella. In the daily double betting combination, the bettor makes a wager on which two horses (dogs) will win the first two races of the day. Both must win for the wager to be successful. The exacta is a combination bet in a specific horse or dog race in which the bettor seeks to predict the first- and second-place finishers in the race in exact order. In a trifecta, the bettor makes a wager on the first three finishers in order. Another combination bet is the quinella. Here the bettor picks the first two finishers, and if they are first and second or second and first, the bettor wins.

faro   A very popular game on the frontier in the western United States in the late nineteenth century. Players make wagers on the order in which cards will be dealt from a deck. It is basically a total luck game.

gambling (used interchangeably with the terms *gaming* and *wagering*) Placing something of value at risk in order to win a prize of value if a chance event (or an event determined in part by chance) occurs. The chance events are usually determined by the outcomes of card or dice games, contests, or drawing of lots. The legal definition of gambling requires three elements: consideration, chance, and prize. The casino industry prefers the term *gaming*, as it sounds more acceptable than *gambling*. *Wagering* is a term that generally applies to betting on horse races and dog races.

gaming   *See* gambling.

grifter   A gambling cheater or swindler. Grifters use many schemes to cheat, including peeking and counterfeit cards, dice, or casino chips as well as collusion with gaming staff members.

gross gaming win   The casino hold over a period of time. The gross gaming win is actually the amount bet minus the prizes given back to the players. This revenue won from the players is the basic amount utilized for most casino taxes.

handicap, to handicap, handicapping   A practice of studying horse races and making wagers according to an analysis of racing situations, the history of performances of specific horses and jockeys, the conditions of the track, where the horse was trained, and the horse's lineage. A serious player at the racetrack is referred to as a "handicapper"—one who handicaps races. The term *handicap* also refers to a system of adding weights to horses who are considered better runners in order to even out the chances of all the horses in a race.

handle, drop, and hold   *Handle, drop,* and *hold* are terms used mainly in casino accounting. The handle refers to the total amount wagered at a game or games in a specific period of time. This amount includes prize money that is won and then bet again. The handle for a slot machine would constitute all the coins put into the machine in a period of time without regard to coins coming out as prizes. Drop is the moneys the gambler brings to the game and plays. For instance, if a gambler brings $100 and plays the money at a blackjack table for several hours, experiencing both winning and losing hands, the drop is $100. The hold is the amount of money the house wins from the player over a period of time. For instance, if the player who wagers $100 leaves the casino with $80, the casino hold is $20.

hazard   A dice game that was very popular in England in the nineteenth century. It is considered the forerunner of craps and chuck-a-luck.

house   *See* casino.

Internet gambling   Systems of gambling conducted through computers on the Internet system. The systems permit people to make bets on races, sports events, or casino-type games such as blackjack, poker, or keno from their home terminals. Although such systems are in existence, they are of very questionable legality in the United States.

jai alai   A game played by two individuals or teams. Players use a scooped racket to hurl a ball extremely fast against a wall. The rules are similar to those of handball or racquetball. People make wagers on the winners, and betting is on a pari-mutuel basis.

junket   A junket is an organized excursion to a gambling location, usually paid for by a casino. The casinos willingly furnish transportation and hotel accommodations as well as meal costs and entertainment to the person on the junket. In exchange, that person agrees to engage in gambling games and make a certain quantity of wagers at the casino. Junkets are usually designed to bring in high-stakes players. They were first used by Nevada casinos in the 1960s.

keno (or Chinese lottery)   A game in which the player selects a set of numbers (typically 1 to 15 numbers), and the casino then randomly draws 20 numbers from a pool of 80 numbers. If all of a certain portion of the numbers drawn match those selected by the player, the player receives a prize.

loan shark   A loan shark is a person who makes loans to gamblers and charges them extremely high interest rates—often as much as 20 percent a week. Loan sharks are attracted to gambling locations, as they prey upon problem and pathological gamblers.

lottery   A game in which the winning numbers are determined by the random drawing of lots. In actuality, almost all forms of gambling games have characteristics of lotteries. In popular usage, the term *lottery* refers to government-run games that exist in two-thirds of the United States, all provinces of Canada, and nearly 100 other countries. Lotteries involve the sale of numbers (or series of numbers) to a player and then the drawing of numbers to determine which players are winners.

lottery, instant   A game in which a player purchases a ticket that has a concealed number (or symbol) upon it. A scratch-off variety ticket conceals the number behind a latex substance; a pull-tab ticket covers the number with a piece of paper. The player then removes the covering and reveals the number. If the number matches a predetermined winning number or symbol, the player receives a prize. These tickets are utilized by both government lotteries and charity organizations.

lotto   In the United States and Canada, lotto refers to a progressive lottery game in which the players select a series of numbers. The lottery agency then draws a series of numbers. If a player has all the numbers drawn, he or she is a winner. If no player has all the numbers drawn, the prize is added to a subsequent drawing after new tickets are sold. The prizes escalate with each drawing in which there is no winner. Some lotto games have had prizes exceeding $100 million.

luck   The experience of having success at games that are essentially determined by chance.

marker   A slip of paper signed by a casino player when he or she borrows money from the casino in order to gamble.

Martingale system   The Martingale system is probably the most popular betting system used by gamblers who think they can "beat the house." The bettor typically makes a wager on a nearly even-odds game (blackjack, red-black at roulette, and so on). If he loses, he doubles the bet. He continues to double bets with each loss. When he finally wins, he recoups all his losses and also has a profit of his original bet. In the short run many gamblers can win small amounts of money with this system. Indeed, when they win, they are only winning their original small stake. However, in the long run a losing streak will occur (this is part of the law of chance, as well). And few gamblers can afford to keep staking doubled bets in the face of a streak of eight, nine, or ten losses. At this point the player is also restricted by house gambling limits. For instance, a player might be at a table that allows bets between $5 and $500. After seven losses in a row, the player would not be able to use the system, as he would have to wager $960 just to have a chance to win his original $5 back. Conversely, when the player wins, he just starts again, so seven wins in a row would result in total wins of $35. If you want to use this system, the casino has only one thing to say: "Come on in!"

numbers game (also called *policy*)   A lottery game in which a player selects a three- or four-digit number. If the number matches a number that is randomly drawn by the lottery organization, the player is a winner. This is the most popular illegal lottery game in the United States.

odds   The advantage one side of a wager has over the other. In house-banked games, the casino will have an odds advantage in an actual game, or it will have an odds advantage in the payoff structure used.

pai gow   Pai gow is a Chinese dominos game. Players are given four dominos face down. They make two hands of two dominos, with the numbers of dots being considered much like the numbers on playing cards. The player's hands are then matched against a dealer's hands. One side either wins both, or there is a tie. It is truly an even match, but where it is played in a casino, the casino discounts a percentage of a player's win at the time of a payout.

pai gow poker   Pai gow poker involves playing cards. A player is dealt seven cards, as is the dealer. They then make their best five-card poker hand and two-card poker hand. As in pai gow dominos, the hands are compared, and one side is a winner if the two hands are better than the two hands of the other. Otherwise it is a tie.

pari-mutuel betting A form of wagering utilized for horse racing, dog racing, and jai alai games. All player bets are pooled together. Prizes are taken out of the common pool and given to those bettors who selected winners of the event (the race or the game). The gambling organization will also take a percentage of the pool as its fee for operating the game. Odds for prizes are determined by the patterns of players' bets. If many bettors place wagers on the winner, the prizes are small; however, if only a few bettors select the winner, the prizes are much larger. The establishment (the casino, house, bank) does not participate in the gambling as a player.

parlay, parlay card A parlay bet is a combination sports bet on several games or events. The player wins only if he wins on all the parts of the combination. Of course, a winner is given multiple odds. In Las Vegas a $10 parlay bet on two games will win a player $26 (that is, a return of $26 plus the $10 wagered). Often casinos have cards prepared with lists of bets, and a bettor can select from three to ten or even more bets on a single card. A three-game parlay will pay 5 to 1; a four-game parlay 10 to 1; a five-card parley 19 to 1. Ties may be counted as wins or losses on parlays, depending on the casino and the cards. As the odds on single-game bets are more favorable than those on cards, professional sports bettors avoid parlay cards.

pathological gambler *See* compulsive gambler.

point spread A term used in sports betting to refer to the betting handicap given to those making wagers on underdog or presumably weaker teams. The point spread is used most often in basketball or football betting. As an example, Detroit may be a 7.5 point underdog at Dallas. Those betting on Dallas will not win their bet unless Dallas wins the game by 8 or more points. Detroit bettors will win the bet if Detroit wins the game or loses by less than 8 points.

poker A nonbanking card game that involves considerable skill in betting behavior. Players make wagers on which one will have the best five-card hand (although there are some games with other hands). Hands are ranked from the highest (a royal flush; that is, ace, king, queen, jack, of the same suit) to the lowest in value. There are many variations in dealing. In stud poker, cards are dealt, and the players must use the cards; in draw poker, the player may exchange cards for new ones. Betting occurs at the beginning (ante and opening bets) and as cards are dealt. In some games some cards are dealt face up; in other games all cards are dealt down. In addition to being a casino game, poker is the most popular social gambling game in the United States and Canada.

policy *See* numbers game.

problem gambler A gambler who gambles excessively, usually more than he or she would like to gamble. Losses exceed amounts of money the gambler can easily afford to lose. The problem gambler maintains some control over his or her gambling activity, being able to stop and then avoid returning to gambling activity. However, most pathological gamblers go through a stage of problem gambling.

professional gambler   The professional gambler is a player who gambles as a livelihood. He or she participates in order to win money and with an expectation that he or she will win money. Professional players usually avoid games that are primarily chance games, as they know that in the long run they will lose at these games. Rather, they will play games that have a skill factor involved, such as poker or blackjack—if the player is a counter. Professional gamblers will also make wagers on horse races and sports events, as it is possible with good knowledge and analytical abilities to make consistent wins at these games. In a sense, a person who plays the stock market regularly may be like a professional gambler.

punter (used interchangeably with the terms *bettor, gambler, player,* **or** *plunger***)**   A term used most often in England. It refers to a person making a wager.

raffle   A form of lottery in which numbered tickets are sold and then placed into a large drum or container. The players are given receipts for their tickets. The tickets are mixed up, and one is drawn out in random fashion. The player who purchased the ticket is given a prize. Raffles are very popular in charity gambling.

rake   A part of the pool of funds that the casino takes from a game such as poker in which the players are competing against one another, with the casino furnishing the gaming table and the dealer. In a sense, it is like the portion of bets at a racetrack that are retained by the track, that is, taken away from the ultimate prize awards.

recreational gambler or social gambler   A person who participates in gambling as a casual activity to fill time with friends or for excitement during leisure time. The player may expect to incur some losses, but these are seen as the cost of the entertainment experience. The losses are moneys that the player can afford to spend on recreation.

risk   *See* chance.

roulette   A very popular casino game. It is played with a horizontal wheel with numbers from 1 to 36 and also either one zero (European wheel) or two zeros (U.S. wheel) around the circumference. Bettors select a number or combination of numbers. The wheel is then spun, and a ball is dropped into it. Eventually the ball settles in a slot beside a winning number. If this number matches the number on one of the numbers bet upon, the player receives a prize.

skill   Skill is an ability of a player to affect the outcome of a game by utilizing a talent either as a result of personal qualities or training. Where skill may be a major factor in determining the outcome of the game, the game is called a skill game. For game players, most athletic contests are considered skill games. Native Americans traditionally gambled on running races. Games like darts are skill games. So, too, are some card games such as bridge or poker. Card-counters have the ability to use skill at blackjack. Handicappers use their skills to pick winning horses at racetracks.

slot machine   A mechanical, electromechanical, or computerized device into which coins are placed and play is activated by a bettor. The machine displays symbols indicating that the player has won or lost the wager, and if the player is a winner, the machine will distribute the prize (or paper or tokens as evidence of the prize). There is a wide variety of slot machines and video devices. The most popular video machines display poker hands and give the player a second chance by allowing another choice of cards. Today, over half of the gross gaming win of casinos comes from machine play. Some state lotteries also utilize slot machines, which they call video lottery terminals.

South Oaks Gambling Screen   A survey that is given to gamblers in order to assess whether they have a gambling problem and, if so, the extent of the problem. A series of questions is asked about matters such as the frequency of gambling, control over gambling, preoccupation with gambling, withdrawal symptoms when not gambling, attempts to stop gambling, and borrowing or stealing to get gambling funds. The number of positive answers to the questions constitutes a score that is used to evaluate the gambler. The screen was developed by Henry Lesieur.

twenty-one   *See* blackjack.

video lottery terminal   *See* slot machine.

wagering   *See* gambling.

win, place, show   Terms used in horse race and dog race betting. A win bet is a bet that a horse or dog will finish the race first. A place bet is a wager that the horse or dog will finish in either first or second position. The show bet is a wager that a horse or dog will finish either first, second, or third.

Index

William N. Thompson is Professor of Public Administration in the College of Business at the University of Nevada–Las Vegas. A noted authority on gambling, he has researched and written extensively on the topic and has served as a consultant on gambling for national and international businesses and organizations. His other books on gambling include three coauthored works: *The Last Resort: Success and Failure in Campaigns for Casinos*; *International Casino Law*; and *Casino Customer Service*. In addition to his work on gambling, he has written *Native American Issues* for ABC-CLIO's Contemporary World Issues series.